Library/Media Center
Carroll Community College
1601 Washington Road
Westminster, Maryland 21157

WITHDRAWN

D0734462

23.33 //92

Pretty Bubbles in the Air

Pretty Bubbles in the Air

America in 1919

WILLIAM D. MILLER

UNIVERSITY OF ILLINOIS PRESS
Urbana and Chicago

© 1991 by the Board of Trustees of the University of Illinois
Manufactured in the United States of America
C 5 4 3 2 1

This book is printed on acid-free paper.

Library of Congress Cataloging-in-Publication Data

Miller, William D., 1916–
    Pretty bubbles in the air : America in 1919 / William D. Miller.
      p.   cm.
    Includes bibliographical references and index.
    ISBN 0-252-01823-0
    1. United States—History—1913–1921. I. Title.
E766.M66   1991
973.91—dc20   91-14399
                                             CIP

To
John Hebron Moore,
gentleman and scholar

Contents

Preface

This is not a work in which I have tried primarily to refine or extenuate either the substance or interpretation of any of the biographical and monographic studies that cover the year following the First World War. My concern has been to get as close to the action of the time as I can, to breathe its air and to stride along with it, as it were. Books I used as references are primarily the memoirs and reminiscences of those who were part of the action.

No source, though, is more immediate to the general picture than the daily newspaper. Because of its concern with reporting issues that have national scope, because of its preeminence in its concern with cultural and artistic matters, and because of its reputation for journalistic integrity, I chose the *New York Times* as a controlling source for social history. A newspaper gives continuity to events and usually imparts to them elements of color that tend to be lost in subsequent recountings. Further, newspapers provide a means of judging the relative significance of events as contemporaries viewed them. In addition to this foundation source, I have used whatever else might help me tell the story—mainly periodicals, novels, and reminiscences, both written and verbal, of people who remember the time.

In the matter of documentation, my principle has been, when feasible, to include the source in the body of the text. This disposition, which especially lends itself to newspapers, has been indulged so as to relieve the text of the sometimes ponderous, and even pretentious, intrusion of a formal footnote structure. Still, some type of note is desirable, not only to designate a source, but to provide information for those who want to pursue a subject in more detail. I therefore included at the end of each chapter a brief note on sources and some suggestions for further reading.

This book is narrative history but it has a point. Inasmuch as I see and judge the significance of the events of which I write in terms of an "idea climate" and its change, the interpretive principle is found in the area of what some choose to call "intellectual history." On the basis of this principle, I see the time immediately after the war as one of transition. The ordered and tempered life, governed by the stability of place and value, that most Americans led in settled forms of community—family, neighborhood, village—would henceforth suffer from an accelerating erosion caused by the advent of machines and a new idea climate. The traditional stability of values and manners that gave order and a hopeful meaning to life began to give way to the new view of an open universe seething with energy, where randomness and indeterminacy were its marks. Within this aborning universe, there were, in the minds of Henry Adams and Nicholas Berdyaev, ominous portents. These two thinkers are given a hearing in the concluding chapter.

It is here fitting to thank those who have, in one way or another, helped me in this work. Professor William W. Rogers closely read the manuscript and then provided a setting of food and drink to offer his counsel. Dennis Downey and Richard Crepeau read—even studied—the work and made good suggestions (which I took) for its improvement. Frank Sicius has been a source of striking insight where intellectual history is concerned, and Marc Ellis set a good example through his passion for human justice. These latter four were my students; all are now professors, and each, in my view, embodies in his person and work the authentic mark of the vocation to teach—the conviction that true knowing makes brighter the vision of what it means to be human.

I thank Rhea, my wife of some forty years. She too is a professor and her creative works have been many—including seven sons, all of whom are gifted and good. Our daughter, Carol Maria Miller, is also gifted and good. She is a Medievalist, who nonetheless handles a word processor with quick authority and has, therefore, been of much help to me in the preparation of this manuscript.

The substance for this work was obtained at the Florida State University Library, the Marquette University Memorial Library, and the Milwaukee Public Library. The chapter-ending notes were prepared at the State Library of Florida, and I thank Louise Brown for her assistance in getting place and date information on publications.

Introduction

This work began out of an impulse to reminisce—a memory that I have of life in America just after the First World War. I was less than a month short of being two years old when the war ended, and I remember one episode from it. My grandparents lived at 751 Oak Street in Jacksonville, Florida, and one night, as they, my parents, and I were having lemonade on the front porch, my grandmother led me into the street to observe some shafts of light darting in the sky. Later I learned that those shifting and crossing beams were from searchlights looking for an airplane, supposedly launched from a German submarine off Jacksonville beach. When I used to tell of this singular recollection, the response was usually, "Oh, you just imagined that." But the Jacksonville newspapers for October 1918 tell of just such an occurrence. The supposed plane, launched from the hypothetical submarine, had as its diabolical mission the bombing of a Jacksonville shipyard. And, no doubt, some of Jacksonville's citizenry would have professed to think that the airplane carried an "infernal machine" wherewith to effect its mission.

So, with this memory as a preface, I began to work on what I intended to be a social history of the year after the war, for some feeling about the character of that year began to impress itself on my consciousness. There was an ebullience about those days, imparted by the nation's having just won a war—a mood that was accentuated by the appearance of dazzling new machines and signs of the carefree modes and manners that went with them.

Machines were among the first objects to intrude themselves into my life's marveling consciousness. We then lived on Post Street in the new "development" of Murray Hill, and one morning, standing on the sidewalk in front of the house, I saw high in the sky the sunlight glinting on the wing of an airplane and I heard the reverberations of the plane's faraway motor. Once I saw a plane tumbling from the sky, like a cross falling end over end. It crashed in the area and sometime later a part of its propeller appeared against the wall over the counter of Mr. Phillips's grocery store, on the corner of Edgewood and Post.

Automobiles were beginning to appear on the streets in increasing numbers, and while my father still rode a bicycle to work, my grandfather had an automobile. On many weekends we all went in his Oldsmobile to a camp house that he had built on Strawberry Creek. We crossed the St. John's River by ferry, either on the *Arlington* or the *Fairfield.* It was quite an adventure, even to get the car on the boat. When the time came to board, women and children got out, and then, with engine popping, the car lurched over the drawbridge onto the deck. The fear was that the car, from brake failure or an overwrought engine, would carry on for a dive into the river—as, my grandfather liked to say, one car had done. On the Arlington side we passed a pavillion of tools and machines where boat engines were repaired and then headed south for several miles on the Arlington Road into the deep shadow of oaks, cedars, and hickories—the area, which my grandfather owned, lying between Pottsburgh and Strawberry creeks.

Frequently it was dusk when we arrived, and to leave the tired, but now quiet, car and step into the low murmur of the night—to breathe a soft air made fragrant by lush vegetation, long untouched—was to be bathed in bliss. Later, more bliss was crowded into the few moments before sleep. Atop the house, facing the creek, was a large screened-in upper porch that was used as a dormitory room. As I and my brother, Richard, lay in our bed on a denim sheet, there arose from the creek below the occasional sound of a fish slapping the water after leaping for an insect. And, less frequently, from the marsh on the other side of the water, a male alligator's deep-voiced grunt could be heard, a suggestion to some nearby female that his hole had room enough for two. One night my grandfather, on hearing some slight noise coming from the rooftop, went out to see a panther astride the ridgepole. To this menace my grandmother directed a firm "Shoo!" and such was the authority in her voice that the animal leaped into a tree and made off.

This experience of taking a deep and sweet-clean breath of nature occurred from the time of my earliest memory through the days of my youth. When I was six years old, all of us, including my great-grandmother and two dear maiden aunts, moved out to The Place, as we called it. But never again would the joy of family community, of living in the harmony of an undefiled nature, be as complete as it was for me in the time just after the war. This Eden-like existence of unspoiled nature ("The river water is so pure you can drink it," my grandfather used to say) and family community is virtually unknown today.

While such natural places, making for community and peace, still existed back then, the air over the land was becoming alive with a new energy and a new spirit. Technology, which by war had been made the instrument of massive killing, began to introduce into life fascinating new creatures, seemingly of such guileless innocence and a willing disposition to free humankind from servile work that the very air one breathed took on a new lightness and sparkle. A popular song of the year 1919, "I'm Forever Blowing Bubbles," told of the pink glow that infused life, and I remember my mother, who was a fine pianist, playing it along with Percy Grainger's "Country Gardens."

Blowing "pretty bubbles in the air" was an image that caught the fancy of the comfortably situated middle class, but it was one that masked a tragic reality. White middle-class America needed to recognize the personhood of American blacks and to accord them their full human due. In the year after a war fought "to save the world for democracy," segregation and discrimination continued unabated where blacks were concerned, as did the atrocities of the lynch mob.

Without overburdening imagery, one perhaps cannot suggest that "pretty bubbles in the air" worked to undo Woodrow Wilson's plan for a world brought into such social harmony by his League of Nations that a lynching would be an unthinkable anachronism. But if the advent of dazzling new machines, and the carefree modes and manners that went with the new cast of things, bespoke the beginning of a new time in life, a time when Marx and Freud would challenge England's dyspeptic Herbert Spencer and Yale's William Graham Sumner, Wilson appears as a contrapuntal element to the main theme. In America especially, the armistice of November 1918 represented an introduction into life of the "open universe" of William James. The new "ether" that people breathed began, almost imperceptibly at first, to produce a response that ran counter to the old Enlightenment assumption of an automatic progress that would culminate in a final form—Spencer's "equilibriation."

Wilson was a classical Enlightenment type. He affirmed an ordered and rational universe, he affirmed "progress," and he affirmed a final harmony in the political life of humankind. These affirmations, it can be added, were entirely in accord with his Calvinist orientation: the political covenant system that the English and American Puritans had worked out.

Perhaps America's failure to join the League was the tragedy that some writers have tended to make it, but it was small compared to a larger tragedy. Western civilization at the close of the war needed to examine itself—to stand back, aghast at what it had just done; to ask how such a demonstration of maniacal frenzy had come to pass, and what it might do—after intellectual and spiritual reexamination—to make amends for its madness. But too little of this self-examination occurred. Abroad, there was the wreckage of war in the lives of wounded and embittered people, full of grotesque notions about how community could be built by exalting "we" at the expense of "they"—other classes, other nations, other religions. The League, perhaps, might touch the ultimate perimeter of a new eruption of violence, but the problem of an inner healing and reconciliation of people to people and nation to nation was acute and would require more than a new form to solve it.

Who might have taken the lead in creating a more generous, a more understanding, a more personalist reconstruction of society at home and abroad? A prophet? A vital intellectual leadership? Religious institutions? There was no prophet in America who had such an audience as Wilson, but his vision rested on a proposition that by June 1919 seemed already to have lost its meaning, as far as the national mood was concerned. The war had, with some few exceptions, enlisted into its cause the leaders of American higher education. But whatever the depths or heights that were reached by the most gifted thinkers in understanding the tragic character of the time, their words were never heard among the hosannahs that were sung to support the great crusade. As for the religious leaders, a few may have had deep misgivings about America's entrance into the war, but the most vocal seem to have tried to outdo one another in identifying their particular religious enthusiasm as the one most sanctified in upholding the cause of the state.

As it turned out, during the months following the armistice it was "business leadership" and its canons that set the standards for the good life in America. Over the years, this new and intrusive development evolved from a form of after-dinner pep rally and sloganeering, as it was during the twenties, into the sophisticated puppeteering of the masses that it has assumed today. The tragedy is not in the sloganeering and puppeteering so much as in the diverting of human vision away from the ideal of community toward the exaltation of the "I."

Yet one cannot blame "business leadership" for creating all of the doom-portending signs that hover over life today. The fault is, perhaps, as some artists and thinkers have suggested, that the mission of the intellectuals and spiritual leaders to keep human life's vision has become lost in darkness and that they somehow have permitted the opening of a Pandora's box in the roilings of history's process. Perhaps it is, as some thinkers have suggested, that the men and women of higher learning no longer think in terms of the subject (the person) but of the object—and that they no longer think in terms of community (the deepest craving of every human soul, as Dostoevski declares) but of counting and sorting. And one might add, of those who have said this, perhaps none has said it more profoundly, nor with such an angelic voice, as has Simone Weil, the French essayist and thinker who died in England in 1943.

Despite these dour reflections on the character of life as it began to change after the war, the age-long institutions and forms that made for community still held in 1919. The family, the veritable model of community, the source of hope for the community's completion, stood unscathed; and community was a reality in neighborhoods and small towns. Yet, amid the confusion and the cacophony that followed the war, there were people who could stand in childish innocence before the new world unfolding and marvel at what they saw.

Now, from the perspective of nearly seven decades, I recognize that if some, such as my mother, could sing of "pretty bubbles in the air," the imagery of that time immediately after the war caught a mood that bespoke the end, not the beginning, of an era. The ordered phase of Enlightenment "progress" was closing, and beginning to emerge was a new universe of randomness that imparted a restlessness and tension to life that was inhospitable to the values of community.

For the moment, though, amid alarms and scares that were almost contrived, there were no imminent menacing signs. It was a frothy and exciting time whose spirit will never return. Where in America is the child who, utterly at peace with creation, can now drift off to sleep breathing an unmolested sweet night air from nature's store and hear an occasional bellow from an alligator? As for those "pretty bubbles in the air," I hope they went beyond the stars to a place where the withering grasp of time does not reach, and that those who sung of them and saw them wafting aloft a dream of community and bliss have all found their dreams come true.

Prologue

W HEN WOODROW WILSON was inaugurated president of the United States on March 4, 1913, the people of the Western world seemed never more certain that they had been providentially chosen to lead on the pathway of progress. Scarcely a day passed that some miracle did not open up a new understanding of nature's workings. Time was not a destroyer; it was a jeweled lord who rewarded the homage rendered it with rich fiefs.

Americans were among the most vocal in affirming their preeminence in the march to glory. Their country, they were taught, had been born at the dawn of the new age of reason and freedom, and it took its character from that age. As a sovereign and rational people, they were, finally, the infallible source of truth and progress. On March 4, 1913, could they not say that the evidence was at hand? Recent changes in the forms of local and state governments had opened the political process even more to the will of the people, and the results had been felicitous. A new type of efficient, reformist, and even scholarly leadership had appeared in political life. Election of the high-minded Wilson, a university president, had been a capstone to the process.

Washington, D.C., was in a festive mood as the inauguration day approached. On Sunday afternoon, March 2, a number of receptions were held for members of the outgoing Taft administration. The main affair was a concert for the Tafts, performed by the Flonzaley Quartet, one of the very distinguished chamber groups of the time. Assistant Secretary of State and Mrs. Huntington Wilson were the hosts.

That night thousands of visitors thronged Pennsylvania Avenue. Above the swell of talk were the voices of vendors, selling pennants decorated with the pictures of Wilson and Vice President Thomas R. Marshall, former governor of Indiana. But there were other banners, yellow ones, bearing the inscription, "Votes for Women." And an attractive young woman, one hand in a white muff, held in the other a blue and white pennant that read, "Kiss me kid. I'm lonely."

Pennsylvania Avenue that evening featured a new addition to the customary inaugural trappings: the street was ablaze with electric lights. Searchlights illuminated public structures, and strings of lights outlined office buildings. The Hotel Willard had a large electric sign that read, "Wilson and Marshall." In front of the White House, a Court of Honor, where Wilson would make his first public appearance, had been set up. It was illuminated by flaring calcium carbide torches.

There was a spirit of togetherness among those who were promenading that night, a spirit that, for those of their class and character, seemed to pervade the whole land. They knew one another by their capacity for work and by the value of their material possessions, which they regarded as testimony of their moral worth. They identified themselves by their skin color and their emphasis on "getting ahead." And, certainly, they found a powerful impulse to community in their assumption that they stood at the forefront of history's process and that all others who could not keep the pace would be passed by. Now, as many professed, they were about to install as president one of their own, a man of a character and scholarly attainment, which the other peoples of the world, with their kings and czars, might well emulate.

Wilson the scholar did indeed affirm and uphold the values honored by most of white America. His view of reality was formed by Newton and Calvin—a formation that contained the prime substances of American life. He believed there was an order in the universe that served as a model for American constitutional government and for the free enterprise system. Since the laws of the universe were immutable, so were the laws of political, economic, and certain aspects of social association. The laws were there, like gravity, to undergird and direct the process of history's unfolding along the path of progress. The politics of statesmanship was to see that these laws were not transgressed.

Religious dispositions among people were a personal matter, but where Wilson the Calvinist was concerned, religious commitment reached its highest expression when it was completed by a covenant enacted between a person and God. Under the covenant principle of the old Puritans, the person, in return for God's favor of special election, committed his or her personhood, personally or corporately, as latterly in a "social covenant," to further on earth a mark of God's kingdom. The attempt to register upon history a form of this latter covenant

constitutes the theme of epic struggle that runs through the year beginning with the end of the war.

The circumstances that attended Wilson's inauguration, from the
bright lights on Pennsylvania Avenue to the optimism that marked the
intellectual climate of the day, must have buoyed his spirit and infused
into his delicately balanced physical state some of the energy that led to
the legislative accomplishments of his first year in office. But his days of
confident accomplishment ended when the illusion of an inevitable,
enlightened progress, under which Europe had lived for almost a century,
was dispelled by a war so deadly and of such scope that few could
comprehend it.

Although the war initially brought shock and dismay to Americans,
many preferred to think of it as an eruption of Europe's chronic ailment
of martial adventure that would have nothing to do with America.
Their president reassured them. As he said, America would be impar-
tial in thought as well as in deed—and for the moment, that view was
accepted.

How the United States became involved in the war is a subject that a
number of historians have examined with great care, scrupulous in
their regard for the ideal of objectivity and in their use of all of the
methodological refinements at hand to support that ideal. Nonetheless,
they have reached conclusions that sometimes are at variance, one with
another, as to what or who was responsible for the war. Perhaps
Dostoevski's Grand Inquisitor in *The Brothers Karamazov* offers an
insight into the causes of World War I that goes beyond the historian's
extensively footnoted explanations. The Inquisitor observes that so
desirous is the human spirit of the feeling of community that people
will accept any idea or program, no matter how irrational or ultimately
inhuman, if they can make it into a holy cause and be together in it. In
the somnolence of the closing days of peace in 1914, war was the
dramatically appearing cause that momentarily lifted people to near-
ecstatic levels of community.

When the First World War cast its shadows across America, it seemed,
or was made to seem, by Allied supporters, that the more ominous
shadows came from Germany. From this initial tilting of the perspective,
and through increasingly strident journalistic interpretations of the war
as an apocalyptic crisis between Good and Evil, many Americans almost
joyously submitted themselves to a prowar sentiment that in some
quarters amounted to a frenzy. They, too, were drinking the frothy elixir
that produced the illusion of community.

President Wilson had his own illusion, that of the absolute character of the legalisms and principles intended to govern international relations. In 1916, while campaigning for his preparedness program, he stated his position in phrases that bespoke his idealism. In one speech he observed that he could not consent to "any abridgement of the rights of American citizens in any respect. The honor and self-respect of the nation is involved. . . . Once accept a single abatement of right and many other humiliations would certainly follow, and the whole fine fabric of international law might crumble under our hands." Wilson likewise held to his notion that Americans were uniquely "a body of idealists, much more ready to lay down their lives for a thought than for a dollar"; that they were the "trustees of the moral judgment of the world"; and that other nations looked to them "to keep even the balance of the whole world of thought." Thus, there was "a price too high to pay even for peace and that was the price of self-respect, of duties abdicated, of glorious opportunities neglected."

Wilson's early biographer, Ray Stannard Baker, wrote in reference to the war issue as it developed throughout 1916 that "events" closed upon Wilson "like the jaws of some monstrous, inexhorable vise." One of these jaws was Wilson's idealism; the other was the rising clamor for war among a growing segment of influential Americans. Wilson's depictions of American high-mindedness contrasted starkly with characterizations of the "Hun," luridly drawn by a large segment of the press. The German people, as it was generally told, had been caught in the toils of a bestial leadership (usually depicted as the Kaiser in a spike helmet) that had caused them to shed their veneer of civilization and revert to a state of savagery whose main mark was blood lust.

Wilson was not a demagogue, not one to run at the head of the pack and yelp the loudest. Still, if run he must, then he must also put the rising wave of passion to the end of an enlightened objective—that is, toward extending and upholding the principles of international comity. On January 22, 1917, insofar as his principles were concerned, he seemed not to have regarded Germany as much more blameworthy than the Allies. On that day he faced the Senate to make a moving appeal for a termination of the war, a "peace without victory." "There must not be a balance of power, but a community of power," he said, concluding that he was "speaking for the silent masses of mankind everywhere."

But nine days later, a rapidly expanding American military and economic aid to the Allies caused Germany to announce the resumption of unrestricted submarine warfare. Wilson was stunned. Germany had taken the action that by his own explicit definition had rent the fabric of international law. Still, he recoiled from the barbarism of war, and it is surely to his credit that during those trying days of February and

March 1917, when every road to peace seemed to be closing, he weighed each action against what he knew would be the judgment of history, a judgment that, when finally rendered, was to affirm the value of peace over that of war.

Wilson's cabinet chafed at his seeming inactivity. Ray Stannard Baker says that "customary mild discussion began to give way to emphatic argument and patriotic oratory." The meeting of February 21 "came as near being a cabinet crisis as the American system is able to produce." In the course of the round of solemn pronouncements, full of high-minded feeling for the country's "honor," Secretary of the Interior Franklin K. Lane asked "whether it was true that German authorities had stripped the wives of American consuls to search for 'writing on their flesh.'" On March 12, after some wrangling over a last-ditch stand taken by a small group of antiwar congressmen, led by Senator Bob La Follette of Wisconsin, Wilson ordered the arming of American merchantmen.

Then came the dramatic news that many Americans took to be the final clarification of the problem of peace or war. On March 15, the Russian czar abdicated. Beneath all the lofty and not so lofty pronouncements on why the war was being fought, a truth seemed to emerge. This was a war of democracy against autocracy. "William of Germany is now the only living exponent of absolutism that the democracies of the world need fear," said Illinois's *Springfield Republican.*

On Friday, March 9, the president went to bed with a cold, and for the next ten days he stayed there, almost isolated. On the nineteenth he conferred with Secretary of State Robert Lansing, who from the beginning never seemed to have doubted which force represented righteousness. Lansing found Wilson "still seeking some way to avoid the final catastrophe." According to Baker, Lansing felt the president was "resisting the irresistible logic of events." Meanwhile, the engines of war increased their speed. Defense committees sprang up and sermons were preached to call Americans to face the larger issue of moral righteousness and to denounce pacifism. The United States was already at war, many were saying.

Finally Wilson's indecision left him. Powerfully impelling him to depart from agonizing indecision to a clear affirmation of war was his conviction that America should participate in, and even dominate, the peace conference. According to Baker, David Lloyd George, the British prime minister, reportedly told Walter Hines Page, the enthusiastically prowar American ambassador to Britain, that he would especially welcome the American entrance into the war because "your Government will then participate in the conference that concludes the peace. I especially desire this because of your President's cool and patient and humane counsel which will be wholesome for us all."

On March 20, at 2:30 P.M., the cabinet met again. Wilson asked two questions: Should Congress be called into extra session, earlier than April 16 when it was to resume? And if so, what should he say to it respecting the crisis with Germany? Each member was asked to give his views. All said they thought a state of war with Germany ought to be recognized and that Congress should be called to meet before April 16. In the course of his comments Postmaster General A. S. Burleson read several telegrams to illustrate the force of a pro-war public opinion. "We are not governed by public opinion," said Wilson. "I want to do right whether it is popular or not." The meeting ended at five o'clock with Wilson still giving no sign of what he would do. But the next morning he announced the convening of Congress for April 2, to consider "grave questions of national policy." There followed a series of actions in the way of military preparation that anticipated war.

While Wilson's conduct of events seemed quick and sure, troubling doubts continued to intrude into his thinking. Sometime on the evening before he was to read his war message to Congress, Wilson sent for Frank I. Cobb, an editorial writer for the *New York World.* He liked Cobb and thought him an intelligent person of acute discernment; occasionally, when he was trying to think through a problem, he would ask Cobb to think it through with him. That night, though, there was some mix-up in the message from Wilson to Cobb and it was not until 1:00 A.M. on April 2 that Cobb got there. Cobb found "the old man" waiting for him, "sitting in his study with the typewriter on his table where he used to type his own messages." Cobb had never seen Wilson so worn looking. He told the president he looked as if he had not been sleeping and Wilson said that was true. Wilson then said he probably would go before Congress to ask for a declaration of war, "and he'd never been so uncertain about anything in his life as about that decision. For nights, he said, he'd been lying awake going over the whole situation." Wilson put his hand on the table and tapped some sheets with his finger. It was his war message. "He said he couldn't see any alternative, that he had tried every way he knew to avoid war. . . . 'Is there anything else I can do?' "

Cobb, as one might suppose, ventured no opposing view. As he saw it, Wilson's hand had been forced. " 'Yes,' Wilson said,

> "but do you know what that means? . . . It means . . . an attempt to reconstruct a peacetime civilization with war standards, and at the end of the war there will be no bystanders with sufficient power to influence the terms. There won't be any peace standards left to work with. . . . Once lead this people into war . . . and they'll forget there ever was such a thing as tolerance. To fight you must be brutal and ruthless, and the spirit of

ruthless brutality will enter into the very fibre of our national life, infecting Congress, the courts, the policeman on the beat, the man on the street."

Then Wilson cried out, " 'If there is any alternative, for God's sake, let's take it.' " Wilson was "uncanny" that night, Cobb said.

It is possible that Cobb, when later recalling his evening's visit with Wilson, put words into the president's mouth that reflected how Cobb himself judged the postwar year. Nonetheless, the large point was doubtless Wilson's, although his appeal to heaven was somewhat hyperbolic. He could not sweep back the tide, remake decisions, and erase solemn pronouncements; nor could he cool the fever for war that had been building for a year.

Moreover, as profoundly as Wilson shrank from an American participation in the conflict, there was *one* condition that would justify it. If nations could be raised to cooperate in a new order of law that would insure justice and equity for all people, then America's entrance into the war would be a moral obligation. Whatever excess of bigotry or intolerance the war fever might produce would be a debit on the ledger book, but what was this against the prospect of a world whose affairs could be brought into final order and peace forever secured. Such would have to be the position of any rational person who affirmed an evolutionary progression toward an enlightened order in the politics of the world.

The night had nearly run its course when Cobb left the White House. When the sun came up, Pennsylvania Avenue was again filled with people, charged with an electric surge of expectation. They carried small American flags, the highest sign of their common unity. Sparsely scattered among them were the few who wore white armbands: pacifists, Socialists, and some students from Columbia University, many of whom were Jewish. The war was not their business. Besides, had it not been in France that anti-Semitism had recently been most virulent?

At 8:00 A.M. Wilson and Mrs. Wilson left the White House to play golf for a while. The exercise, it was thought, might enable Wilson to sleep before going up to the Capitol. After that, he remained secluded, assuming that by mid-afternoon Congress would call to say it awaited him.

At the Capitol, one of the noisiest advocates of war, Republican Senator Henry Cabot Lodge of Massachusetts, was sitting in his office when he was summoned to the door. A group of young people wished to register their opposition to the war. An argument developed. One of the group called Lodge a "coward." "You are a liar," Lodge reportedly said, and then struck his accuser a sharp blow to the face. The young man was a recent graduate of Princeton, where he had excelled in athletics. His face bloodied, he retired from the scene. Lodge had given "the only appropriate reply," declared the *Washington Post*. The *Post* also thought it significant that Lodge's critic "was said to have a German name."

Congress assembled at noon, while at the White House Wilson restlessly awaited the news that the body was organized and ready to receive him. It was after 4:30 P.M. that the word came: Wilson would be received at 8:30 P.M. the message said. At 8:10 P.M. Mrs. Wilson left to sit in the gallery with the wives of the cabinet members. Wilson left ten minutes later. With him were his personal physician, Cary T. Grayson; his secretary, Joseph P. Tumulty; and an army colonel.

Some three hours previous, Secretary of War Newton D. Baker had received a message from Secretary of State Lansing. In the interest of the president's safety, could an army cavalry unit be provided to supplement the usual police escort to the Capitol? The procession provided a sight that raised the spirit of patriotism to near ecstatic heights. Wilson, his features set in grim lines, looked straight ahead. The cavalry troop, moving with him, added the motif of war. A light rain fell, causing the streets to glisten and reflect the electric lights above them. Ahead the newly illuminated Capitol shone under the dark sky.

At 8:30 P.M. the Speaker of the House announced, "The President of the United States." All rose and applauded vigorously. Wilson walked in crisply, placed his manuscript on the podium, and with a hint of impatience, waited for the applause to cease. The hint brought immediate silence. Wilson then began to read, deliberately and without oratorical flourishes; only occasionally did he look up from his text, and then briefly.

The president began with a recitation of the injuries that Americans had suffered as a result of the German policy of unlimited submarine warfare. It was this action that had so clearly violated international law. Germany was "throwing to the winds all scruples of humanity or of respect for the understandings that were supposed to underlie the intercourse of the world," Wilson accused. It was a war against all mankind that cut to the roots of human life.

There was, the president insisted, one choice the nation could not make. It could not "choose the path of submission and suffer the most sacred rights of our Nation and our people to be ignored or violated." He therefore advised Congress to "accept the status of belligerent" that had been thrust upon the government and the people of the United States. The remainder of the address was a statement of the ends for which America would fight: "Our object . . . is to vindicate the principles of peace and justice in the life of the world as against autocratic power."

America was not fighting the German people, it was fighting a system. The system must be changed so that the voice of the people everywhere could be heard by those who governed them. Wilson noted that Russia had recently made itself fit for the new world that was coming. He concluded with a soaring statement of the absolute selflessness with which America fought:

> The world must be made safe for democracy. Its peace must be planted upon the tested foundations of political liberty. . . . We are but one of the champions of the rights of mankind. We shall be satisfied when those rights have been made as secure as the faith and freedom of nations can make them. . . . [These rights are] more precious than peace, and we shall fight for the things which we have always carried nearest our hearts, for democracy, for the right of those who submit to authority to have a voice in their governments, for the rights and liberties of small nations, for a universal dominion of right by such a concert of free people as shall bring peace and safety to all nations and make the world itself at last free.

When Wilson had finished he received a great ovation. Ashen-faced, he leaned heavily on Secret Service Agent Edmund Starling as he made his way to the president's anteroom to wait for Mrs. Wilson.

The president advanced with forceful certainty on the issue of remaking the world. In a series of addresses from January to December 1918, he defined the ends for which the nation fought. On January 8, he set forth his Fourteen Points, the first thirteen being conditions of a new world order that should exist for subject and occupied peoples as "the only possible program." Point Fourteen was the bedrock for the world revolution America was leading: "a general association of nations . . . formed under specific covenants for the purpose of affording mutual guarantees of political independence and territorial integrity to the great and small alike."

On February 11, Wilson gave the world his "four principles." On July 4, at Mount Vernon, he defined "four ends" that had to be realized before peace could come—ends he summarized in one sentence: "What we seek is the reign of law based upon the consent of the governed and sustained by the organized opinion of mankind." On September 27, in a speech in New York, he referred again to the Fourteen Points, putting a particular emphasis on the League of Nations as "an indispensable instrumentality": "Without such an instrumentality, by which the peace of the world can be guaranteed, peace will rest in part upon the word of outlaws, and only upon that word."

Meanwhile, George Creel, the head of the Committee on Public Information, worked with great energy and imagination to make sure that Wilson's ideas were heard and understood the world over. So effective was he that the American flag became, for many people of the world, the symbol of their redemption.

In their soaring idealism Wilson's speeches were noble and dramatic, but, tragically, ascended far beyond the reality that characterized the treatment of many white Americans toward their black compatriots. Nothing is so contradictory, or so painful to contemplate, as the fact that as Wilson launched his Great Crusade, mob violence against blacks radically increased.

One such incident occurred just a month after the war began. In May 1917, a sixteen-year-old white girl was raped and then decapitated in a river bottom just outside Memphis, Tennessee. Suspicion was directed at a half-witted Negro named Eli Persons, who was picked up and taken to Nashville for safekeeping. On Saturday, May 19, the sheriff of Shelby County demanded Persons's return. Sunday word circulated around Memphis that the criminal court was trying to find a lawyer to defend Persons, but none could be found.

By daylight on Monday, armed men in "hundreds of automobiles" began positioning themselves along the railroad line leading from Nashville to Memphis. Even the Illinois Central train that ran from Chicago to New Orleans through Memphis was stopped and searched on the far-fetched assumption that Persons might be on it. Throughout the day automobiles and wagons began to converge at a point in the lowlands near the site of the crime. By Monday night a crowd estimated at four thousand had gathered. "Fully 500 cars" from Memphis were parked on each side of the road for a mile or more. A "long lank countryman," brandishing a pistol in one hand and a swinging lantern in the other, supervised the parking, ordering vehicles to line up off the road or he would "shoot them in line."

That night hundreds of men left their cars, descended the embankment, and sat around campfires. As they drank their whiskey the euphoria of the cause that bound them took hold. They talked obscenely of the grisly prospect of the next day. A story circulated among them that the proof of Persons's guilt was in a photograph taken of the dead girl's eyes. The last thing she had seen, it was said, would be registered on the film, and when the film had been developed, the image of Persons appeared.

Before daybreak on Tuesday, a hundred men in some twenty automobiles headed for neighboring Holly Springs, Mississippi, to intercept the Frisco train from Nashville. Anticipating this, however, deputies took Persons off the train at Potts Camp, a small community outside Holly Springs. So informed, the mob went to Potts Camp, seized Persons, and placed him in the fastest automobile for the return trip to Memphis.

Back at the riverbottom there was a prefiguring enactment of the event about to occur. At 8:00 P.M. the mother of the murdered girl was brought on the scene, and a minute or two later the car carrying Persons arrived. One of the men in the car stood up and raised his hand for silence. Then he asked the mother to speak.

"I want to thank all my friends who have worked so hard in my behalf. Let the negro suffer as my little girl suffered, only 10 times worse."

"Burn him," the crowd cried.

"Yes, burn him on the spot where he killed my little girl," said the mother.

Several men began to tie Persons to a stake, but one of the leaders objected because not all the spectators could see what was happening. So Persons was taken down the embankment and chained to a log, where all could see. As brush was piled around him the mob jeered. Then, in the midst of the milling crowd, a large man called Brother Royal, a leader of a rural religious sect, held up his hand for attention. "It has been suggested that prayer be offered," he said, "but I am opposed to that because he didn't give the little lady an opportunity for prayer."

Persons silently suffered the flames as the mob went into an ecstasy of screaming obscenities and gibberish. Later, when the fire had died, some of the leaders cut the heart from the body and dismembered the charred remains. On Beale Street, Persons's head and a leg were thrown among a group of blacks, and a barber shop displayed a burnt remnant.

Two days after Persons's murder one of the leading citizens of Memphis addressed a bond rally in the city's Court Square. He proposed to define the great issue facing the people of Memphis. That issue was, he said, "whether the Germanic powers should trample upon and fling to the winds the rules of international law. We could not, with honor and self respect, let the hands of civilization be set back a hundred years." Another speaker said that "Germany is the Judas among the nations of the earth."

Yet less than a year later Jim McIllheron, another black, was tortured with red-hot irons and burned alive at Estill Springs, Tennessee. A written protest by blacks was sent to President Wilson; but the response came from Attorney General Thomas W. Gregory. He said that the federal government had no jurisdiction in the matter because the crime was in no way connected with the war effort.

But in the full tide of war, these atrocities were blotted from the national conscience. What a swell of power and unity the war brought to white America the summer of 1918. Thomas Wolfe, in "The Four Lost Men," described the exultation he felt from the war as he returned home to Asheville from the University of North Carolina: "The war seemed to have collected in a single image of joy, and power, and proud compacted might all the thousand images of joy and power and all-exulting life which we had always had, for which we had never had a word before. Over the fields of silent and mysterious night it seemed that we could hear the nation marching, that we could hear, soft and thunderous in the night, the million-footed unison of marching men. And that single glorious image of all-collected joy and unity and might had given new life and new hope to all of us."

It was a war for singing: Irving Berlin's "Oh, How I Hate to Get Up," Zo Elliott's sentimental "There's a Long, Long Trail," and Geoffrey O'Hara's "K–K–K–Katy." The rallying song of World War I, however, was George M. Cohan's "Over There," dashed off by Cohan as he rode from Long Island into Manhattan on the morning after Wilson's message. Enrico Caruso, wherever he went, sang it—a verse in English, a verse in French, and a concluding verse in English that ended with the rousing line, "And we won't be back til it's over over there!" Caruso's wife, Dorothy, to whom he had just been married, taught him the lyrics of the song, reading the words over to him several times until almost every problem of pronunciation had been overcome. Caruso first sang "Over There" at an Ocean Grove concert on July 27, "his audience cheering and waving flags, many of its members in tears despite the rolled Italian *r*s and words which emerged strangely as 'Hover Dere.' "

Louise Homer, the American-born contralto who sang Wagnerian roles at the Metropolitan, also placed her art at the disposal of patriotism. On a concert tour in the fall of 1917, she opened each appearance with "The Star-Spangled Banner." Coming on stage, she would move to where the American flag stood in its standard, resolutely remove it, and with its folds pressed to her ample bosom, move to the center of the stage. It was verily, as her biographer says, "a breathless moment." Then, "when she had sung one verse, and had her audience poised in a moment of supreme vulnerability, she would command them to sing, and while her own far-flung, ringing tones led the way, there would be a spontaneous outpouring of emotion."

Still, even the best singing could not mute the discordant note of hysteria. In his war message Wilson had said, "We have no quarrel with the German people. We have no feeling towards them but one of sympathy and friendship." True, it was at the person of the German soldier that Wilson had declared the American soldier should aim his gun, but this was the only way to get at the "system," and changing this system was the object of America's crusade. Many Americans were incapable of making that distinction. The president's vivid portrayals of American high-mindedness contrasted with the increasing darkness of a press-created baleful image of the "Hun."

Unquestionably, the most effective piece of propagandist image making was written by the Spanish novelist Vicente Blasco-Ibanez. *The Four Horsemen of the Apocalypse* was read throughout the Allied countries in 1917 and was then published in the United States in 1918 by E. P. Dutton. The book was a great success, establishing "the world's record for sales." Blasco-Ibanez, although thought by many to be a prophet, was actually a meretricious person who apparently affirmed nothing except his own variant of Republicanism and the sale of his books. Yet his portrayal of the war in apocalyptic terms, and his depiction of Germans as essentially subhuman, must have confirmed in the minds of those many Americans who read his novel a conviction that the struggle pitted the hosts of heaven against those of hell.

The epitome of the "Hun" was the Kaiser. No figure was put to more frequent use in inflaming the public mind to exalted reaches of patriotic excess than that of the German emperor. Commercial artists portrayed him in magazines and newspapers as a beast in whose glittering eyes lurked the fires of murder and rape. And in 1918 the subject of rape was one best calculated to rivet the attention of those seeking to plumb to new depths the hellishness of the "Hun." In *McClure's Magazine* for December 1918 was a full-page illustration depicting an intense moment in the story it accompanied. Somewhere in Europe the delirious heroine lay cringing in her bed, while above her stood a spectral Kaiser. " 'You— Monster—you Kaiser!' she cried out." As she uttered these words the musing physician standing nearby began to suspect the source of his febrile patient's malady. She had been a victim of the unbridled lust of the Hun. No doubt it was all deliciously thrilling and, of course, gave a transcendent aura of godliness to the crusade "over there."

But what of Americans of German descent who were over here, more than one-quarter of the nation's population? Louis P. Lochner, in *Always the Unexpected*, provides a litany of the barbarous cruelties of war hysteria: Pastor Hebert S. Bigelow of Cincinnati was forcibly taken into Kentucky "where he was horsewhipped for praying that the soul of the Kaiser might be redeemed from pride and lust of power." A German coal miner, Robert P. Prager, was lynched at Collinsville, Illinois, "for alleged remarks derogatory to President Wilson." At Salisbury, Pennsylvania, Charles Klinge was beaten and made to walk along the street with a dog chain around his neck for making supposedly disloyal remarks. And so it went.

In times of public hysteria there is usually one voice that soars above the others in execrating the presumed menace to community well-being. In 1918 that peerless patriot was Arthur Guy Empey, reportedly one of the first Americans to have gone "over the top." In any case, once over he did not tarry but returned shortly to the United States to inform Americans of the despicable character of the enemy. Empey, "the soldier with a message," had an article, "Our Real Enemy," in the "Win the War" issue of *McClure's Magazine* of July 1918. The "real enemy" was American apathy, and when the time came—"and it will, as sure as there is a God in heaven"—when 95 percent of the American public ask themselves the question, " 'Why don't *I* do something?' then and only then will victory loom in sight."

What was it Empey would have Americans do? They must recognize that they were not fighting a system but were "*at war . . . with the German people, and everything connected with Germany* and the sooner we realize this, the sooner our boys will come marching home, with German helmets stuck on the tips of their bayonets, and with that baby-killing, crucifying Kaiser, and his idiotic son, the Crown Prince, by the scruff of the neck." A big order, yes, but Empey had even more to recommend. He told every American to "constitute yourself a secret-service agent, and if at any time you hear a remark against our Government or against our Allies . . . either arrest that person, or report to your nearest police station. . . . Perhaps after the war we will see him again, and perhaps we won't. Let us hope we won't, for the United States will be well rid of a parasite on the folds of the Star Spangled Banner."

Was Wilson concerned about this vulgar and strident anti-Germanism that seemed to possess so many Americans and that such a large element of the press cultivated? The historian Eric Goldman says that the president "raised not a finger." Perhaps Wilson thought the inhumane consequences of this hysteria were part of the overall price America had to pay to achieve a humane world. With victory, all could be made new; the ledger could then be balanced. One may presume that Wilson thought this, but at the same time it is a fact that the public Wilson, war or no war, showed a general insensitivity to human injustice in his own native land, and it may have been that the anti-German madness concerned him no more than the inhuman consequences of America's traditional racism toward blacks.

What of those luminous names in higher education? Did any publicly appear to advise reflection and moderation in the face of the excesses that the war fever had reached? Most, it appears, put the current affairs segment of their classroom oratory to support of the Great Crusade. One of the most significant endorsements came from Professor John Dewey of Columbia University. In an article in the *New Republic* during the summer of 1917, he endorsed the position that the war objectives Wilson had set down made the conflict morally acceptable and necessary.

Dewey's position as one of the foremost philosophers in academic life made his endorsement of the war significant, but to one intellectual the article was a knuckling under to popular pressure. Randolph Bourne, thirty-one years old, with a disfigured face and a curved spine, saw the intolerance and hysteria allowed by Wilson and his academic followers as the first tragedy of the war. In an article in the October 10, 1917, issue of *The Seven Arts,* entitled "Twilight of Idols," Bourne wrote of his antipathy for "a philosopher who senses so little the sinister forces of the war, who is so much more concerned over the excesses of the pacifists than over the excesses of military policy, who can feel only amusement at the idea that any one should try to conscript thought, who assumes with it the mob fanaticisms, the injustices and hatreds, that are organically bound up with it, is speaking to another element of the younger intelligentsia than that to which I belong."

Bourne was appalled at "the relative ease with which the pragmatist intellectuals, with Professor Dewey at the head, have moved out of their philosophy, bag and baggage, from education to war." There seemed to have been "a peculiar congeniality between the war and these men. It is as if the war and they had been waiting for each other." America, Bourne concluded, was in the war because it had practiced an "instrumentalism" (Dewey's phrase denoting a social pragmatism) for uncertain objectives, "instead of creating new values and setting at once a large standard to which the nation might repair."

What was this "large standard" that Bourne talked about? He did not say, but one can presume he meant a standard by which the people of the world could better their lives and grow in the spirit of community without having to go to war or to burn a man at the stake. Bourne died of the flu several days after the Armistice, but had he lived through that unbelievable year following the end of the war, he would surely have been at an even greater loss to find his standard.

Thus America went to war, and the engines of war began to run with increasing momentum. The bigotry and hysteria Wilson had professed to fear, according to Cobb, he feared no longer because its energy was aimed at a God-sanctioned end, and all the powers of persuasion that the country's masters of rhetoric—politicians, teachers, and pulpiteers—could contrive was fuel for war's throbbing power. Wilson led them. He spoke ringingly of destiny, fulfillment, and a transcendent selflessness. With an implacable will he pursued the course he had set, refusing to see anything but the luminous vision ahead. The deceit, lying, and killing that war brought did not desecrate that vision. It was the sacrificial offering to time's promise, made with a faith such as Abraham had shown when he offered to God the sacrifice of his son, Isaac.

SOURCES

Information about the city of Washington on the eve of Wilson's inauguaration and the armistice celebration is from the *Washington Post*. Wilson's statements, bespeaking the idealism of his prewar neutrality, are quoted in William L. Langer, "From Isolation to Mediation," in *Woodrow Wilson and the World of Today*, ed. Arthur F. Dudden (Philadelphia, 1957). The account of Wilson's late-night musings with journalist Frank I. Cobb is from *Cobb of the World, a Leader in Liberalism, Compiled from His Editorial Articles and Public Addresses*, comp. John L. Heaton (New York, 1924). Another journalist, the head of the Press Bureau of the American Peace Commission and a man who had begun his distinguished career on the old *Chicago Record*, was Ray Stannard Baker. The material on Wilson's Cabinet meetings and the war declaration is from Baker's *Woodrow Wilson and World Settlement* (New York, 1922).

The description of the burning of Eli Persons is from William D. Miller, *Memphis during the Progressive Era* (Madison, Wisc., 1953). The section on Caruso singing "Over There" is from Stanley Jackson, *Caruso* (New York, 1972) and from Dorothy Caruso, *Enrico Caruso: His Life and Death* (New York, 1945). Louise Homer's contribution to wartime music is from Ann Homer, *Louise Homer and the Golden Age of Opera* (New York, 1974). Information on the sales of Blasco-Ibanez's *Four Horsemen of the Apocalypse* is from *Twentieth Century Authors: A Biographical Dictionary of Modern Literature*, ed. Stanley J. Kunitz and Howard Haycroft (New York, 1942).

FURTHER READING

The subject of Woodrow Wilson and America's entry into the First World War has been treated by historians in a succession of interpretive works that began to appear almost as soon as the war ended. The first was John Spencer Bassett, *Our War with Germany* (New York, 1919), followed two years later by John B. McMaster, *United States in the World War*, 2 vols. (New York, 1918–20). These early chronicles, which at that time could not but entirely justify the war, were succeeded in the mid-1930s by a critical view of America's participation. Walter Millis, *Road to War, 1914–1917* (Boston and New York, 1935) and C. C. Tansill, *America Goes to War* (Boston, 1938) were the principal voices in presenting this major revision. Their main point was that the United States, by permitting the financing of a significant Allied arms supply by American capital, was responsible for triggering in early 1917

Germany's resumption of unrestricted submarine warfare. A second theme was that America entered the war because of an inept diplomacy, the worst feature of which was the fawning susceptibility of its diplomats to the smooth-talking British.

In more recent years, books on Wilson and America's entry into the war have examined the subject with respect to its more complex character. See, for example, John Milton Cooper, *The Warrior and the Priest* (Cambridge, 1983). The barbaric elements of anti-Germanism that were a part of the domestic scene during the war are described in David Kennedy, *Over Here* (New York, 1980).

CHAPTER

1

Peace

AFTER JULY 1918, the German command recognized that the war had been lost, and on October 1, General Eric Ludendorff asked his government to negotiate an armistice. On October 6, the United States government, through the Swiss Legation in Washington, received a note from the new German chancellor, Prince Max of Baden, asking for an immediate armistice preparatory to peace negotiations. Further, as a pledge of its good faith, the note stated, the German government "accepts, as a basis for the peace negotiations, the program laid down by the president of the United States in his message to Congress of January 8, 1918 and in his subsequent pronouncements." That is, Germany accepted the Fourteen Points.

A month of note interchange followed. On October 8, President Wilson demanded the evacuation of invaded territory. The next day, the three Allied prime ministers, meeting in Paris, telegraphed Wilson that they wanted not only evacuation but assurances that Germany would be militarily incapable of resuming the war.

On October 14, Washington received German assurances that invaded territory would be evacuated. Wilson replied that same day, adding to his demand for evacuation the further condition that the German army disarm to a point that would be acceptable to the Allied military leaders. With this condition "Professor" Wilson added a moralizing lecture: not only must the German army be rendered incapable of further action, but

the President feels that it is also his duty to add that neither of the Governments with which the Government of the United States is associated as a belligerent will consent to consider an armistice so long as the armed forces of Germany continue the illegal and inhumane practices which they still persist in. At the very time that the German Government approaches the Government of the United States with proposals of peace, its submarines are engaged in sinking passenger ships at sea, and not the ships alone but the very boats in which their passengers and crews seek to make their way to safety.

Finally, Wilson wanted to know "beyond a peradventure" with whom he was dealing. He cited the words of his Fourth of July Mount Vernon address that there must be a "destruction of every arbitrary power anywhere that can separately, secretly, and of its single choice disturb the peace of the world." Peace, he insisted, must come "by the action of the German people themselves."

Germany responded on October 20, evading the issue of disarmament but asking Wilson to do nothing "which would be irreconcilable with the honor of the German people, and with opening a way to a peace of justice." The note protested Wilson's charges of inhumanity and concluded with a statement of the changes in process in governmental structure that would assure all that the German government did indeed rest on a popular base.

Wilson responded on October 21, and two days later he read his response to the "President's War Council," among whose members present that day were Bernard Baruch, chairman of the War Industries Board; Vance McCormick, chairman of the Democratic Committee; and Herbert Hoover, War Food administrator. The president reiterated the necessity of German disarmament and added that he deemed it "his duty to say again . . . that the only armistice he would feel justified in submitting for consideration would be one which should leave the United States and the powers associated with her in a position to enforce any arrangements that may be entered into and to make a renewal of hostilities on the part of Germany impossible." Much discussion followed Wilson's statement, with McCormick observing that he would like to see a complete surrender with an occupation of Berlin. Hoover rejoined that he wanted the war ended and that he "took no stock in a triumphal march down the Unter den Linden."

From Hoover's account of the armistice negotiations, it appears that for Wilson the biggest obstacle to an armistice declaration was his concern that he was dealing with a government that truly represented the German people. As Hoover reported, it did not appear to Wilson "that the principle of a Government responsible to the German people has yet been fully worked out." In fact, said Wilson, he would have to use "harsh words" to insure this. If he, Wilson, had to deal with "the military masters and the monarchical autocrats of Germany," then an armistice agreement "must demand, not peace negotiations, but surrender."

In the meantime, young men by the thousands continued to die daily. Colonel E. M. House, Wilson's adviser and detail man for the large issues, thought that the president was getting on shaky ground. On October 24, House noted in his journal that he was "disturbed" by Wilson's concern over the finer points as to who was speaking for the German people. The president had gone "into a long and offensive discussion which may have the effect of stiffening German resistance and welding the people together back of the military leaders. . . . The Germans may accept the President's terms without question, but if they do not and the war is prolonged, he has taken the entire responsibility upon himself."

The German government responded to Wilson's message of October 21 on the following day. It said that the authority to make decisions was now in the hands of "the people," both "actually and constitutionally," and that the military powers were subject to this authority. The implication was that Wilson should stop his moralizing and lecturing and transmit to Allied associates "the proposals for an armistice, which is the first step toward a peace of justice, as described by the President in his pronouncements."

Wilson did just that, and in Paris, Colonel House worked feverishly for a reconciliation of differences. Finally, on November 3, the president sent the German government, through Secretary of State Lansing, a general statement of the conditions for an armistice. Yes, an armistice could be arranged on the basis of the Fourteen Points and subsequent pronouncements, *but* there were three conditions: the German government would have to accept the sweeping conditions for disarmament prepared by the Allied military leaders; it should understand "that compensation will be made by Germany for all damage done to the civilian population of the Allies"; and the Allied governments would interpret freely for themselves the meaning of the "freedom of the seas" provision of the Fourteen Points.

On the fighting front the war was ending almost blithely, according to a rhapsodic report on November 3 from a *New York Times* correspondent. There had been nothing in the war "more picturesque" than the fifty or so American trucks "with our doughboys, with ready rifles, perched on the hoods and machine guns mounted above the drivers' heads, filled with fighting men on tiptoe for a fight, roaring northward on a grand hunt for the Germans."

On November 7, German representatives met with the Allied Military Commission at General Foch's headquarters. Possibly it was this meeting that caused the celebration of the "false armistice." A dispatch, cabled from France, picked up and circulated throughout the country by a news agency, declared that an armistice was to be signed at 11:00 A.M. and the fighting would end at 2:00 P.M. It was around noon in New York when whistles suddenly began to blow. Everyone knew what it meant: Germany had surrendered. Newsboys were immediately on the street shouting that the war was over.

Harold Stearns, the young "bohemian" who had taken an unexcited and even critical view of the war, described the occasion as he recalled it some years later. He had been to visit his publisher, Horace Liveright, and the two of them, having decided to lunch together, left the Liveright office on Fortieth Street and walked up Broadway toward Forty-second, when bedlam broke out. At that time the old Knickerbocker Hotel stood on the southeast corner of Forty-second Street and Broadway. Looking high up, Stearns and Liveright witnessed the object of a growing crowd's attention. On a small balcony outside his apartment stood Enrico Caruso and his wife, Dorothy, throwing flowers to the crowd below.

Dorothy Caruso also described the episode. She and her husband were having lunch in their apartment when they heard voices in the street shouting for Caruso. So the great tenor went out on a balcony that was draped by two huge flags, Italian and American. In this setting he sang the national anthems of America, England, France, and Italy. The crowd roared "More!" and Caruso invited the people to sing with him. Dorothy Caruso described the ecstatic thrill of hearing thousands of voices welling up as Caruso's voice soared above them all. In response, she phoned the florist in the hotel lobby to ask that he send up all his flowers—red roses, white carnations, and blue violets—which she and her husband then threw to the crowd.

That afternoon Americans learned that, for the moment, their excitement had been premature. Nonetheless, the collapse of Imperial Germany was at hand. Revolutionaries had already taken over the naval bases at Kiel and Wilhelshaven and the cities of Lubeck, Bremen, and Hamburg. The most shaking event in those early days of November, however, was the fall of the established order in Munich. King Ludwig III, of the House of Wittelsbach, whose family had claimed the fealty of Bavarians for a thousand years, left the royal residence in the dead of night, a tottering and befuddled old man with a box of cigars tucked under his arm. As he departed, the Socialist Kurt Eisner, drama critic, was released from prison, to become the minister president of the Free State of Bavaria. What followed that—to anticipate the continuing drama in Munich—was the public emergence of Adolph Hitler.

The revolt in Berlin began on November 9. Military units stationed in the city to keep order joined with the revolutionaries. In the course of the day, Prince Max handed over the chancellorship to the chairman of the Majority Socialist party, Fritz Ebert. The new German Republic was proclaimed from the steps of the Reichstag.

At Spa, a Belgian resort, the kaiser consulted with army leaders. They could assure him nothing. In the early hours of November 10, the King of Prussia and Emperor of All Germany boarded his cream-and-gold private railroad car and crossed into Holland. The next morning, just as dawn was breaking, another railroad car, drawn up in the forest of Compiègne, became the scene of the first action of the day that would mark the end of the war. At 5:13 A.M., the German armistice delegation, headed by Matthias Erzberger, signed the articles prepared by the Allied command.

For five hours and forty-five minutes more men continued to die. Two hours after the armistice provisions had been signed, the American Second Army attacked in force just east of the Meuse River. The attack was preceded by an artillery barrage that the Germans answered in kind. For three hours the Americans swept forward, hurling themselves against the wire entanglements and taking a devastating fire. Then, as the *New York Times* of November 13 reported, "at exactly one minute of eleven, like a final thunder crash at the clearing of a storm, the guns on both sides abruptly ceased" and, more slowly, rifle fire diminished. For an instant there was silence, and then cheers came from the trenches on both sides of the line. "Against the skyline figures were suddenly silhouetted. They appeared cautiously at first, but soon growing bolder all along the line they stood upright." It was not more than one minute past the hour when "the rolling plain was alive with cheering, shouting men, friend and enemy alike. . . . Germans and Americans were coming along the narrow stretch of ground so fiercely fought over, some shyly and awkwardly, like schoolboys."

After four years and three months, after the sacrifice of ten million lives—a sacrifice ordered by the warring states for all of the holy causes they had claimed as uniquely their own—where was that final truth proclaimed in the perfervid utterances by a legion of patriotic orators? Those visions of a new dawn of peace in the unity of this presumed truth seemed nowhere at hand against the darkening turbulence of the breakdown of old forms and systems. In Russia, a new vision had been raised out of the seeming destitution and wreckage of the past, and to many it appeared that what had occurred in Russia would also occur in Germany.

In America spirits soared. Had not all that had been prophesied come true? Had not this war, like all previous wars fought by America, demonstrated that Americans were more surely in accord with the "right and true" than any other people in the world? Jubilant and hastily robed, people appeared on porches and in yards to exclaim over the news, and a few of the more ecstatic citizens brought forth pistols from behind the clock on the mantelpiece to fire into the air. As the day progressed, crowds gathered in the streets, formed impromptu parades, and listened again to patriotic declamations.

That night was the opening of the Metropolitan Opera season, and the program appropriately featured a French work, Camille Saint-Saëns's *Samson and Delilah.* No opening night was ever more moving. Ann Homer described the occasion as one in which "throughout the evening a victory mood shimmered up and down the rising tiers of red and gold." At the end of the first act, the singers staged a "victory pageant" for an audience thirsting for some action to express its jubilation. Unexpectedly, the curtains parted, displaying the entire company massed on the stage. Nothing could have been more appropriate than the presence of Louise Homer, the "Delilah" of the evening, standing just behind the footlights grasping the standard of a large American flag. To her right and left stood other principals in the cast holding the flags of Britain (Ananian), Italy (Caruso), France (Rocher), and Serbia (Reschiglian). Behind them stood the chorus, each member waving an American flag. Beginning with "The Star-Spangled Banner," the company sang in stirring succession the national anthems of the victorious nations. One presumes that by comparison the rest of the opera was relatively dull.

In Washington, Wilson announced the armistice to Congress and then proceeded to read its terms. He concluded with some observations regarding the revolution in Russia, directed to the revolutionary leaders but applying equally well to America and the world at large. The people of Russia, he said, would "never find the treasures of liberty they are in search of if they look for them by the light of the torch. They will find that every pathway that is stained with blood of their own brothers leads to the wilderness, not to the seat of their home." To Wilson, it may be said, brotherhood seemed to be a matter of national and even racial definition. But he was not pondering the subject at the moment. "Everything for which America fought has been accomplished," he told Congress.

That night "a spectacular climax" to the capital's peace observances occurred on the White House grounds. Forty-eight huge bonfires were kindled, and the crowd, according to the *Washington Post,* went into a state of near frenzy, "singing patriotic songs, tooting horns, clanging bells, and otherwise giving vent to their jubilation." Wilson joined the crowd for a few minutes and even participated in the singing. Joseph Tumulty, Wilson's aide and secretary, stood by the president and later recalled "how happy he looked," his face illumined with "a glow of satisfaction of one who realizes that he has fought for a principle and won."

There were some in the capital city who, preferring a more tasteful and solemn celebration of victory, conceived of a massive pageant, a kind of "hymn to victory" to be sung by the populace as a whole. The event was set for December 7. It was thought that a hundred thousand would attend to raise their voices in thanksgiving and triumph, but probably no more than thirty thousand actually showed up. Even so, there was a problem of how to get them all to sing in unison. This was solved by having twelve subleaders, on stands positioned around the field, who received their direction from the main leader on a central stage.

One of the features of the afternoon was the performance of a cantata, "The Spirit of Victory," sung by a choir from Howard University. This composition, "especially written for the occasion," was rendered as army planes wheeled and dove overhead. Presumably, the cantata was to well out of an inspirational genius induced by the mood of triumph and thanksgiving, but artistic immortality was not its fate. For many it seemed that the celebration of the armistice had been going on long enough.

SOURCES

As the text indicates, newspapers were the main source for this chapter. The recitation of negotiations leading to the armistice is standard textbook fare to which has been added material from Herbert Hoover's *Ordeal of Woodrow Wilson* (New York, 1958). On Wilson's response to the armistice, see the recollections of the president's personal secretary and assistant, Joseph P. Tumulty, in *Woodrow Wilson as I Knew Him* (New York, 1921). Harold Stearns's armistice recollection is from *The Street I Know: Reminiscences of Greenwich Village* (New York, 1935). Also used was Dorothy Caruso, *Enrico Caruso: His Life and Death* (New York, 1945).

FURTHER READING

Since the armistice celebration was a spontaneous affair the nation around, the source of its history is now primarily local newspapers. Research in any one of them on the armistice would be interesting work, conceivably productive of good reading.

2

The Soldiers Come Home

FOR A SHORT PERIOD, it would appear, the end of the war brought relief that it was over and expressions of gratitude to the soldiers who would soon be returning. Two days after the "false armistice," the Elgin Watch Company took out a full-page ad in the *New York Times* to give its "welcome home." "Victory," it proclaimed, and then came the exulting message: "Brave boys! Do you think we don't know the biggest thing that's issued from this awful struggle? Ah, but we do. It has purified and burned clear the high white flame of true Americanism. Through you and with you the world has found Brotherhood—the world has found God." And now for the other job, the statement continued, one that was "unparalleled in the constructive history of this world—the task of building up to the level of our new-found ideals and blood-bought vision of Brotherhood." In light of what was to come in the year ahead, that statement now sounds completely fatuous. Yet at the time it recognized that the war had to be put to an end higher than self-congratulation—that it could be justified only, if finally, the peoples of the world could be brought to a new level of unity.

On December 16, 1918, the *Leviathan* tied up at Pier 4 in Hoboken, New Jersey, with more than eight thousand returning soldiers aboard.

The *Leviathan* was herself a story. Built for the Hamburg-American Line, and christened the *Vaterland,* she was one of those luxurious and ornate giants of the sea of the early twentieth century. The shadow of war pursued the *Vaterland* across the Atlantic on her maiden voyage, and the ship reached New York just in time to claim the haven of a neutral port. Then, when the United States entered the war, the German crew that had remained aboard for three years subjected her to a thorough sabotage. Eventually, she was brought up to what was thought to be cruising order, and the American government, claiming the ship as a prize of war, rechristened her the *Leviathan.*

Reincarnated, the ship almost became the instrument of depriving the American public of some of the excitement of movie-going in the thirties and forties. The German crew that had sabotaged the ship had been clever; they had reversed the fans on the exhaust system. As a result, some of the crew members on the ship's trial run almost suffocated in their bunks. Young Humphrey Bogart was one of them.

The *Leviathan* was soon back in France, then returned to the United States on March 6, 1919, bearing ten thousand men of the New York 27th Division. It was a gray, rainy day, but from the moment the outline of the huge ship became discernible in the harbor mists, the air was rent with the sound of whistles, and the water churned as small craft capered about. At 12:12 P.M. the ship was again at Pier 4, as a band played the popular songs of the war, among which surely was "Over There." For most of the soldiers who lined the decks and whose faces were framed by every porthole, a solemn and even tearful moment came when the band played "Home, Sweet Home."

On May 6, the 77th Division paraded in New York City, from Washington Square up Fifth Avenue to 110th Street. Even though the day was chilly and rain threatened, over a million people watched. The march was preceded by a cortege in honor of the dead, and then came the twenty-seven thousand men of the 77th, marching in battalions, each of which stretched out for a little more than the length of a block. As the men marched abreast, from curb to curb, along the cavernous streets, their glittering bayonets rose and fell rhythmically. From a distance, noted the *New York Times,* "the bayonets . . . seemed thick-standing as a field of grain, and the battalions appeared like huge rectangles of olive drab cloth with a steel gray metallic mixture." Among the marchers were "men of every color of skin and cast of countenance," yet they were all stamped with "Americanism."

Compelling as was this feeling of national solidarity that came from witnessing these soldiers in battle array, the "Americanism" that presumably included the black soldier was something different in the minds of white Americans. A curious feature of the war had been the way in which American blacks, facing second-class citizenship at home, accepted the official pronouncements of the government concerning the war's purpose. Or, perhaps, their leadership had affected to accept them, thinking that finally they might turn them toward an easing of their own plight at home. In any case, over forty-thousand blacks went to France, more than one-third of the entire American Expeditionary

Force. Mostly they served in work battalions, unloading ships and constructing railroads behind the front lines. They performed prodigies of work and earned for themselves the picturesque sobriquet "jazzboes."

There were also black combat troops who were placed in battalion strength with the French army, and all served well. But even the black soldier's effective performance was not accepted simply as that of an American. He was praised, but praised for attributes that, in popular fancy, were characteristic of his race. The *New York Evening Sun,* for example, in giving the black soldier his due, boasted that "the negroes were, perhaps, the most proficient bayonet-fighters in the American Army. They simply doted on cold steel. . . . It was not long before the fame of the negro bayonet wielders spread among the Huns, and it was seldom that German troops would hold out when the yelling, sweating negroes, jumped into their trenches."

Of particular note was the story of a wounded black soldier who hurled himself into a German trench and was killed, but not before "he got at least one Hun with a good old southern shaving implement pressed into service for the occasion." "Yes sir," said the black who purportedly narrated this story, "We all did our share and we are all glad we did it. This was democracy's war. The negro troops assumed the burden of democracy along with the white and red troops. We did our share to keep America unchained, and we are all proud we did it."

There was also the inimitable humor that blacks supposedly brought to the war. The *New York Times Magazine* provided examples in a feature article, "Comic Anecdotes Brought Back by Negro Soldiers":

"What would you do if a pack of Germans suddenly came down right on top of us?" asked a Sergeant.

"Dey aint gwine to know where I is," replied the private.

"How is that, Sam?"

"Well, you see dey might know whar I wuz, but not whar I is."

And:

"Would you like to be in the airplane service?" an officer asked one of the negroes while he was watching a French machine sailing overhead.

"No Sah, not fo' mine," was the rejoinder.

"Why?" the officer persisted.

"Well, you see, ef I was up in dat dah machine an' de officer got kilt I'd have to get out and crank up de engine, wouldn't I? I wouldn't have nothin' to stan' on."

In January 1919, Columbia Records, aware of the attention being given the black soldier, released a record called "Dixie Song." Said Columbia: "Here's a Van and Schenck . . . [record] with a decidedly novel slant. 'Instead of picking melons off the vine, they're picking

Germans off the Rhine.' " The record was to be a "real tribute to the 'Smoke Brigade' that fought so bravely Over There."

The peerless hero of the war was, of course, Alvin C. York of Pall Mall, Tennessee, who on October 8, 1919, killed twenty Germans, captured 132 prisoners, and put thirty-five machine guns out of action. In the spring of 1919, Americans were given in detail, in newspapers, magazines, and a hurriedly constructed biography, the story of their great war hero. The picture was, in every detail, just as they knew it had to be. "Have you ever seen a gunman of the old Southwest?" the readers of the *Saturday Evening Post* were asked. "A real gunman, not the loud, quarrelsome, spurious saloon hero? Well, that's York. The same rather gentle voice in ordinary conversation, with a vibrant note when he is stirred that fairly trumpets danger; he has the same gray eyes, flecked with brown—eyes which can harden to pinpoints. He has the same unhurried, half-indolent confidence of manner. In his steady gaze is absolute sureness of self."

Other bits of biographical information ideally fitted the picture. York had been born on December 13, 1887, on a small farm in the Cumberland Mountains, one of eleven children. As a young man, he admitted, he "used to drink and gamble some" and when drinking he was "kind of liable to fight." Sometimes in his fights he used a pistol or a rifle— "peculiarly American weapons." There was a story told around Pall Mall about York's handiness with a pistol, a "true" story, interjected the author of the *Post* article. "Once, years ago, in a tavern row ... York averted bloodshed by suddenly clipping the head off a tree lizard with his six-shooter as the lizard was running up the base of a persimmon across the road. They just naturally quieted down after that."

Then York took stock of himself and his rowdy life, and in 1913 he joined the Church of Christ and Christian Union, a sect so lacking in theological subtlety that it opposed fighting in any form. Thus, when he was drafted he faced a difficult decision: Should he ask for an exemption as a conscientious objector? No, he decided, he wouldn't. He belonged to a church with a pacifist doctrine, "but he was not going to back out of serving his country." York told the *Post* interviewer how his fellow church members used to plead with him.

"I remember one day especially. A man had been arguing quite a while, so I said to him, 'If some feller was to come along and bust into your house and mistreat your wife and murder your children, maybe you'd just stand for it?' "

"And what did he say to that?"

"Well, he looked down at the ground and kind of studied a while, and then he says: 'No—I believe I'd kill him.' "

York also told the *Post* interviewer how he had killed the twenty Germans. "The whole bunch came charging down the hill at me. . . . I had my automatic out by then, and let them have it. Got the lieutenant right through the stomach and he dropped and screamed a lot. All the boches [Germans] who were hit squealed like pigs. Then I shot the others."

"You killed the whole bunch?"

"Yes sir. At that distance I couldn't miss."

York was discharged on May 29 and immediately was besieged with offers to tell his story on the lecture circuit. No, he said, "this uniform aint for sale." He just wanted to go home and marry his sweetheart, Grace Williams.

So now, in the last days of May, York was going home to his family and sweetheart. Arriving at Crossville, Tennessee, he was awaited by a fleet of six Model T Fords from Jamestown, the entire automobile population of the town. From that point, because there were no roads for automobiles, he rode in a mule-drawn wagon the remaining thirteen miles to his home. When the procession arrived, it was dark and the whippoorwills were calling. There, in the doorway of the cabin, stood the pastor of his church. For some time he and York talked alone. When they finally stepped out on the front porch, a *New York Times* reporter noted, "Nothing indicated that the peaceful head of the church had any grudge against the war-like member of the flock."

York married Grace Williams on June 7, and over the years they raised five sons and two daughters. He devoted himself to the civic life of Pall Mall, founding and directing a vocational training school for the young people of the area. Otherwise, he occasionally yielded to the frequent calls directed at him to appear at political rallies and parades. As World War II loomed, York was widely quoted as saying that what Hitler and Mussolini needed was "a good whuppin'." During that war he presided over the local draft board, sending two of his sons into the service.

York tried to live quietly but found himself embroiled in a tax suit with the federal government over royalties he had received from a movie based on his lifestory, made in 1941 and starring Gary Cooper. The government contended that York had received $172,000 on which he had paid no taxes. But York said he had given all the money to his school. Finally, the government agreed to settle for $25,000, a sum beyond York's reach but which was paid through a popular subscription. York's comment on the affair was that "them tax folks been hounding me so long and I been fighting them so long I thought it'd never end."

He died on September 2, 1964, after a succession of strokes and heart attacks.

Alvin York was a guileless soul who never thought himself a legend, hardly knowing what one was. But his fellow Tennessean, Luke Lea of Nashville, did think about the political advantages of such a reputation and tried unsuccessfully to provide the substance for it. Or, perhaps, Lea simply took too seriously the popular World War I song that included these lines:

> Goodbye Pa,
> Goodbye Ma,
> Goodbye mules with your old hee-haw.
> I don't know what this war's about,
> But I bet by gosh I'll soon find out.
> I'll bring you a Turk and a Kaiser too,
> And that's about all that a feller can do.

The part about bringing home a kaiser seemed to Lea to have possibilities. A former senator from Tennessee, defeated in 1916 by a young Democrat, Kenneth McKellar, Lea joined the armed services when the United States first entered the war. As a colonel, he commanded the 114th Field Artillery of the 30th Division, the "Old Hickory Division." Languishing in Paris after the armistice, and with Christmas approaching, he decided to kidnap Kaiser Wilhelm and present him as a Christmas present to President Wilson. The attempt was made on December 21. About a dozen officers and men in an automobile party, led by Lea, headed for the castle in Holland where the kaiser was sojourning. As Lea reported later, he had gotten close enough to the kaiser "to hear his voice," but the plot was "foiled by the sudden dispatch of Dutch guards to the castle, a contingency . . . which forced the American officers to make a quick retirement."

The ground war of World War I was too massive and too positioned to provide much latitude for personal heroics. In the air, it was different. During the course of the great conflict, a new note had pulsed. Through the titanic heaving and groaning of the struggle, there had been the roar of engines, putting into battle the fury of their energy and raising clear-eyed young men into the sky, where in brightly painted planes they dueled as had the knights in an era long past. Each nation produced mighty warriors in this form of conflict, men who, in the eyes of an entranced public, took on the character of demigods. America had a taste for the aerial jousters and wanted to see and hear them. On February 14, 1919, an audience at Carnegie Hall heard Canadian Billy Bishop, "The World's Greatest Ace," with an "official record" of shooting down "72 Hun machines," give a personal account of his exploits to whoever was willing to pay for a seat that ranged in price from thirty cents to two dollars.

The hero of the American air service was a former racecar driver and military chaffeur named Edward V. Rickenbacker. He was given his "welcome home" on the night of February 3, at a banquet at the Waldorf-Astoria. There, in a setting that glittered with the wealth and prestige of those who attended, Rickenbacker heard himself eulogized by Professor Henry van Dyke of Princeton University, in "an oration filled with poetic phraseology and delivered in an impassioned style."

Newton D. Baker, the Secretary of War, also spoke, and though he did not reach Professor Van Dyke's oratorical heights, his words still rang with the spirit of lofty patriotism. In his autobiography, Rickenbacker says that Baker pronounced him "one of the real crusaders of America— one of the truest knights our country has ever known." Baker predicted that when Rickenbacker reached "the evening of his life," he would "never forget the thrill of combat in the clouds where it was his life or his adversary's. He will always know this thrill even when he awakes from his deepest sleep. But his life will always be gladdened as he looks about him and sees men and women and children walking about free and unafraid."

Baker then presented Rickenbacker with a pair of diamond-studded wings and asked the flyer to address the audience. Said Rickenbacker: "I held out the jeweled wings . . . and said, 'For you, Mother.' Then I sat down. Everyone present . . . rose to his feet and applauded. Some stood on chairs and tables. I saw tears on the cheeks of both men and women."

The unscathed hero might stand, accepting the cheers of his compatriots, but he and the rest of the world lived in the shadow of ten million who had died in the conflict. In the brief lives of how many of those dead had there been ablaze a creative potential that had beauty and not war as its objective? Certainly, this was true in the case of David Hochstein, a violinist, from Rochester, New York. He had studied in Vienna, where he was a prize pupil in the Meisterschule of the Imperial Academy, and where he made his debut in 1911. One can assume that during his years in Vienna he grew to appreciate the city's beauty and life, and this appreciation must have cooled whatever ardor he had for the war. Apparently he was drafted and on October 15, 1918, he was killed in battle, at a time when his reputation as one of the finest violinists that America had ever produced was becoming established.

SOURCES

Newspapers and magazines constitute the principal sources for this chapter. The story of the *Leviathan* and Humphrey Bogart is from Malcolm Brinnin, *The Sway of the Grand Salon: A Social History of the North Atlantic* (New York, 1971). The *New York Evening Sun's* comments on the fighting qualities of black soldiers is quoted in *The Literary Digest* (January 18, 1919). The story of Alvin York that appeared in the *Saturday Evening Post* (April 26, 1919) was written by George Pattullo and is titled "The Second Elder Gives Battle." On Luke Lea's supposed attempt to kidnap the kaiser, see John Berry McFerrin, *Caldwell and Company: A Southern Financial Empire* (Chapel Hill, N.C., 1959). See also William D. Miller, *Mr. Crump of Memphis* (Baton Rouge, La., 1964). The Rickenbacker segment is from Edward Rickenbacker, *Rickenbacker* (Englewood Cliffs, N.J., 1967). On David Hochstein, see *The Literary Digest* (February 1919).

FURTHER READING

Jesse J. Johnson, *Black Armed Forces, 1736–1971* (Hampton, Va., 1971).

Samuel Kinkade Cowan, *Sergeant York and His People* (New York, 1922).

David Lee, *Sergeant York, an American Hero* (Lexington, Ky., 1985).

3

Forgiving the Enemy

DAVID HOCHSTEIN WAS one of over forty thousand Americans killed in the war, a relatively small number when compared to the total of ten million who lost their lives in battle. Among these millions, from both sides, there were surely others who would have contributed to the beauty of the world if they had lived out their lives. This thought alone should have muted the disposition of the victor to crow over the defeated enemy and to indulge in vaunting and witless name-calling. Yet throughout the year 1919 the American press continued to show this spirit. Gerald Stanley Lee, in an article in the *Saturday Evening Post* on January 4, 1919, said, "I believe in being magnanimous with the Germans when we strike bottom and have something solid to be magnanimous on. . . . So far as can be seen with the naked eye not a single German soul in all Germany has been thrashed yet. I cannot bear to have the Germans step up to us so promptly, so glibly, and begin a new world with us."

Seven weeks later, *The Literary Digest* quoted a letter from journalist Frank Crane to "Kaiser Bill" that had appeared in the *New York Globe*:

> You suggest that we get together, bury the hatchet, smoke the pipe of peace, let bygones be bygones, and everything. . . . but I do not want to be friends. . . . I can conceive of no greater calamity. And please don't speak to me again. I may speak to you, but I don't want you to speak to me. And please don't write. My man Pershing will be over to your house pretty soon and he will hear what you have to say. For I don't like your face.
>
> Still I am kinda glad I met you. You are so darned low-down and contemptible that it makes me love my fellow man the more. I want to go out and kiss all the chicken thieves and murderers in the county jail

when I think of you. . . . Yes, when I think of you, Bill, I say to myself that surely everybody outside of your bunch of thugs and pirates is going to heaven.

The theme of the "unrepentant" German was one the press was fond of playing upon in the months immediately after the war. The *Washington Post* repeatedly offered "new evidences" of the "unrepentant spirit." It cited the crowds of people in Berlin that had greeted the returning troops and, worse, the flowers and cigarettes thrown to them from the city's balconies and windows.

It would appear to have been an opportune time in those first months of peace for some of America's church leaders to step forward and urge an end to this kind of alley-gang name-calling, and to remind Americans that, after all, the Germans, on the subject of religion, professed as they professed and that at the heart of this profession was an ideal that transcended all others—the community of believers. One cannot doubt that many in the United States recognized this, but their thinking was not widely reflected in the press.

A German theologian did make the point, however, and his statement was carried in *The Literary Digest* of January 25, 1919. Professor Gustave Deissmann asked the "Christian circles of all belligerent nations" to bring about "an age of mutual forgiveness and conciliation in order to fight in unison against the terrible consequences of the war." Professor Deissmann said that he was appealing to all of the Christian leaders "whom I know in the belligerent countries, to use all of their influence, so that the approaching peace may not contain the seed of new universal catastrophes, but, instead, release all available conciliatory and rebuilding powers between the nations." Professor Deissmann's letter was sent to the archbishop of Canterbury and to the Federal Council of Churches of Christ in America. Although the archbishop's reply was lengthy and avoided self-righteousness, he admitted to no hope for the reconciliation of Christians just then. "Righteousness," he said, "must be vindicated, even if the vindication involves sternness."

If the Federal Council of Churches replied, it did not make public what it said, but its record during the war, according to one Christian minister, had been altogether negative on the score of reconciliation. Writing in the February 1919 issue of the *New Republic*, the Reverend John Hayne Holmes of New York City said that the churches that made up the council had, throughout the war,

with shocking unanimity, prostituted themselves to the work of hate. That they should oppose the war was not to be expected. That they should devote themselves, so long as the tragedy of the war was with us, to preserving some measure of understanding and goodwill in the world, to preaching unfalteringly that ideal of brotherhood to which mankind must soon or late return if it would live, to seeking those ways and means of constructive spiritual reconciliation through which alone a society shattered by the shock of war can be permanently rebuilt—this was certainly to be expected!

To the contrary, charged Holmes, the churches of the council had "rivaled the security leagues and national defense councils in the . . . business of fostering hate, sowing bitterness, and persecuting nonconformity. There was not an atrocity against the soul of man, not a blasphemy against the holy spirit of God, of which they were not guilty."

Charles S. Macfarland of New York answered for the council in the following month's issue of the *New Republic.* It was true, he was happy to say, "that the Federal Council and its constituent churches did give unmeasured support to our nation and its allies and their soldiers, who fought for the highest ideals of justice and righteousness for which a people ever contended, and, we may rest assured, they would do so again under the same sense of moral obligation."

So that was that.

At the University of Chicago, Professor Shailer Mathews had doubts about an easy reconciliation. Writing in the University of Chicago's *Bible World,* Mathews declared: "We want no good natured peace. Forgiving that which permits a criminal to continue to prey upon his victim is immoral. There must be criminal trials and punishment for those both high and low who have been guilty of the unspeakable atrocities of Germany." *The Bible World* editorialized: "The most unhappy man in the world today is the Pope." His "political universe is tottering. Despotisms are crashing to destruction in the struggle with freedom, and with the victory of the Allies despotisms must disappear. . . . It [the papacy] is not only a medaeval [*sic*] despotism but it professes to teach authoritatively the principles that must govern social structures of states." The editorial further stated that the Pope saw in the war "a chance to impose once more the political teaching of Rome upon an unwilling world. The existing despotisms allied with the Papacy would be strengthened; the temporal power of the Pope would be restored; France would be punished and the monarch and church reinstituted." And so on.

In New York, the Reverend Dr. S. Edward Young of the Bradford Presbyterian Church expressed his thoughts on reconciliation in the *New York Times* of June 23. He said that those who had been favoring "a soft peace . . . are springing up, and talking louder and louder, and soft-headed and treacherous-hearted Americans are daily more willing to echo their sentiments." The Reverend Charles Edward Jefferson, also of New York, offered his thoughts on Germany and the war in *What the War Has Taught,* a compilation of his sermons delivered in the Broadway Tabernacle on Sunday evenings from January 1 to Easter 1919. One of his profundities was that "Germany gave us our first insight into the malignity and awfulness of sin." Beyond this, Reverend Jefferson filled his two hundred pages of text with various "lessons" that the "Supreme Commander," through the use of the war, had taught: "self-discipline" and "pulling together," for example.

The subject of the effects of the war on the religion of the soldiers was one that commended itself to what was presumed to be the concern of many Americans, one that the press allayed with reassuring interviews with Y.M.C.A. directors and chaplains. Of the latter group, the *New York Times* of April 22 provided the testimony of Father Francis Duffy, "the fighting chaplain of the fighting 69th, and one of the war's individual heroes." Father Duffy thought that "the war has deepened the religious convictions of the soldier." America had been in the war "just long enough to benefit in a religious way."

In the March issue of *McClure's,* an article by one Coningsby Dawson entitled "We're Coming Back to You" gave this hard-line theology: "We shall not come back to you as we went," the author-soldier, professing to speak for the entire American Expeditionary Force, declared. "Had the Hun proved his God to be existent, we could never again have worshiped. . . . We rarely spoke of religion 'Over There.' . . . We did not pray—at least, not the way you taught us to say our prayers; we listened, and believed that God spoke through our hands when for righteousness we struck the enemy and when for love we shared with our pals."

During the war, several prominent academicians, mostly historians, had been suspected of harboring "radical," or pro-German, sympathies. On January 24, 1919, a U.S. Senate committee investigating pro-German propaganda made public a "Who's Who in Pacifism and Radicalism" in which the names of Professors Charles A. Beard and Harry A. Overstreet were listed. Beard emphatically denied that his name belonged on the list and insisted in a letter to Senator Lee S. Overman, chairman of the committee, "I am not and never have been a pacifist. . . . I was never 'too proud to fight.' " Indeed, said Beard, when "Mr. Wilson was ordering his countrymen to be neutral in thought and deed . . . I was denounced at City College for a speech in which I attacked the Central Empires as responsible for the war." Overstreet's defense consisted of citing a conversation he had recently had with a "high official" of the War Department wherein he had explained his position on the war. Then the War

Department official reportedly said to Overstreet: "You are exactly the same kind of a pacifist that I am."

Others, too, denied that they had ever harbored pro-German sentiments. David Starr Jordan, chancellor emeritus of Stanford University, averred, "Any statement by German agents or any one else that I was actively or passively pro-German during the war or at any other time is an unqualified falsehood." Albert Bushnell Hart, the dean of American historians, declared that, rather than having any excess of zeal where charity toward Germans was concerned, he had "been continuously active in the National Security League . . . and for a long time chairman of the committee on patriotism." John W. Burgess, a Columbia University historian, said that he had done nothing other than to attend strictly to his duties as an American citizen. Professor Herbert Sanborn of Vanderbilt University insisted that he, too, was "clean."

One prominent historian, Carl Becker, who had once professed to be prowar, had second thoughts about that profession. In May 1917, he had published an article in the *Minnesota Historical Society Bulletin,* entitled "The Monroe Doctrine and War," in which he said that "it is the part of wisdom as well as fitting that we should do our share in making the world safe for democracy." But in 1920 Becker confided in a letter to the historian William E. Dodd that the war had been "inexplicable on any ground of reason, or common sense, or decent aspiration, or even of intelligent self-interest; on the contrary it was the most futile, the most desolating and repulsive exhibition of human power and cruelty without compensating advantage that has ever been on earth."

With the passage of time, other concerns and enthusiasms moderated the disposition of most Americans toward arrogant, moral self-righteousness with respect to the war and Germans. For most the war, as a subject for florid expostulation, was soon forgotten. But for one person, an English journalist who arrived in America two months after the armistice, the war would never be forgotten. On the morning of February 13, the stately old Cunard liner *Carmania* approached New York City bearing the widely read war correspondent, Philip Gibbs. As the ship passed Staten Island and neared the Statue of Liberty, Gibbs stood at the bow rail, staring intently into the mists, trying to get his first glimpse of New York. He wanted to see "that view which had been described a thousand times by many great writers." Gradually he saw it, "a phantom city towering faintly through the sun-lit mists . . . [which] then appeared in sharper outline, but still vague and ghostlike out of the water. I drew my breath and felt a queer excitement and awe. It was more wonderful and more beautiful than any description I had read. This great city with its high, straight towers and immense masses of architecture upon which the sunlight gleamed between gulfs of blackshadow-worlds, was like some visionary's dream of a new world capital not yet materialized."

That evening Gibbs walked to the theater district. "I felt more afraid of the city of New York than when I had walked through other cities like Arras. . . . There were fountains of light leaping above the topmost stories of fantastic buildings which seemed to touch the skies and cascades of light railing down steep walls and lights that wriggled and squirmed and whirled in marvelous combinations." The power of New York, in whose spirit coursed the sun-tipped reaches of soaring technology, with its intimation of the world to come, continued to awe Gibbs. "I am having a fairy-tale time in America and I am not at all sure at present that it is not a fantastic and delightful dream," he wrote in the *New York Times*.

One night Gibbs was the guest of honor taken to the City Club, and at the banquet table where he sat, a group of men arose and serenaded him. The men were from a glee club, and they sang two songs that would have appealed to Gibbs: "Love Me and the World Is Mine," and the traditional "John Peel." Gibbs was scheduled to address the City Club members, but halfway through his talk he was stopped, escorted out of the club and into a taxi, and taken to the stage door of the Forty-fourth Street Theater, where he was conducted down the corridors and into the middle of what he thought was an Oriental harem. "There were many beautiful . . . ladies dancing about in a white light and gossamer garments, while a gentleman with a black face, the famous Mr. Al Jolson," danced and sang. Gibbs had been taken backstage during a performance of *Sinbad*, which was enjoying a long run on Broadway. Somewhat uneasy in the company of the dancers, who were hurrying on and off stage, some of them greeting him cheerfully, he was relieved to be taken back to the City Club, where he concluded his talk.

Compared to the gray desolation that he had witnessed for so long in Europe, New York, full of life and action, repeatedly amazed Gibbs. Continuing his diarylike reporting in the *New York Times*, he told of going one night to Carnegie Hall to hear the talk that Billy Bishop was giving about his exploits in the air. But Gibbs did not dwell on Bishop's lecture. He left Carnegie Hall before it was over to go out into the blaze and sound of the city and then to the Plaza Hotel, which was "like some magician's palace, with a wonderful facade rising to the stars and with all its hundreds of windows shining in the darkness." It was a ball night, and he was caught in the excitement of the crowds of men and women in evening dress as they walked into the huge salon of the Plaza.

He noted that the girl's dresses were "fluffy and shimmering," and that their eyes "sparkled out of bright, audacious little faces."

This was the New York of F. Scott Fitzgerald and George Gershwin, and Gibbs stayed there for two months, during which he was much sought after as a lecturer. He did some public speaking, but it was not an occupation to his liking. As he said on several occasions in his reports to the *New York Times,* he felt inadequate as a speaker. Moreover, he was not disposed to give glowing recitals of the war's glory. The danger, he said, was that "in a generation, or less, the memory of what this war meant in human suffering may fade out, leaving only the remembrance of heroism, touched by romance."

Before he returned to England, Gibbs tried to tell Americans what the war had been like. "The misery and beastliness and the terror of it all should be stripped of all their romantic 'camouflage,' " he declared, "so that the truth should be etched deeply in the pages of history." Who, he asked, could describe the terrors of a battlefield, "the suffering of spirit and body to each individual before he lay quiet below a wooden cross or went home with a blighty wound?" He could not describe it, although he had "gone through those fields on days of great battles and seen . . . our dead and German dead, headless, with arms and legs flung far from their bodies, with dreadful mangled faces or with no faces." He had seen "not once but scores of times, the long trail of the walking wounded, staggering back under shellfire with their arms about each other's necks, or hobbling along until they dropped, to wait for the stretcher bearers or to die, so patiently that they hardly groaned—men with ghastly wounds revealed nakedly, blind men groping forward miserably with one hand tightly clutching a wounded comrade, men so hideous in masks of clotted blood that I dared not look at them after the first glance."

One time, Gibbs said, after a long night following a battle, he could hear the voices of the wounded wailing about, "and as the light of dawn paled over those gray fields of slime," he could see "figures raising themselves out of their pits like dead men risen from their graves." Lost and hurt, they clung to each other and "held hands like children." For these reasons and more, Gibbs concluded, the soul of the world was crying out, "Never Again": "For God's sake let us devise some new philosophy which will cut out this horror. Let us get at the root causes of war, so that we may kill them, and let us establish safeguards against any nation likely to let loose the old devils of international hatred in bloody conflict. That is the present mood of civilized mankind and I think it is out of that general emotion of revolt against the sacrifice and agonies of its manhood that a new philosophy of life, based upon a new international relations may be evolved."

Gibbs wanted to say something positive about Woodrow Wilson's League of Nations. America had embarked on "one of the greatest missions in history," he told an audience at the Forty-fourth Street Theater. It could not turn back, but should it do so, it would have "missed a call that is divine." Gibbs believed, though, that more than just a new political form was needed to prevent a recurrence of the horror through which Europe had just passed. A religious man, he felt that peace had to be made by overcoming hatred with understanding and charity. Throughout the twenties he wrote novels aimed at establishing a community sense of idealism between young Germans and Britons. He thought if war could be presented as it was, stripped of its romance, then the world would have no more of it. In 1921 his book *Now It Can Be Told* was published, a history of trench warfare.

In the fall of 1939, Gibbs was again on the western front. Taking a tour in a British tank, he quickly recognized the terrain. "In this very field," he mused, "once lay the dead bodies of German soldiers," Speaking to an officer who had been in the first war, he remarked, "Do you know, I can hardly bring myself to believe that it may happen all over again.... The damned folly of life has caught us again."

Gibbs died on March 11, 1962, at the age of eighty-four, one of the few men in English history to be knighted for wartime reporting.

SOURCES

The theme of this chapter, unlike the question of who started the war, was not one to evoke much study. The sources here are from contemporary newspapers and magazines and most are indicated in the text. The charges made by the Reverend Holmes concerning the warmongering of the Federal Council of Churches of Christ in America are from the "Correspondence" section of the *New Republic* (March 15, 1919). Shailer Mathews's truculent "hard-line" attitude is evident in "Some Ethical Gains of the War," in *The Bible World*, n.s. (January–November 1919). Various professorial prowar declarations are found in the *Washington Post* for December 7, 1919. Carl Becker's initial prowar position, stated in the *Minnesota Historical Society Bulletin*, is quoted in Burleigh Taylor Wilkins, *Carl Becker: A Biographical Study in American Intellectual History* (Cambridge, Mass., 1961).

FURTHER READING

After the war, Philip Gibbs became a Catholic. Some of his novels of the 1920s emphasize the theme of travel exchange and reconciliation where the youth of Germany and England were concerned. His principal work, *Now It Can Be Told,* published in 1926, is a graphic depiction of the grotesque nature of French warfare.

4

Wilson Goes to
Europe

JUST AS THE WAR was ending, Professor John Dewey noted that
some troubling distortions had entered into those otherwise scientifi-
cally constructed pragmatic equations by which he had justified America's
entry into the great conflict: that a world blessed by a final peace would
come after it. His "good" war, Dewey perceived, was producing an
irrationalism that "has striven to persuade us that a military defeat of
Germany has only to be complete enough to be of itself a winning of the
war irrespective of any further consequences." It was thus easy to foresee,
he said, that the authors of the present cult of the irrational "will come
forward with frank disparagement of the League of Nations, and will
propose for the prevention of future wars as a substitute a more assidu-
ous devotion to those principles of exclusive and militant nationalism.
. . . Cultivated irrationality," he wrote in the *New Republic,* "is a hate-
ful thing, which easily gets out of all control."

If the fact of World War I may be taken as a cataclysmic sign of
"cultivated irrationality," Dewey's endorsement of war means that he
had erred grievously in assessing one of the values of his equation. But
what might he have anticipated other than a continuation of the
overheated and inflamed sensibilities that the war had produced? An
"exclusive" nationalism and an upsurge of inhumanity at home? In any
case, on the grounds that the war had been a mistake, by the time the
year 1919 had begun, Dewey and like-minded others who had supported
the war seemed to have washed their hands of an obligation to support
the League of Nations.

Still, there was after the war, the world over, a considerable idealism
that focused on the word "reconstruction." "Old Europe is dead and a

new world is slowly emerging," observed Jan Christian Smuts, the South African statesman. "We saved the soul of civilization; now let us care for its sick body." But the idealism of the reconstructionists, either at home or abroad, seemed never to have made the attainment of the League the primary objective. The new world that Smuts saw emerging was one in which the spirit of nationalism was taking on a new momentum, and idealism found its expression in this spirit.

In the closing days of the war, a tired Woodrow Wilson seemed to become possessed with apprehension that his objective could founder in a growing chasm of irrationalism. Surely, he sensed what Dewey had sensed; else how does one explain his surprising and in the view of many, uncharacteristic appeal to American voters on October 24 for the election of a Democratic Congress, an appeal that he accompanied with an attack upon Republicans and their representatives in Congress?

The document, appearing in the nation's newspapers, had a plaintive and weary tone. "If you have approved of my leadership and wish me to continue to be your unembarrassed spokesman in affairs at home and abroad, I earnestly beg that you will express yourself unmistakably to that effect by returning a Democratic majority to both the Senate and the House." America's friends abroad "would find it very difficult to believe that the voters . . . had chosen not to support their President." He would "beg" again that the electorate sustain him "in a way which it will not be possible to misunderstand, either here at home or among our associates on the other side of the sea."

Wilson's attorney general, Thomas W. Gregory, has given an insightful explanation of the matter. "It seems probable to me that Wilson decided to write the letter in a moment of extreme weariness, for those were harrowing days, at the end of a long session when his nerves were taut and his intellectual sentinels were not on the lookout for danger." Gregory thought that had the president not interjected this partisan appeal into the congressional elections for the fall of 1918 "the Democrats would have carried the elections easily, on the basis of Wilson's prestige and the fact that the war had been won." As it turned out, the Republicans won control of both the Senate and the House.

The consequences of a Republican victory were inauspicious for the League, especially since one of Wilson's well-established enemies, Henry Cabot Lodge, would become the chairman of the Senate Foreign Relations Committee. Lodge and his friend Theodore Roosevelt might declare that a world free from war was an objective to be sought, but they both stood steadfastly opposed to the proposition that the League was the key toward reaching this state. When Roosevelt learned of the president's appeal, he appeared almost ecstatic. "I am glad Wilson has come out in the open," he wrote to Lodge. "I fear Judas most when he can cloak his activities behind a make-believe of non-partisanship." Lodge replied with similar enthusiasm and with a similar literary touch: "The President has thrown off the mask. The only test of loyalty is loyalty to one man."

Wilson then made what some have regarded as a second mistake. He decided that he would go to Europe to participate in the process of treaty making. Colonel House had advised him to go, but then House was inclined to "advise" according to Wilson's already defined position. An imposing array of others, however—Secretary of State Lansing, War Trade Board Chairman Vance McCormick, Fuel Administrator Harry Garfield, and Bernard Baruch, chairman of the War Industries Board, advised him not to go. His effectiveness, they felt, would be enhanced by distance.

Frank Cobb, Wilson's journalist friend who, at the time of the armistice negotiations was assisting House in Paris, thought at first that the president should go to Europe. But on November 4, he gave House a memorandum on Wilson's proposed trip which House sent on to Wilson. "When we left New York," Cobb said, "I believed that it was not only desirable but necessary for President Wilson to come to Europe. Since our arrival here, my opinion is changed completely." Cobb thought that the "moment President Wilson sits at the council table with these Prime Ministers and Foreign Secretaries he has lost all the power that comes from distance and detachment. Instead of remaining a great arbiter of human freedom he becomes merely a negotiator dealing with other negotiators."

Wilson was not persuaded. His private secretary, Charles L. Swem, gave to Herbert Hoover, who knew Wilson well and who was party to the events of the time, what he thought was the best explanation for Wilson's position: "To one of Mr. Wilson's mind, this situation left him no alternative . . . His inability . . . to clothe others with presidential authority, led inevitably to the decision to go himself." Perhaps also in Wilson's mind was the unstated "other" side of the Cobb position. Worried about the erosion of his influence at home, he may have considered the prestige that surely would come to him in the minds of the American people as they saw their president across the sea, beyond the political tempests of Washington, settling the world's fate. He may also have thought that it would be worth a great deal if he could get beyond the fusillading of Lodge and Roosevelt.

Wilson told Congress of his decision on December 2. He was going to Europe, he said, because he believed it was his duty to play his full part in making secure the objective that the men of the armed forces of the nation had offered their lives to attain. "May I not hope, gentlemen of the Congress, that in the delicate tasks I shall have to perform on the other side of the seas in my efforts truly and faithfully to interpret the principles and purposes of the country we love, I have the encouragement and the added strength of your united support?" The president was again the supplicant and again he was rebuffed.

The announcement received an embarrassingly cool reception. "Its unpopularity . . . was manifest," reported the *New York Times* the next day. Republican Senator Lawrence Sherman of Illinois offered a resolution declaring the office of the presidency vacant while Wilson was out of the country. On December 3, while preparing for his departure, Wilson summarized his feelings to his assistant: "Well, Tumulty, this trip will either be the greatest success or the supremest tragedy in all history; but I believe in a Divine Providence." Furthermore, it was his faith "that no body of men however they concert their power or their influence can defeat this great world enterprise, which after all is the enterprise of Divine mercy, peace and good will."

The odyssey began on the evening of December 3. The President and Mrs. Wilson left the White House at 10:30 P.M. and minutes later were at Union Station, entering into the great concourse through what was known as the "President's Entrance." A crowd had gathered; there was applause, but Wilson did not linger. The party moved through the gate and out to where the train, with Wilson's Pullman, named "Ideal," awaited. When dawn came the train was parked on a sidetrack near the piers at Hoboken, New Jersey, and from there the Wilsons and a host of advisers and experts boarded the old American liner *George Washington.* Ray Stannard Baker, head of the Press Bureau of the American Peace Commission, described the departure: "Three weeks and three days after the last victorious shots of the great war had been fired . . . the American peace argosy . . . with accompanying warships dropped down through the bedecked and beflagged harbour of New York and a new *Santa Maria* [was] on its extraordinary voyage of discovery to an unknown world."

Almost from the moment of departure, life for the Wilsons settled into a pleasant and restful routine. The ship was scarcely underway before lunch was served in Mrs. Wilson's suite, with Edith Benham, Mrs. Wilson's secretary, and Dr. Grayson as guests. In her memoirs, Mrs. Wilson recalled that it was a particularly "marvelous lunch." And well it might have been, since Louis Ceres, the chef at the Biltmore Hotel, with his staff and a crew of waiters, was making the trip especially to please the president's palate. It was, however, Chef Ceres's only crossing, since Wilson objected to such royal treatment.

After lunch, Wilson crossed to the other side of the ship to his own suite and slept for three hours. He did this daily, as well as sleeping late into the morning. Already, it appears, his physical reserves were low. Working hours—conferences with various members of the peace delegation—were in the late morning and the evening. His walks around the deck with Mrs. Wilson before dinner were his exercise.

Wilson's real moments of relaxation came with his nightly viewing of motion pictures. Two areas on the ship were equipped with movie projectors, one below for servicemen, known as The Old Salt Theater, and the other on the upper deck, used by members of the Peace Commission. Wilson went nightly to The Old Salt, perhaps because he thought, and wanted others to think, of himself as one of America's fighting men, fulfilling the mission "over there." Then, too, perhaps he wanted to avoid fraternization with all the college professors aboard, having had enough of that when he was president of Princeton.

Since he was an ardent fan of the actress Alla Nazimova, three of her pictures were shown: *Revelation, Toys of Fate,* and *Eye for an Eye.* Additionally, Wilson saw "Romeo and Juliet" starring Francis X. Bushman and Beverly Bayne, and then something presumably in the vein of light whimsy, called *Blue Jeans,* featuring Viola Dana. Wartime themes held the prominent place in the programming. Rita Jolivet, a survivor of the *Lusitania,* starred in *Lest We Forget.* Then there was *My Own United States, Draft 255,* and "a patriotic superfeature, depicting the contrasting and dramatic life-story of Woodrow Wilson, the builder, and Wilhelm, the Kaiser and wrecker." After the movie there was singing—"Pack Up Your Troubles," "Keep the Home Fires Burning," and, as always, "Over There."

Meanwhile the *George Washington* continued to creep along at about seventeen knots, with five destroyers running alongside and the battleship *Pennsylvania* heading the procession. Admiral Henry T. Mayo, commander of the Atlantic Fleet, directed the flotilla. "I anticipate no trouble," Mayo told a *New York Times* reporter before leaving New York. Of course, there was "the faintly possible exception of a stray floating mine," but if one were encountered, it would hit the *Pennsylvania.* "Our men will understand that the life of the President . . . is more precious than the lives of any of us." But nothing out of the ordinary occurred, and on December 12, the last night of the voyage, a chorus of bluejackets serenaded the president at the conclusion of the program at The Old Salt Theater. "God Be with You 'Til We Meet Again," they sang.

During the early hours of December 13, the *Pennsylvania*'s wireless picked up the information that American naval vessels from European waters were approaching from the north. The *New York Times* graphically described what then occurred: "The night was partly cloudy, with the moon visible now and then. Suddenly, the *Pennsylvania* got a series of rapid signals from a destroyer, hovering off on the skyline. . . . With the searchlights pointing a long illuminated finger into the sky, she wrote a message in flashes on the big black clouds. In a few seconds the answer, written on the sky by a battleship away over the horizon, began to come back." Sometime later, the lights of the approaching fleet began to rise over the horizon. By daylight all the ships of the convoy were in their appointed places. At 11:00 A.M. a French fleet was seen approaching from the south, and when its units had taken their places, there were more than forty vessels lined up on either side of the *George Washington*, reaching as far as the eye could see.

Led by this triumphal procession of naval might, the president of the United States approached the French coast. Of the world's leaders, Wilson was at that moment peerless as the incarnation of the Enlightenment precept that the will of the people, when freed from arbitrary power, would effect a rational and humane order in society. In the wave of exultation that came as the war ended, the acclaim given Wilson in Europe was that given a messiah. After he landed at Brest, a Spanish newspaper called him "a citizen of the world." Another Spanish paper declared that he was the "most humane man of the century." An Italian paper insisted that no man in Europe was more loved than Wilson. Ray Stannard Baker, who witnessed the adulation given the President, described it as follows: "His pictures were in every window. I was even told, in that time of exaggerated speech, that the peasants in some parts of Italy set candles to burn before them." And in Poland, "so strong was the feeling for him . . . that when university men met each other—one of them told me this—they struck hands and cried out 'Wilson!' as a greeting."

For a week, the president met dignitaries, attended receptions, and waited on generals. On Saturday afternoon, December 21, Wilson was given an honorary doctorate at the University of Paris. In the university's great amphitheater, Lucien Poincaré, vice-rector of the university and brother of the French president, gave the testimonial. History would recount, he said, how Wilson, listening to his own conscience and that of the American people, "reached one glorious day the decision which is one of the greatest events recorded in the war, and in your own words, placed the blood and all the power of America at the service of the principles which have given her life."

Yes, that was why he was in Europe, Wilson would have agreed, to bring to the whole world those principles that had given life to America. He wanted immediately to begin work, to begin sorting out the problems and proposing solutions that conformed to the new rules for international reconstruction that were the first thirteen of his Fourteen Points. And he, personally, wanted to begin the work of giving substance to Point Fourteen, the League of Nations.

But Wilson was like a guest who had come to dinner too early. To accommodate an election in Britain, the opening of the Peace Conference was put off until January 18. To pass the time, it was arranged that the Wilsons would visit the king and queen of England and then go to Rome as guests of the Italian monarchs. Their journey was a round of presentations, banquets, and speeches, the sort of thing that interested Edith Wilson. In her memoir she gives two chapters to those weeks, providing impressions of members of the royal families, what they said, what they wore, what she said, what she wore. She found King George V a diffident and nervous public speaker but very entertaining at an informal dinner, where he delighted in telling stories about the guileless rusticity of the American troops. According to Mrs. Wilson, one of the king's stories told of the time when he and the queen went to the opening of the Liberty Hut in London. " 'One of your privates,' said the king, 'came forward and said: "Excuse me, but am I right that this is the king of England?" I said 'Yes,' at which he extended a horny hand and said: "Put it there!" ' "

Mrs. Wilson found the royal ladies of Britain punctilious and well schooled in their roles but lacking in a self-assurance that allowed spontaneity and warmth. However, in Margot Asquith, wife of the British cabinet officer Herbert Asquith, she found self-assurance to the point of brashness. "I found her . . . clever, egotistical and exceedingly plain. . . . she smoked one cigarette after another, striking matches as I have seen certain men do, on their own anatomy." Mrs. Asquith seemed to have felt that since she and Mrs. Wilson had both been twice married, she possessed a platform for a discussion of the sexual aspects of matrimony. "She . . . launched into a detailed and intimate narrative to which she warmed as she proceeded; and by the time luncheon was over the veil had been stripped from the most personal and sacred things."

The trip to Italy, in terms of a personal triumph, was the high point of Wilson's European experience. "Our arrival in Rome will always be the most brilliant canvas in all the rich pictures in my memory," Mrs. Wilson wrote. "The ancient beauty of Rome needs no tribute from me, but those who know and love it must picture the added brilliance of streets covered with the golden sands brought from the Mediterranean Sea, a time-honoured custom accorded to returning military conquerors and to visiting heads of States." Crowds of people lined the streets; the long windows of every house along the route were opened and from them hung "rare old brocades or velvets with arms embroidered on them.... And the flowers! From the roofs, the windows and balconies, poured a veritable shower of purple violets and golden mimosa. From baskets filled with them, from white arms laden with them, they fell about our stately coaches, a libation fit for the gods."

For King Emmanuel and his queen, Mrs. Wilson held fond feelings and much admiration. "We came away with a very vivid impression, not that of a king and queen living in lonely state, but husband and wife with mutual interests in a real home made doubly dear by the presence of lovely children. It was all so unostentatious and genuine." The Wilsons, however, seemed to have overlooked the Vatican.

On January 7, 1919, President and Mrs. Wilson returned once more to Paris. For four days Wilson consulted with his advisers and delegations, and then on Sunday, January 13, they held a long session with the Allied leaders to prepare for the opening of the conference. After that, Mrs. Wilson says, her husband was caught up in such mounting demands on his time that she "scarcely saw him, except perhaps for meals."

SOURCES

The Dewey article, "The Cult of Irrationality," is in the November 9, 1919, issue of the *New Republic.* A discussion of postwar idealism is found in James R. Mock and Evangeline Thurber, *Report on Demobilization* (Norman, Okla., 1944). Attorney General Gregory's statement on Wilson's "appeal" is quoted in Herbert Hoover's *Ordeal of Woodrow Wilson* (New York, 1958). Further discussion of the "appeal," including journalist Frank Cobb's comments, are also from Hoover. The Lodge-Roosevelt exchange is from Alden Hatch, *The Lodges of Massachusetts* (New York, 1973). Details of the voyage to Europe are from the *New York Times,* Ray Stannard Baker's *Woodrow Wilson and World Settlement* (New York, 1922), previously cited; and *The Literary Digest* (February 22, 1919). Edith Wilson, in her *My Memoir* (Indianapolis and New York, 1939), provides the atmospherics.

FURTHER READING

There is scarcely any form of writing more effective and interesting in the way of bringing one close to a person and the times than the reminiscence or memoir. In addition to those named above, read Cary T. Grayson, *Woodrow Wilson, An Intimate Memoir* (New York, 1960), and Joseph P. Tumulty, *Woodrow Wilson as I Knew Him* (New York, 1921).

5

Edith Wilson

IN JANUARY 1919, Woodrow Wilson entered into a contest, first with the Allied leaders and then with some members of the United States Senate—a contest that would break him and hasten the end of his life. Throughout that year Edith Bolling Wilson emerged as a woman of vital strength, a woman who, as her husband began to lose his hold on his affairs, was increasingly his refuge and, finally, almost the only person standing between him and those who would destroy him. Beneath a surface appraisal—that of Woodrow Wilson as a man of steel, temperamentally equipped to sustain with a stout heart some verity in the universe, and that of Edith Wilson as a woman of the South, conforming to the popularly conceived images of what such a woman should be—there was a deeper truth. The president was strong willed, but inside he trembled; he would ask for quarter. The memoirs written by people who were close to Wilson contain references to the signs of severe distress that would show whenever he was confronted by someone, or whenever pressures of decision making mounted. His face would "drain," turn "ashen," "gray," "pallid"; his hands would turn "icy-cold," "white"; they would "shake." He fainted from within; his body chemistry curdled, and the degenerative process of aging seemed rapidly to pick up momentum, especially during his critical year.

Edith Bolling Wilson seemed to have a certain strength that he lacked. Born at Wytheville, Virginia, in 1873, she came from a family that had deep roots in the Southern tradition, and this circumstance gave a quality to her character that she gracefully lived out. Attractively vivacious, she was a good conversationalist, and she rigidly lived by the canons of propriety and good taste that were prescribed by her heritage.

She knew what it meant to be a lady, and she was one. But if there ever was, even in literary fancy, an image of the Southern woman as a bloodless creature who took fainting refuge from the seething strife of the male world, Edith Wilson did not conform to it. She did not suffer trespassers upon her standards, and if anyone wantonly violated them she was likely to shoot from the hip. She was tough.

In the presence of women, something of the president's real self appeared. He saw them within a framework of ideal delineations provided by the time in which he lived. He believed that it was the woman's role in marriage to bring to man the quieting solace of a peculiarly feminine steadfastness, to stand like a breakwater between him and the tempestuous world.

The women who were Wilson's family when he was governor of New Jersey and who moved with him into the White House in 1913 had fulfilled this function.. There was his first wife, the former Ellen Axson of Rome, Georgia, a person of culture and strong character. There was a cousin, Helen Bones, who as an orphaned child had been raised by Wilson's mother and who later came to serve as a kind of personal secretary to Ellen Wilson. The Wilson daughters were Jessie, Eleanor, and Margaret. Before them Wilson could recite the events of his "day at the office," or when he was in a festive mood they served as an appreciative audience for an exercise of his latent talent as a vaudevillian. He sometimes liked to play the fool—to distort his face into a clownlike mien, to wiggle his ears, to imitate an ape hulking along. He could tell entertaining dialect stories and dance the jig to the accompaniment of a phonograph. He was also, according to Secret Service Agent Edmund Starling, who had the opportunity to witness Wilson's antics, "an accomplished buck and wing artist."

But all of this occurred during the president's early days in the White House. Ellen Wilson had come to Washington suffering from the nephritis that she knew would take her life, and on August 8, 1914, after showing great fortitude and patience, she died. The Wilson daughters soon left, too. Jessie married Francis Sayre, and Eleanor married the secretary of the treasury, William G. McAdoo. Margaret was a roamer. As Agent Starling put it, she "ran with a crowd of liberals, and was apt to show up with all sorts of long-haired, wild-eyed persons as her guests." Although Margaret had ambitions to become a concert singer, in Starling's view her voice was "not too good. Often it flooded the White House . . . creating a strange tension among the members of the staff."

After his first wife's death, Wilson was increasingly alone except for the company of Helen Bones. Subject to a "nervous" stomach and "declines," Wilson was a worry to his devoted physician, Carey T. Grayson. Because Grayson had recommended golf for Wilson, usually every morning for an hour or so he dutifully played golf. In that lonely period Wilson also indulged himself in his favorite pastime of going to the theater. "Almost nightly," says Starling, Wilson went to Washington's Rialto Theater for vaudeville or musical comedy. Starling said that Wilson "wanted to laugh at the clowns, admire the pretty legs of the chorus girls—like any normal man he had a deep and sincere appreciation of the female form. . . . Often I took him back-stage to meet some of the performers, particularly the good-looking ladies. I knew he enjoyed the experience of seeing them at close quarters, observing their charms, and inhaling their perfumes."

It seems apparent that Grayson perceived a connection between the president's indifferent health and the lack of a female presence in his life. Wilson might go to the music hall to observe and appreciate the dancing and the radiant flesh of the girls, but there seemed to have been no disposition to expand his interest into clandestine areas of activity. So Grayson, the complete physician, essayed a venture in romance making. In 1915 the object of his own romantic aspiration was an attractive Virginia girl, whom he shortly would marry, named Altrude Gordon. In her company as frequently as possible, Grayson got to know Miss Gordon's older widowed friend, Edith Bolling Galt. In time, Grayson came to hold a high opinion of Mrs. Galt, her intelligence, her level-headedness, and her cultural attainments.

Born on October 15, 1872, Edith Bolling was married as a young woman to Norman Galt, owner of an old and prominent Washington jewelry concern. In January 1908 she was widowed. Thirty-five at the time, she moved, on the basis of an income from her husband's business, into a pleasant existence of indulging her taste for clothes, concerts, and travel in Europe. At forty-three, she possessed a robust comeliness. "A fine figure of a woman," was the way Agent Starling described her— "plump by modern American standards, but ideal from the viewpoint of a mature man." Starling thought her face was "not only lovely but alive." She laughed easily, but she was especially attractive, he thought, when, with "her eyes dancing and her lips trembling," she tried to hold back laughter.

Much later, Starling permitted himself the indulgence of a crush on the president's second wife—from afar, of course. "She is a dear, gracious woman and I like her better each day," he wrote to his mother. His decorous infatuation, however, was not always confined to the sweet attractiveness of trembling lips or dancing eyes. He told his mother how he had assisted Mrs. Wilson over a barrier to enter a room and added,

"Well, I can truthfully say that I could help her . . . all day, for she had on a narrow skirt and owns a beautiful leg."

Grayson began his matchmaking early in 1915. His approach was oblique. Visiting Mrs. Galt, he adverted to affairs at the White House and especially to the isolated life of Miss Helen Bones and the consequent lassitude into which she had fallen. "Poor thing," Grayson mused, she so badly needed someone to talk to. Could Mrs. Galt see her way clear to take on this kindly ministration? Responded Mrs. Galt (as she recorded in her memoirs): "My dear Doctor, as you know, I am not a society person. I have never had any contacts with official Washington, and don't desire any. I am, therefore, the last person in the world able to help you."

Grayson was not deterred. Several days later he appeared at Mrs. Galt's home at 1308 Twentieth Street, N.W., with Helen Bones and Eleanor McAdoo. The four of them took an automobile ride through Rock Creek Park. Other rides followed, and then Mrs. Galt, in her "little electric," took to picking up Helen Bones at the White House. Parking the car under a tree in Rock Creek Park, the two would walk along a path while Miss Bones told Mrs. Galt all about "Cousin Woodrow" and the late Mrs. Wilson.

One afternoon in March 1915, after the customary walk, Miss Bones insisted that her new friend accompany her to the White House for tea, since "Cousin Woodrow" had only the other day asked her why she never brought her friends to the White House. As it turned out, just as the two ladies were exiting from the elevator at the second floor, they quite accidentally ran into the president and Grayson, returning from a game of golf. Everybody laughed at the sudden meeting, but, as Edith Wilson later put it, "I would have been less feminine than I must confess to be, had I not been secretly glad that I had worn a smart black tailored suit which Worth had made for me in Paris." As for Wilson, she noted, he was "not so well attired." She found out later that his golf suit had been made "by a cheap tailor the President had known years before and whom he was trying to help by giving an order."

On April 7 the now customary ride was planned, but this time a White House car picked up Mrs. Galt and then returned for Miss Bones. There in the doorway stood Wilson, too, hat in hand. He sat in the front and the ladies in the back where they chatted merrily. As for Wilson, "I don't think he spoke from the time we left until our return about five-thirty," Mrs. Wilson recollected.

April 30 was a highlight: the president double-dated. He invited Mrs. Galt to dinner, and with her Altrude Gordon and Grayson. To each of the women he had sent a corsage of roses, yellow for Mrs. Galt and pink for Miss Gordon. For Miss Gordon, the color selection threatened the smooth unfolding of the evening's affairs: pink did not match the dress she had chosen. So while the White House car, with Grayson in a state of nervous agitation, waited, Miss Gordon, with Mrs. Galt's cool assistance, dressed again. "My own dress," said Mrs. Wilson, "was a princess black charmeuse Worth had created for me, with a panel front of jet forming a very slender line. The golden roses with gold slippers made all the colour I wore."

"Oh, dem golden slippers," Wilson may have sung after the evening was over. But maybe it was the "black panel" that had fascinated him. Four days later, Mrs. Galt was again at the White House for dinner. After the meal the attendant retinue of ladies discreetly slipped off to the garden for a walk, leaving Woodrow and Edith together on the south portico. In her reminiscences Mrs. Wilson records what then occurred. "Almost as soon as they were gone he brought his chair nearer to mine, and, looking directly at me with those splendid, fearless eyes . . . he declared his love for me." Responded Mrs. Galt, with a level look into those splendid eyes, "Oh, you can't love me, for you don't really know me; and it is less than a year since your wife died." Yes, Wilson rejoined, he knew how she felt, but, "little girl [a figure of speech, since Mrs. Galt was five feet, nine inches tall] in this place time is not measured in months, or even in years, but by deep human experiences; and since her death I have lived a lifetime of loneliness and heartache." It was a matter of principle with him, he continued, to tell her of his feeling. It was the manly, honest thing to do.

Mrs. Galt preferred not to be swept into the conjugal state on the basis of a schoolboy profession of love. Anxious though Wilson might be to relieve his life of its "loneliness and heartache," she wanted time to achieve a more settled view of things. Nonetheless, his declaration was a memory to treasure. "I still keep the dress I wore that night," she noted in her memoir, "a white satin with creamy lace, and just a touch of emerald-green velvet at the edge of the deep square neck, and green slippers to match."

Three months passed in yachting and sojourning at vacation retreats, during which time the romantic pair were much together and Wilson's sighings became more insistent. On the afternoon of September 3, while driving through Rock Creek Park, he delivered himself of a particularly long reflection on the weight of the burden he had to carry, on his loneliness, and so on; and how, in view of it all, he could not honorably ask anyone to share his life with him. Whereupon Mrs. Galt responded with decision. Turning abruptly to him, she put her arms around him and said, "Well, if you won't ask me, I will volunteer, and be ready to be mustered in as soon as can be."

So it was settled—almost—until Colonel House and Wilson's son-in-law, William McAdoo, heard about it. Back when Wilson was president of Princeton University he had been enamored of a certain Mrs. Peck, a vivacious conversationalist who, alas, was unhappy in her marriage. There had been walks, lunches, and long conversations, which Ellen Wilson had been aware of but had, apparently, tried to ignore. Innocent enough, except—perhaps—for some letters that later would be referred to as "compromising." Now, House and McAdoo had come to say that there were rumors that Mrs. Peck planned to reveal the contents of those letters if the engagement of Wilson to Mrs. Galt were announced.

At most, the assumption that Mrs. Peck might "tell all" was based on the flimsiest of rumor. Yet whatever this "all" had been, it was enough to throw Wilson into a state of shock. He imagined a likely chain of events: the announcement of his engagement, publicity that breathed the odor of scandal, the sacrifice of Mrs. Galt's good name to the backstairs gossipers. No, he concluded, he could not in honor do anything but explain the situation to her and free her from her promise to marry him. He sat down to write her accordingly, but he could not. In *My Memoir*, Edith Wilson quotes Dr. Grayson, who stood watching the president: "he went white to the lips, and his hand shook . . . his jaw set. . . . but after a long time he put the pen down and said: 'I cannot bring myself to write this; you go, Grayson, and tell her everything.' "

So "the little Doctor," as Edith Wilson called him, did just that. "What shall I tell him?" he finally asked Mrs. Galt. "Tell him I will write," she said. Her letter, after a night's reflection, was an understanding and tender reaffirmation of her love for him and a pledge to stand with him, gossip or no gossip. Dispatching the letter, she awaited what she presumed would be Wilson's glad response. To her confusion there was no word from the president. She waited three days and then, finally, Grayson came again. Would Mrs. Galt go to the White House and see the president? He was ill; he needed her. Yes, she said, she would go. She had promised when she said that she would marry him that she would stand by him no matter what.

Wordlessly, they drove to the White House and on that afternoon in late September 1915 the doctor led her to a darkened second-floor bedroom. There she saw "a white, drawn face with burning eyes dark with hidden pain. . . . No word was spoken, only an eager hand held out in welcome, which I took to find icy cold, and when I unclasped it we were alone." The president and Mrs. Galt decided then and there to announce their engagement soon, and, surely, if all went as the *Memoir* suggests, the patient's burning eyes ceased to burn, color returned to his hitherto pallid cheek, and that hand, so icy cold, became positively feverish at the touch of his lady's.

They were married at 8:30 P.M. December 18. After the ceremony, they were taken by automobile to Alexandria, Virginia, where at an isolated railroad siding Agent Starling blinked his flashlight three times to direct the newlyweds to their waiting Pullman. At 7:00 the next morning the train reached its destination, Hot Springs, Virginia. It was an area that Edith Wilson had known from her childhood. Starling relates that when the train stopped he went back to the president's private car. "I entered quietly and walked down the narrow corridor flanking the bedrooms. Suddenly my ear caught the notes of a familiar melody. Emerging into the sitting room I saw a figure in top hat, tailcoat, and gray morning trousers, standing with his back to me, hands in his pockets, happily dancing a jig. As I watched he clicked his heels in the air, and from whistling the tune he changed to singing the words, 'Oh, you beautiful doll!' "

That afternoon, sitting before a fireplace, Wilson drew an unopened letter from his pocket. It was the one that his now wife had written to him some five weeks earlier, assuring him of her steadfast support in the face of the rumored revelations by Mrs. Peck. Until that moment, Wilson, fearing the worst, had not had the courage to read it.

It was three years later—in mid-January 1919—at the Paris peace conference, Wilson, sixty-one and tired, girded himself for the battle that he thought of as Armageddon. Had his decision to go to war been glorious, as the vice-rector of the University of Louvain had said? Perhaps now he began to doubt it. While walking the decks of the *George Washington* on his way to the great confrontation, Wilson said to George Creel, the man who had so flamboyantly publicized to the world the idealism of America's war aims, that "the hungry expect us to feed them, the roofless look to us for shelter, the sick of heart and body depend upon us for cure. . . . You know and I know, that these ancient wrongs, the present unhappinesses, are not to be remedied in a day or with a wave of the hand. What I seem to see . . . is tragedy."

SOURCES

The sources for this chapter are the statements of the principals: Edith Wilson's *My Memoir* (Indianapolis and New York, 1939); Cary T. Grayson's *Woodrow Wilson, an Intimate Memoir* (New York, 1960); and Thomas Sugrue's account of Secret Service Agent Edmund Starling's White House association with the Wilsons, *Starling of the White House* (New York, 1946), written from Starling's papers, letters, and oral reminiscences.

FURTHER READING

The attractiveness and strength of the person of Edith Bolling Wilson is suggested by the many books about her. Some of these are: Alden Hatch, *Edith Bolling Wilson, First Lady Extraordinary* (New York, 1961); Ishbel Ross, *Power with Grace: The Life Story of Mrs. Woodrow Wilson* (New York, 1975); and Tom Schactman, *Edith and Woodrow, a Presidential Romance* (New York, 1981). The emphasis on Edith Wilson should not shadow the strength and character of the president's first wife. Frances Wright Saunders has written a fine biography of her, *Ellen Axson Wilson* (Chapel Hill, N.C., 1985).

6

The Four Horsemen

IN JANUARY 1919, as Woodrow Wilson stood ready to anoint history with his League of Nations, he could, and no doubt did, think of his task as the culmination of a century and a half of progress, the world over, toward those principles that had been enunciated at America's birth and that gave the nation its remarkable life. It had been one of the propositions of Enlightenment political theorists that there was an ideal natural order in political association and that when societies observed this order people would be free. Wilson believed that his Fourteen Points recognized this order and that the League would secure its beneficent reality on a global basis. Wilson's belief in this was absolute; his belief in his ability to give form to those laws was apparently absolute, too. In his mind, it was a belief whose purity could not be tainted by procedural adjustments or concessions to unworthy motives— else how could the war be justified?

Something more profound than a few tactical errors was, however, beginning to undermine the fulfillment of Wilson's vision. The old order that was presumed to have existed at the heart of history was breaking down; a change was occurring in those mystic ethers that hover above the battleground of history's action and that give to it a characteristic sign and value. A new time was at hand, and people's spirits began to bend to a new force. It was a force that took its energy from the decay of the old, for it is almost always true that the evil dragons which are slain by war leave a trail of blood that attracts a horde of new monsters.

In 1919 the Four Horsemen of the Apocalypse galloped across Europe. Death, Destruction, Famine, and Pestilence came with the aftermath of war, and with these, the unleashing of national and class enmities that were provoked by a flaming mood of revolution. Herbert Hoover, director of the American Relief Association, which was organized at the end of the war to combat hunger and disease in Europe, said that as the year 1919 began his organization was "confronted with about 215,000,000 people of Central and Eastern Europe in acute famine, and another 185,000,000 people of the Allies and neutrals, urgently in need of large imports of overseas supplies to survive."

There was mass starvation in Russia—"hundreds of thousands were dying monthly." In Latvia, where a Soviet republic had been set up, the communists had "looted every store, every house. . . . Literally hundreds of innocent people were executed daily without trial in a sadistic orgy of blood of which the world has known few equals." Then a White Terror succeeded the Red Terror, causing Hoover to threaten a suspension of food shipments until the executions abated.

In Armenia, whose Christian population had suffered periodic massacres at the hands of the Mohammedan Turks, the situation was disastrous. Writing to Wilson on June 20, Hoover said, "The daily reports that we have . . . are of the most appalling that have yet developed out of the war. I need only to mention that the eating of the dead is now general." Hoover added that if "anyone wants material for a treatise on human woe, intrigue, war, massacre, incompetence and dishonesty, he can find ample source material in the mass of reports from our American officers on Armenia."

Hunger and starvation were not confined to these areas, of course. The problem was acute and widespread in Hungary, Romania, Czechoslovakia, Yugoslavia, and Germany. Then came pestilence.

Late in March, word came to his office in Paris that typhus was sweeping westward out of Russia. Reports indicated that there were possibly one million cases, with one hundred thousand people dying each week. Typhus was a fever transmitted by lice, and what with populations debilitated by hunger and cold, and the squalor to which life had been reduced, there was no telling where it would stop. Some two decades later, people might talk of Hoover's insensitivity to human suffering, but in 1919, through stupendous feats of red-tape cutting and organization, he may have saved the lives of five times the number of people who had been killed in battles. "We formed a line of battle in front of typhus areas hundreds of miles long—a 'sanitary cordon,'" Hoover reported. "With the aid of local police, traffic was stopped across this line except to persons with 'deloused' certificates or with assured recovery beyond the infection stage." Then, in a general movement eastward, village after village was deloused "until . . . the fire was out."

Hoover, valiant humanitarian that he was, fought the Four Horsemen wherever their gaunt visages appeared; however their presence bespoke not only physical suffering but the appearance of a volcanic change in political forms. On November 1, 1918, Theodore Roosevelt made a speech at Carnegie Hall for Negro War Relief in which he warned against an "overoptimism" on achieving universal peace. "Now we have got to steer a straight course equally distant between Kaiserism and Bolshevism," he said.

Two months later, on January 7, the headlines of the nation's newspapers announced that the former president had died from a heart attack sometime during the previous night. For the moment, tributes and recollections of the more dramatic episodes of Roosevelt's life crowded front page reports of Wilson's triumphal visit to Rome. That day, as his train was returning to Paris, Wilson got the news at a station stop. Reporters on the platform saw the telegram handed to him and the look of surprise on his face as he read it.

Roosevelt's death was reported on a Monday, and all that day rotating flights of army planes circled over his home, Sagamore Hill, on Oyster Bay, Long Island. On Wednesday afternoon, his coffin was lowered into a grave near the top of a steep hill overlooking a cove across from Sagamore Hill. It had snowed that morning and the automobile procession, which had come a mile and a half from Christ Episcopal Church, had stopped at the bottom of the hill at the cemetery gate, only a few feet from the water. A small group, including a few Rough Riders, climbed the hill for the final rite, held in the lowering light of the afternoon sun.

So Roosevelt died the kind of death he seemed to have been protesting all his life—alone, and in bed. He had been a mighty actor for an era that adored great defenders of the conviction that Columbia was indeed the Gem of the Ocean.

On the day after Roosevelt's death, the *New York Times* published the "last known letter written by Col. Roosevelt" and expressed an editorial opinion that his "words are clothed for us now with a deeper significance and solemnity"—words from the grave, as it were. "There must be no sagging back in the fight for Americanism merely because the war is over," Roosevelt had written to the American Defense Society. "Our principles in this matter should be absolutely simple. . . . we should insist that if the immigrant who comes here does in good faith become an American and assimilates himself to us he shall be treated on an exact equality with everyone else." But "if he tries to keep segregated with men of his own origin and separates from the rest of America then he isn't doing his part as an American. There can be no divided allegiance here. . . . We have room for but one language here, and that is the English language."

Roosevelt was concerned lest the zealots of turmoil born of Europe's desolation should make their way to America and infect its life with their ideas and propensity for violence. And in the winter and summer of 1919 things were happening that to most Americans seemed to lend, as the *New York Times* suggested, a special weight to Roosevelt's words. The Bolshevik menace appeared to increase.

The Russian Revolution, arising out of military defeats, a profound war weariness, and a breakdown of internal order, began on March 8, 1917, when thousands of factory workers, moving as a desperate, irresistible force into the streets of Petrograd, chanted "Give us bread!" The rebellion spread and the Cossacks and troops that were supposed to have put it down themselves joined the forces that pressed against the crumbling structure of the old order. On March 15, Czar Nicholas abdicated. "May the Lord God help Russia!" were the final words of his document of abdication.

The Romanovs were gone, but the war continued, the successful prosecution of which was still the cherished hope of the liberal parliamentarians who, for the moment, were in control. Reacting to their hard-pressed circumstances, the German government took an action that could have been one of the turning points of twentieth-century history. Fully aware that one of the demands of the extreme revolutionary groups in Russia, the Bolsheviks, was an immediate peace, the Germans undertook to deliver Nikolai Lenin, Russia's leading revolutionary in exile, from Switzerland, across Germany, and through the battle line to Petrograd. On April 9, 1917, with Lenin and some thirty other Russian exiles aboard, the legendary sealed train left Zurich, arriving at the Petrograd station on the night of April 16. Half expecting to be arrested when he arrived, Lenin was greeted by "vast thousands of the people" standing outside the station in the illumination of searchlights. Briefly welcomed by the president of the Petrograd Soviet, Lenin addressed the crowd in words startling and prophetic: "Dear Comrades, soldiers, sailors and workers. I am happy to greet in you the victorious Russian revolution, to greet you as the advance guard of the international proletarian army. . . . The war of the imperialist brigandage is the beginning of civil war in Europe. . . . The hour is not far when . . . the people will turn their arms against their capitalist exploiters."

Later that night at the Bolshevik party headquarters, Lenin delivered a savage assault on his fellow party members for their collaboration with those revolutionary elements that wanted to continue the war against Germany. In brutal language he ruled out any kind of compromise with the revolutionary moderates. Henceforth, where Lenin was concerned, total power was the revolutionary objective of the Bolsheviks.

During the summer of 1917 the tide of revolution rose, ebbed, and rose again. The government of moderate parliamentarianism held on, irresolute and wavering. Whatever hope there might have been for its success was cast into the shadows by its persistence in continuing the war. The complete disaster that befell the Russian army in the closing days of June spread over the country a darkening pall of despairing anguish that provided an irresistible vitality to the Bolshevik cause. Lenin, who had gone into hiding in Finland during a period of counterrevolution, sensed in September that the time had come to complete the revolution, and he urged the Party Central Committee to organize immediately an armed insurrection for the seizure of all state power. With Trotsky aggressively and tirelessly securing arms for the revolutionaries, the Bolsheviks were able, at 2:10 A.M. on November 8, to seize the members of the Provisional Government and imprison them in the Fortress of Peter and Paul.

That night at 8:40, Lenin, amid "a thundering wave of cheers," stood before a mass of humans welded together in the bond of community by their expectancy of peace. John Reed, the American journalist who was among them, provides, in *Ten Days That Shook the World,* a graphic picture of Lenin at that moment:

> A short, stocky figure, with a big head set down in his shoulders, bald and bulging. Little eyes, a snubbish nose, wide, generous mouth, and heavy chin; clean shaven now, but already beginning to bristle with the well-known beard of his past and future. Dressed in shabby clothes, his trousers much too long for him. Unimpressive, to be the idol of a mob; loved and revered as perhaps few leaders in history have been. A strange popular leader—a leader purely by virtue of intellect; colourless, humourless, uncompromising and detached, without picturesque idiosyncrasies— but with the power of explaining profound ideas in simple terms, of analysing a concrete situation. And combined with shrewdness, the greatest intellectual audacity.

Lenin, "gripping the edge of the reading stand, letting his little winking eyes travel over the crowd as he stood there waiting, apparently oblivious to the long-rolling ovation . . . said simply that 'we shall now proceed to construct the Socialist order!' " and that the first step was "the adoption of practical measures to realise peace.' "

"And before him," wrote Reed, "a thousand simple faces looking up in intent adoration."

Peace, bread, and community! In the Marxist view, the construction of the socialist order would quiet history's convulsions and humankind would at last find its resting place in time, the only reality a person could know. God and heaven were imaginative creations to make bearable the anguish of existence; history was the true bearer of grace. But in 1917 the community of socialism was a long way off, even if one could think that somewhere along time's route community was really there. Lenin got his peace with Germany: the Treaty of Brest-Litovsk of March 1918, a harsh settlement, but at last, where Russia was concerned, the war was over. Still the consolidation of the revolution went on, along pathways drenched with the blood of those who were thought to represent the final barrier to socialist order. In this killing there was nothing new—only the exercise by states and systems of that ancient policy to kill in order to achieve community.

John Reed shared with the masses who heard Lenin the night of November 8 the ecstatic sense of togetherness. He was, however, far from being a proletarian. Born on October 22, 1877, into circumstances of modest wealth, he attended Harvard University and there distinguished himself for his literary accomplishments as a poet and playwright. Sometime in his college years—it is said through the influence of writers Ida Tarbell and Lincoln Steffans—he became concerned with social issues. What moved him to the extremes he took as a rebel against the conventions of bourgeois culture—as an advocate of radical causes and a restless seeker of those areas of the world where conflict flamed: in Mexico before the beginning of the war in Europe, then to the battlefronts of Europe, and finally to Petrograd in 1917, to witness the culmination of the Russian Revolution—is a question whose answer is buried in those hazy areas where personality is formed. Perhaps he found in the passion of cause-ridden masses some glancing and refracted ray of paradise that vitalized his person with an almost spiritual energy. In the masses he surely found his sign of heaven, for as two of his biographers have said, his participation in a revolutionary action seemed to loose in him an exaltation that was "almost demonic."

Reed returned to the United States in 1917 and quickly involved himself in radical activities that included writing for the *Revolutionary Age*. His great concern was to produce an account of the Russian Revolution as he had witnessed it, but the State Department had seized all of his papers on his return, promising to release them "as soon as they are examined." Two months elapsed and Reed, still without his papers, wrote to his friend, Lincoln Steffans, seeking his intercession in the matter. Without his papers, Reed said, he was "unable to write a word of the greatest story of my life, and one of the greatest in the world. I am blocked."

Shortly thereafter his papers were returned and Reed set about writing *Ten Days That Shook the World,* "a slice of intensified history— history as I saw it." The book was published by Boni and Liveright in January 1919, with nine thousand copies sold in the first three months of publication. It would be difficult to conceive of any medium that could have depicted more faithfully the drama of the tragedy and glory of those days than Reed's prose. It was like an earthquake shuddering and groaning into a cataclysmic climax. Reed described faithfully the events he had witnessed, but beyond question he, personally, had found the cause that was greater than the fear of death. At the conclusion of his chapter "Moscow," he gives a moving account of a mass burial of those who had been killed fighting for the revolution:

> Through all the streets to the Red Square the torrents of people poured, thousand upon thousands of them, all with the look of the poor and toiling. A military band came marching up, playing the *Internationale,* and spontaneously the song caught and spread like wind-ripples on a sea; slow and solemn. From the top of the Kremlin wall gigantic banners unrolled to the ground; red, with great letters in gold and white saying, "Martyrs of the Beginning of World Social Revolution," and "Long Live the Brotherhood of Workers of the World."
>
> A bitter wind swept the square, lifting the banners. Now from the far quarters of the city the workers of the different factories were arriving with their dead. They could be seen coming through the Gate, the blare of their banners, and the dull red—like blood—of the coffins they carried. . . .
>
> Through an irregular lane that opened and closed again the procession slowly moved toward us. . . . The band was playing the Revolutionary Funeral March, and against the immense singing of the mass of people, standing uncovered, the paraders sang hoarsely, choked with sobs.

It was then, said Reed, that "I suddenly realized the devout Russian people no longer needed priests to pray them into heaven. On earth they were building a kingdom more bright than any heaven had to offer, and for which it was a glory to die." Reed's little sermonette on priests, praying, and heaven was, of course, a statement of his personal disposition, a disposition greatly strengthened by his having witnessed the revolution. For him it had been as moving as any great frontier revival meeting had been for the abandoned sinner who had found salvation.

On February 20 Reed's wife, the darkly intense and romantic Louise Bryant, made news. Senator Lee Overman's Committee Investigating Bolshevism had begun "a second phase of the inquiry . . . which has for its principal purpose the disclosure to the people of the United States of the identity of various persons who are operating in this country as official or semi-official agents of the Lenin-Trotsky Government." The Committee room was packed when Louise Bryant Reed appeared, and, as the *New York Times* reported, "Bolshevist sympathizers, mostly women, applauded Mrs. Reed; the patriots hissed," whereupon Senator Overman ordered the room cleared.

"Can I stay; I am the husband of the witness," said Reed.

"Yes, you can stay," said Senator Overman.

"Do you believe in God?" asked an unnamed senator.

"There may be one," replied Bryant.

"I asked if you believe in God. A person who does not believe in God has no conception of the sanctity of the oath," pursued the senator.

"I will concede," replied Bryant, "that I believe there is a God."

When the committee appearance was over, Reed and his wife once again said good-bye. "There was a fateful rhythm to their separations that would continue to their final parting," stated Barbara Gelb, who chronicled their love story. Later in the year Reed had himself spirited out of the country in an adventure-fraught return trip to Russia. There he had seen a faith breaking through into the process of history, and the vision called him back. Later, his wife joined him, but this time the golden moments were few. The suffering of the people continued unabated, and Reed experienced no further moments of revolutionary elation. Made into a bureaucratic pawn, he suffered the shackles of socialist organization. On October 19, 1920, he died of typhus. His ashes were placed in the Kremlin wall.

After Reed's death, Emma Goldman, who was then in Russia, asked Louise Byrant about her husband's last moments. "Didn't he speak at all?" she asked. "I could not understand what he meant," Bryant replied, "but he kept on repeating all the time, 'Caught in a trap, caught in a trap.' Just that." Goldman was amazed. "Did Jack really use that term?" she asked. "Because that is exactly how I have been feeling since I looked beneath the surface. Caught in a trap. Exactly that."

SOURCES

The account of the desolation in postwar Eastern Europe is from Herbert Hoover, *The Ordeal of Woodrow Wilson.* (New York, 1958). Theodore Roosevelt's Carnegie Hall speech is from the *New York Times,* November 2, 1918. John Reed, *Ten Days That Shook the World,* was first published by Boni and Liveright in 1919 and again in 1935 in a Modern Library edition. Most of the structuring facts of the biographical material on John Reed are from Dale L. Walker, *The Last Revolutionary: A Biography of John Reed* (New York, 1967).

Some sense of Reed's character, and of Louise Bryant's, was imparted by Dorothy Day, founder of the Catholic Worker movement. During the summer of 1917, as editor of the expiring *Liberator,* Reed was part of the company that Day kept. Over the twenty years I knew her, she would sometimes briefly reminisce about Reed. Of Louise Bryant, her view was somewhat deprecatory.

For the full "love story" of Reed and Bryant (after the latter had fled the bower prepared for her by her dentist husband), read Barbara Gelb's *So Short a Time* (New York, 1973). Lincoln Steffans, in *The Autobiography of Lincoln Steffans,* tells of Reed's anxiety over the State Department's siezure of his papers. Emma Goldman, in *Living My Life* (New York, 1970), quotes Bryant for Reed's dying words.

FURTHER READING

On the postwar desolation in Europe see Herbert C. Hoover, *An American Epic,* vol. 2 (Chicago, 1929). See also Hoover's *Hoover-Wilson Wartime Correspondence, September 24, 1914, to November 11, 1918* (Ames, Iowa, 1974). For an added dimension on the life of Emma Goldman, see Richard Drinnen, *Rebel in Paradise: A Biography of Emma Goldman* (Chicago, 1961).

CHAPTER

7

Shadows of Revolution
at Home

JOHN REED APPEARED to have little doubt that the United States would enter into the final days where the expectations of his revolutionary faith were concerned. In 1919 he told one of his friends who was being sent to jail as a conscientious objector that he would be freed by the workers long before the sentence had been completed. Just a few more acts of social repression, Reed predicted, and "there will be a revolutionary movement in this country in five years."

Reed's hopes were shared by a number of similarly minded persons. Nineteen-year-old Dorothy Day, who fifteen years later would found the Catholic Worker Movement, recalled that on March 21, 1917, she had "joined with those thousands [in Madison Square Garden] in reliving the first days of the revolt in Russia. I felt the exultation, the joyous sense of victory of the masses as they sang . . . the worker's hymn of Russia"—the hymn that *Call*, the New York socialist newspaper, described the next day as a "mystic, gripping melody of struggle, a cry for world peace and human brotherhood." Granville Hicks said that to America's revolutionary radicals it "seemed certain that the era of world revolution had begun."

Who were these radicals? They came from the old Industrial Workers of the World (I.W.W.), whose members had been hounded and persecuted during the war; and they came out of the radical left-wing labor organizations of immigrant groups, many of which published foreign-language revolutionary journals. Some radicals were also native-born white Americans from middle-class backgrounds, people like Dorothy Day and John Reed, who would storm heaven and bring community to earth, building it on the secure foundation of working-class solidarity.

The high expectation of radicals that the revolution could not be far away was matched by apprehension on the part of many Americans that the radicals could be right. In the weeks following the war revolutionary currents had swept across Germany into Eastern Europe. In its issue of November 23, 1918, *The Literary Digest* said that no one could be certain "that the war for democracy is not to be followed by a war against anarchy." It quoted Frank H. Simonds, a writer on military matters for the *New York Tribune,* as saying that "if the recent course of events in Germany be not promptly changed, nothing seems more certain than we shall at no distant time be facing eastward over the Rhine upon a vast seething mass of anarchy, extending from the Rhine to the Siberian wastes and including within its limits the 300,000,000 people of Russia, Germany, and Austria."

There was in the reading fare of Americans throughout 1919 a continuing reference to the Bolshevik danger. In the *New York Times* of January 15, under the heading "The Red Menace," the subject was set to dubious verse:

> Red is a hue of splendor when controlled
> By Nature; but, when used by man,
> grows bold
> And, running rich under freedom's name,
> seeks to destroy
> what it cannot enjoy—
> Balance, reserve, sobriety of aim—
> Tyrannical as roaring, unchecked flame.
> The pillar of His cloud has served us
> well.
> But the Red Sea begins again to swell.
> What rod can split its waters if they
> spread
> Despite the hands
> Lifted by No Man's Land's
> Millions of chosen, freedom-martyred
> dead?
> It is no god, but Satan, who wears red!

As the readers of the *New York Times* turned the pages of the March 24 edition, they must have been startled to see a full-page depiction of a gorilla-like form advancing out of a background of carnage with a sword in one hand and a flaming torch in the other. "Is Bolshevism coming to America?" the caption asked. The advertisement was the work of the *Christian Herald,* a widely read Protestant periodical. The answer it provided represented a degree of enlightenment that most

Americans had not attained. What was needed to combat Bolshevism was "a new spirit in industry; a spirit that will recognize and respect the personality of each man, so that each man may have freedom for self-expression through his work."

The *Saturday Evening Post* kept the subject on a level that gave substance to those with a taste for the lurid. In its issue of April 3, the *Post* included a story by George Kibbe Turner titled "Red Friday." It was about one Planganov, "the brain of the proletariat, the one great secret mind such as exists behind all movements, within the social revolution of the east of Europe; wise with the wisdom of a catastrophic era, and as secret and pitiless in his movements as he was wise." Planganov was a composite of Lenin and Trotsky, with the addition of some sinister flourishes—"his fire of hatred, his harsh and antagonistic voice, his striking head, his peasant hands, the pits of peasant smallpox in his face; and the long gray faded overcoat, thrown open now and hanging down—that dingy mantle of the proletariat." He was "the personification of the new power in the world— the bitter voice of the proletariat come to judgment, cursing their old master."

Planganov's cunning could be discerned in the breathtaking but awful simplicity of his plan for taking over America. He would effect his ends through an alliance with the Christian Socialists, headed by a Wall Street magnate named Stephen Black. Private capital would be eradicated in a great pincers movement, one side of which included Black and his Christian Socialists; the other side was represented by "the competition of the Government against private corporations." (The shadowy character who narrated the plot interjected here an editorial opinion that "the success of the opening campaign is far too familiar for me to detail. The taking over of the railroads by the national Government was a foregone conclusion.")

So that was it, the millions of readers of the *Post* might have said to themselves. The plan was to disseminate liberal ideas via the churches and the creeping socialism of the federal government! But it had already happened. Walter Rauschenbusch's *Christianity and Social Crisis,* which had begun publication in 1907, was followed by the formation of the Federal Council of Churches, and now its socializing effects could be seen in the ideas of some church leaders. As for the government, one of its potent weapons was "ruinous taxation," and already it was being used mercilessly. On February 24, President Wilson had signed the Revenue Act of 1918, which increased the prevailing tax burden by almost 250 percent and put four-fifths of the load on large income, profits, and estates. Further, there was a continuing agitation among labor circles for the government wartime Railroad Administration to continue the management of the railroads.

What further diabolical plans remained to be revealed by Planganov? Many, to be sure; but unfortunately the story was "To Be Continued."

The next *Post* alarm came in Emerson Hough's "Fool's Paradise." Hough wanted to know what Americans were thinking "just at this time," when news dispatches were filled with accounts of looming threats of a Soviet government in the United States. Had Americans paused to ponder "what this means to your home, your property, your womankind"? If they had not, they had better start because Hough had just "recently" talked "to the head of the largest detective agency in the United States" and had asked him if he thought there was a real Bolshevik threat. The agency chief had "studied for some time before he answered" but then had said, "You can bet your life there is! ... A lot more than people seem to think. It's worse than just bad. Myself, I think that America is getting ready for a revolution ... the worst that ever was." Presumably, millions of Americans gasped.

Such stories lend credence to a statement by the American socialist James Maurer: "I was often asked by people of means when the revolution would start. As a well-known radical I was supposed to know." Maurer related that "one nice old lady" had told him that she hoped that "when the revolution comes they won't torture me. If I must die I hope they kill me with a bullet." It was "hopeless" to attempt to reassure them, Maurer said.

Zane Grey, the prodigious writer of westerns, whose heroes always triumphed and whose unblemished heroines were likely to have long eyelashes and wear triple-A shoes, quickly put his literary talent to the cause of alerting America to its danger. In the *New York Times Book Review* of March 16, Harper Brothers advertised Grey's *Desert of Wheat* thus: "Out West today are new dangers threatening America—dangers far blacker than ever threatened the cowboys." At that very moment, "red-blooded Americans" were fighting these dangers. "Read this fascinating novel of a brave man, a plucky girl and the I.W.W. plots to burn the great wheat fields."

The subject of the Red takeover was irresistible for orators. Vice President Thomas R. Marshall, whose impact on the history of the times went no further than his registration of the need for a nickel cigar, approached another historic breakthrough in a speech to the National Press Club on February 7. He offered the country a new American creed: "I believe that America belongs to American citizens ... and I believe that all others should be taught, peacefully if we can and forcibly if we must, that our country is not an international boarding house nor an anarchist cafe." Nicholas Murray Butler, Columbia University's president, who could always be counted upon to contribute his ringing oratory to support the verities of the Republican Party, said in a speech in Cincinnati on April 19 that the battle for socialism would be half won when Americans were led "to give up their historic patriotism for a sentimental humanitarianism."

It was, of course, the Russian Revolution and what most Americans, by the spring of 1919, had come to regard as its appalling character that produced the alarmist mood and gave license to those who would have their compatriots mount the breastworks and turn back the tide before their lives had been reduced to ashes. But against whom and what was their campaign to be waged? Radical labor seemed the most likely target, but in one celebrated instance the web of circumstances may have wrongly entrapped one of its members. The Mooney case, which reached its most explosive potential in January 1919, was from 1915 until 1939, when Mooney was released from prison, a continuing focus for the rallying of not only radical but much temperate sentiment against the irrational excesses of World War I and after.

Born on December 8, 1882, Thomas J. Mooney became a dedicated and energetic radical. His father was a coal miner, born of Irish immigrant parents in a railroad construction camp; his mother was an immigrant from Ireland. Mooney's early years were spent around the coal mines of Washington, Indiana. When he was ten, his father died of tuberculosis and his mother, in order to survive, took the family to Holyoke, Massachusetts, where she found employment working sixty hours a week sorting rags in a paper mill. Dutifully, she sent her children to a parochial school, but Tom, thrashed by a priest for lying, left and went to a public school.

In 1907 Tom Mooney worked his way to Europe and there became involved in the ferment of radical labor. His socialist position, one is inclined to think, was not so much a matter of philosophical conviction as it was of providing a platform for his restless and energetic nature. Armed with a cause, he left Europe for California, where, in the area around Stockton, he hawked socialist literature and made soapbox declamations on the evils of capitalism. In 1908, to support the presidential campaign of Eugene V. Debs, he raised seventy-five dollars and was thereby elected a delegate to the Socialist party convention in San Francisco. In time he became one of the standard fixtures in the upper echelons of California Socialism.

Mooney's difficulties began on July 22, 1916, the day of a monster preparedness demonstration in San Francisco. Planning for the parade had begun as early as May and was subjected to increasing denunciation by Socialists on the grounds that the affair was being staged in the interest of financiers, munition makers, and newspaper sales. On the appointed day the parade began at four minutes past one o'clock with a group of veterans of the Grand Army of the Republic moving out onto Market Street. The head of the column had not proceeded very far when, about twenty feet ahead of it, a bomb exploded among the spectators, killing ten and wounding forty. Of the radical suspects who were rounded up, the circumstances of evidence appeared to point to Mooney and Warren Billings as the perpetrators of the crime. Brought to trial, Mooney was convicted of prime responsibility and was sentenced to be hanged. After the appeal process had been completed, the execution was set for December 13, 1918.

In the year's time between Mooney's trial and the appointed execution date, American radical and labor papers were bitter in their denunciation of the kind of justice Mooney had received. The evidence on which he had been convicted was all circumstantial; perjury had been proven in the case of one of the state's witnesses; and the trial judge, T. J. Griffin, had recommended a new trial on the grounds that the credibility of other witnesses against Mooney had been questionable. As the judicious *Literary Digest* said, even some conservative newspapers were admitting doubt "whether Mooney was granted justice in the California courts."

As the day for Mooney's execution approached, the outcries of radicals increased. "In New York and in San Francisco, in Chicago and Milwaukee, in Hartford, Conn., and Laredo, Texas, the red flag has been raised," said *The Literary Digest.* In the latter part of November, Woodrow Wilson, preparing for his European journey and wishing to allay radical hostility abroad, asked the governor of California to commute Mooney's sentence to life imprisonment. The governor complied, explaining that his action had come solely at the insistence of the President.

If this action was also intended to dull the mounting exhilaration among radicals as they contemplated the salutary effect on the "cause" that a martyr would provide, it did not completely do so. Neither Mooney nor radicals in general were happy. On January 18, 1919, the Socialists and assorted radical enthusiasts opened the National Labor Congress at Chicago to consider a program for liberating Mooney and Billings. Americans, indignant and alarmed, read in their newspapers of speakers at the congress who "demanded the organization of an American Soviet." The climax of the meeting was reached when a moving picture was shown on the Mooney case. One scene, showing soldiers carrying an American flag in the San Francisco Preparedness Day Parade, brought hisses from the delegates.

Perhaps some of the residents of suburban America were surprised when January passed and there had been no revolution. February had not been long born before the horizon was darkened again. On Thursday, February 6, forty thousand workers at Seattle, Washington, under the direction of a "Central Labor Council's Strike Committee" went on strike to back up the demands of twenty-five thousand striking shipyard workers. At midnight on the night before, Seattle's mayor, Ole Hanson, had been summoned by strike leaders to the Labor Temple for a final conference. Hanson went, but his response was, "No compromise, no recognition," whereupon he armed three thousand special policemen and got the backing of U.S. Army detachments. In two days the "revolution" was over. Said Hanson: "The people were ninety-five percent loyal to our flag and government, and the troops and our police force greatly outnumbered the other five percent. . . . Bolshevism, soviets, anarchists and the red flag will not be tolerated."

Hanson had been born in a frontier cabin in Wisconsin in 1863. Suffering partial paralysis from a train wreck in Texas, which also had claimed the life of one of his children, he decided to try to regain his health by crossing the continent in a prairie schooner. In 1902 he, his wife, and three of their children left Racine for Seattle. It was said that when he pitched his tent in the woods on a hill outside Seattle he remarked that, "by and by," he would be mayor of the city. In March 1918 he achieved his objective.

Because of his decisive action against the strikers, Hanson was bedecked overnight with the mantle of the conqueror-hero who had turned back the Red tide. He did not wear it modestly. Over the next six months he was pleased to become America's strong voice calling for decisive confrontation with all radicals. *McClure's Magazine* named him "one of the most remarkable men in America to-day. The manner in which he settled the Seattle Revolution will go down in history." The magazine, "wishing to present to its readers the most authentic account of this affair," had asked Hanson "to send his own story and held the presses for his answer." Hanson, "feeling it was his absolute duty to warn the people of this country of the very much underestimated danger of Bolshevism," had telegraphed an article "which was dictated from his bed at midnight." The Seattle mayor named the leaders: "Leon Green, Russian, alien, slacker, liar, Bolshevik, I.W.W.; the head of the Electrical Workers' Union, who had said to me on the day of Roosevelt's death, 'I am glad he is dead; he stood in our way!' " He also said that a woman was involved, Anna Louise Strong, who had been "recalled from the office of school director on a patriotic issue by vote of the people of Seattle."

Anna Louise Strong was, at the time, a young journalist who had been caught by the vision of a new socialist order of humankind, where war and injustice would exist no longer. In the twenties she moved to Russia, where she hoped to work in the new Soviet state toward the realization of her dream. But witnessing the Stalinist murders in the thirties and forties produced a reaction that led to her expulsion in 1949. Yet the vision remained, and in China she found signs that she believed upheld her faith. From there, until her death in March 1970, she posted periodically an interpretive newsletter to friends in the United States, one of whom was Dorothy Day of the Catholic Worker Movement. Writing to Day toward the end of her life, Strong said that she, too, had once held hope for life in the heavenly city and perhaps it was that for which she had really struggled over the course of her years.

As for Hanson, the applause from audiences and the fees that went with his lectures on the "Bolshevist menace" were so sweet to his ears and pocketbook that he shortly resigned his office as mayor and took to the lecture circuit. From this work he quickly faded into oblivion.

In late April 1919, the sense of crisis and popular indignation mounted, where covert radicalism was concerned. On the twenty-eighth, a small package was delivered by mail to Mayor Hanson's office in Seattle. Because the mayor was out of the city in patriotic service, for some time the package lay near his desk, finally exuding a fluid that on examination proved to be an acid detonater for a bomb. On the twenty-ninth a package was delivered to the home of former Senator Thomas W. Hardwick in Atlanta. His maid, who opened the package, lost both of her hands in the explosion that ensued and Mrs. Hardwick was burned.

On April 30, a New York postal clerk, Charles Kaplan, reading of these events as he rode home on the subway, remembered that he had put aside for insufficient postage some packages similar to the ones described in the news account. He immediately informed his superiors of his strong suspicion that the packages contained bombs. He was right. There were sixteen cartons addressed to various persons prominent in government and finance. Among them was Associate Supreme Court Justice Oliver Wendell Holmes, Jr. It was, of course, widely assumed that the person or persons who had mailed the bombs were immigrants aflame with radical ideas that had been inspired by the Russian Revolution. Aside from the particular instance of the bomb mailings, a belief prevailed that revolutionary agitation in general was of Jewish origin. Between 1870 and 1914, two million Jews had come to America from Eastern Europe and Russia. They came for the two standard reasons: poverty and persecution. Among the major immigrant groups that came to America, only the Irish were poorer when they arrived. And as for persecution, no immigrant group had suffered more than the Jews had as a consequence of the insane, periodic outbreaks of murderous anti-Semitism that occurred in Eastern Europe and Russia.

It was, then, only to be expected that Jews everywhere, but especially those American Jews of Russian origin who had packed themselves into New York's Lower East Side, looked upon the Russian Revolution as possibly the beginning of a new era in Jewish life. In December 1918, the first American Jewish Congress was convened at Philadelphia, described by the *New Republic* as "a loose aggregation of mutually distrustful delegates." The congress adopted resolutions concerning programs and boycotts to assist fellow Jews in Poland and in hope of securing full civil rights for the Jews of Russia and Lithuania. It further urged "a final disposition" on the issue of Palestine as a homeland for dispossessed Jews.

One participant at the meeting, a firebrand orator named Chayyim Zhitlowsky, threw the deliberations into an uproar by declaring that Jews should, in effect, cease to be Jews. For many centuries, he said, they had "been distinguished as a religious body," but "now this will no longer hold. Religion is not the test. It is nationality that makes a Jew." After this pronouncement, there was pandemonium. For a moment, a subdued muttering rose "from the benches of the Mizrachi, then . . . the whole right was on its feet in a deafening uproar. A dancing dervish in a skull-cap rushed up in front of the platform and screamed, and waved his fists in Zhitlowsky's face, and finally succumbed to tears."

The urge to give up the character of Jewish particularity, to become like the rest, had been throughout history one of the main threats to Jewish identity—the temptation, as Jewish orthodoxy might have it, to break the covenant Abraham and Moses had made with God. It was a temptation that many young East Side Jews, thinking of themselves as living in a new age, would find not only attractive but seemingly logical.

Most East Side Jews were ardent socialists, apparently due to the repression and suffering they had experienced under autocratic political and social systems, systems that historically had enhanced their power by claiming a divine sanction, by identifying themselves as a central and vital part of the spirit and body of Christ's Church—Catholic in Poland and Orthodox in Russia. Themselves victimized by these systems, and seeing the victimization of large classes of others by them, East Side Jews of Polish and Russian origin were likely to think of socialism as not only the instrument of their own redemption but that of humankind in general. No wonder, as Robert Murray wrote in *The Red Scare,* they were "awed and revitalized" by the success of the Russian Revolution.

To most Americans, New York's East Side was a foreign land. But in

1919 many knew about two East Side anarchists, Emma Goldman and Alexander Berkman. In 1892 Berkman had tried to assassinate steel magnate Henry Clay Frick during the Homestead Strike crisis, and for his not quite successful attempt he served fourteen years in prison. Goldman, Berkman's lover before the Frick assassination attempt, continued a fraternal association with him in the anarchist cause after his release. Together, they put out two anarchist publications, *Mother Earth*, a literary and philosophical journal that was primarily Goldman's, and a newsletter called *The Blast*. Goldman, an effective orator, gave lectures on anarchism, mainly to immigrant labor groups.

Obviously, neither of these two, nor whoever else on New York's East Side shared their views, had anything to do with the Russian Revolution. Yet that was an assumption made by one witness before the Senate's Overman Committee investigating Bolshevism, an assumption that was given wide publicity in *The Literary Digest*. "Are Bolsheviki Mainly Jewish?" the *Digest* asked in December 1918. It answered in part by quoting *The American Hebrew* as being disturbed by the "persistent harping, on the part of many writers, on the generally accepted opinion that Jews and Bolsheviki are synonymous and that, therefore . . . the Jews 'are the real rulers of Russia.' "

In February 1919, the Reverend Dr. George A. Simons, who from 1907 to October 1918 had been in Russia as the head of a Methodist mission college, "brought out the fact that Russian Bolshevism was largely a product of New York's lower East Side and that its membership was almost entirely Jewish." Simons went on to say that in December 1918, "the Soviet of the northern commune in Petrograd . . . consisted of sixteen Russians and 265 Jews from New York." If Reverend Simons had truly affirmed the presence of American Jews in the Petrograd Soviet, it should not have been altogether surprising. The East Side harbored many Russian Jewish expatriates who probably felt an obligation to return to the old country and help in the reconstruction of a new society that would end the horror of the pogroms.

What is somewhat curious about the response of some, if not most, Americans to the turmoil at home and abroad was the assumption that Germany was responsible for it. Perhaps a shift in the devil figure from the Hun to the Bolshevik required a moment of transition. "We know this is not a Russian Government. It is German first and Jewish next," declared *The Literary Digest* in February 1919. The assumption that Bolshevism was of German origin is, of course, attributable to the German role in returning Lenin to Russia in 1918. The charge that it was Jewish, which in some vague way was connected with Germanism, must take into account two considerations. First, Jews of Germanic background, since they had more generally moved into the mainstream of German life than they had elsewhere in Europe, were not at all accepting of the sweeping generalization that the Allies were fighting the battle of humanity against inhumanity. Second, if the American Jew, whether of German background or from one of the Slavic countries, was inclined to have a favorite in the great war it would not have been Russia, because of its history of murderous outbreaks of anti-Semitism. So obviously many American Jews, who likely were recent arrivals anyway, were inclined to sit out the "great crusade."

Plans for new systems of social radicalism were usually not part of the cultural baggage of old-world Jews, to be immediately opened when they came to America. They came from Russia with little more, materially, than their few immigrant trunks, and because of their poverty they settled almost where they put their first step ashore—on New York's Lower East Side. Spiritually, though, they brought something unique into the history of humankind: a life, witnessed to in its forms and manner and in the patient weariness in their faces, of concern that they remain faithful to the covenant that Abraham had made with God.

For many of the young Jews, however, growing up in America, the new time and the new air they breathed produced a new vision. Young Hyppolyte Havel, an East Side writer and intellectual, was one of them. The sons and daughters of Israel, he wrote, had always been revolutionaries, for it had been to the Jews that God had first given the vision of the heights to which humankind might aspire. Sometimes, he said, the longing to give substance to that vision had driven "the young generation away from hearth and home . . . just as this spirit once drove out the revolutionary breeder of discontent, Jesus, and alienated him from his native traditions."

But mainstream Americans knew nothing of Hyppolyte Havel and his ideas. The question most of them were asking during the postwar era was, What should be done about the radicals of foreign origin—the illiterate Italians and those East Side Jews who spoke Yiddish and who seemingly were all socialists? In the latter part of January, the *New York Times* asked a number of state governors to recommend corrective action. J. P. Goodrich of Indiana favored "creating an American atmosphere in communities made up of foreigners" where all would be "taught to speak and to think in our common language, which is the Declaration of Independence." W. L. Harding of Iowa had the same thought: "Sad, indeed, was the plight of the country when, engaged in a great world war, it found it necessary to stop its preparation of men to fight to teach them to speak and even to read and understand the language of the country well enough so that they could be drilled and take or give orders." If the immigrants did not attempt to learn English and become Americanized, they should be told, "You may tarry for a time . . . and then you must go back." Other governors thought likewise: learn to speak English, become "Americanized," or go back to Europe.

One concerned American, the Reverend Christian F. Reisner, bethought himself not to wait for state intervention but to take direct action in the particular instance of the notorious and otherwise impenetrable Lower East Side of New York. His action was so direct and so "American" that he was featured in an article in the *American Magazine* for December 1919. The article rose to ecstatic heights in its description of Reisner and his work. He was "six feet of muscular Christianity," the speaker for "the largest church audience of New York City." His theme was exultant patriotism: "Promptly at eight o'clock the singing of 'The Star Spangled Banner' by Louise Homer brought the audience to its feet." Then Reisner, backed by wartime spellbinders like Arthur Guy Empey, Gipsy Smith, and "Private Pete," made the call for a conformity by all to the practices and values of mainstream America.

For Reisner, it was the East Side where the crisis was most urgent. As the *American Magazine* article pointed out, so intense was Reisner's concern that he personally "campaigned vigorously on the East Side in a recent election." Reisner was "the only speaker not a Socialist. . . . To him patriotism and religion are so interwoven they cannot be separated." We do not know how Jews reacted to Reisner's presence among them, but uptown his audiences were thrilled by what they were led to believe was his courage and the loftiness of his commitment. How had Reisner been able to raise the number of his Sunday night assemblages from fifty to over fifteen hundred in just a few years, the *American Magazine* wanted to know. "Advertising!" Reisner said.

The Reisner phenomenon was peculiar to the character of New York City: the Sunday assembling in some hall of rootless people who wanted to be told how good it all was and how they deserved it and could have it. But the effrontery contained in Reisner's assumption that the East Side Jews, whose passion lay in the quest for justice, could be instructed by his flag-waving and bully-posturing kind of religious indoctrination was considerable. It was about this time that a Russian exile living in Paris, Nicolas Berdyaev, wrote the following concerning the communist challenge to Christianity: "the only thing to pit against integral Communism . . . is integral Christianity—not rhetorical, tattered, decadent Christianity, but renascent Christianity, working out its eternal truths toward consistent life, consistent culture, consistent social justice."

In the growing confusion of the postwar months, when the white heat of wartime unity had cooled and a new menace seemed to be mushrooming in the world, some persons looked back to the war with something like nostalgia. An advertisement by the Columbia Trust Company in the *New York Times* on June 25 compared the confusion of the first six months of peace with the solidarity of the war years. Then, "everybody pulled together—for America. National need erased party lines and class lines. Hyphenates largely disappeared. Foreign-born Americans became *real* Americans. Polyglot peoples fought and died under one flag—the American flag." John Dewey wrote in the *New Republic* that some Americans lamented the war's end on the grounds that the country "has not been in the war long enough to experience the intensity of suffering that purchases this elevation of feeling, this spiritual exhilaration, which is sometimes referred to as the priceless boon conferred by the war."

Grover C. Loud, in a kind of meditation in the *New Republic* of March 1919 called "Battle Song," took the subject into the realm of theology. Why was it that people were singing no more "as once they sang?" Must a world at peace be one "that no longer marches and sings? Nothing to march for, nothing to sing for, there is nothing to stir the hearts of men?" The world needed to return to a vision of human unity that transcended nation and race, Loud said. "And as that brotherhood joins to advance into the growing light of new days, toward the nearer realization of the Kingdom of God on earth, it shall sing a new song."

Loud's hope was one that history seemed destined not to tolerate, at least in 1919. There certainly were no new songs to tell of the stirring of hope for a new world community as represented by Wilson's League of Nations. Already the vision was fading. In April the Washington, D.C., Board of Education suspended Miss Alice Woods, English teacher, because she had been talking about Bolshevism and the League to her pupils. The suspension order said that all teachers were to refrain from taking up the League or Bolshevism for the "current topics" discussions. Miss Woods, it added, was not qualified to speak on these subjects.

SOURCES

The sources for this chapter are mainly from contemporary periodicals named in the text. More on John Reed has been taken from Granville Hicks, *John Reed: The Making of a Revolutionary* (New York, 1937). The quotation from Dorothy Day, who at the time was a reporter for the *Call*, is from *The Long Loneliness* (New York, 1952). James Maurer's comments are from his *It Can Be Done: The Autobiography of James Hudson Maurer* (New York, 1938). The source of the biographical material on Tom Mooney is Richard W. Frost, *The Mooney Case* (New

York, 1968). A contemporary survey of the Mooney case can be found in *The Literary Digest* (December 7, 1918). Biographical information on Ole Hanson is mainly from Paul C. Hedrick, "Ole Hanson and the Big Strike," *Saturday Evening Post* (April 5, 1919) and "Ole Hanson on the Job!" *McClure's* (April 1919), written by Hanson himself. The meeting of The American Jewish Congress at Philadelphia in December 1918, is described in the *New Republic* (December 28, 1918). Berdyaev's statement on the ideal response of Christianity to communism is from Nicolas Berdyaev, *The Russian Revolution* (Paris, 1919).

FURTHER READING

The standard and near definitive work on the alarm produced by radicalism abroad and at home is Robert Murray's *The Red Scare: A Study in National Hysteria, 1919–1920* (Minneapolis, 1955). Jewish East Side life is described in Michael Gold, *Jews without Money* (New York, 1938), and in Dorothy Day, *The Long Loneliness* (New York, 1952). Some very fine stories of life on New York's East Side were written by a Russian Jewish émigré, Anzia Yezierska. One, "The Fate of the Land," was declared "the best short story for 1919" in a collection by Edward J. O'Brien. Her story "Hunger" can be found in H. C. Schweikert, ed., *Short Stories* (New York, 1925).

8

A Puritan Abroad

LLOYD C. GARDNER, in *Wilson and Revolutions, 1913–1921,* begins his essay on the Russian Revolution with a brief description of the events that signaled its beginning. It was 2:00 A.M. November 7, 1917, when small bands of armed workers and sailors left their hiding places and went about the city of Petrograd seizing vital segments of its operational life. "By ten o'clock in the morning all were taken and secured." Thus began the Bolshevik action that three years later ended in the establishment of a totalitarian power that would last for seventy years.

President Wilson welcomed the March revolution in Russia because it appeared to affirm the progressive democracy he had advanced as America's stake for entering the war. But in spirit and method the Bolshevik cause was profoundly at odds with his ideals. In Gardner's words, those ideals were "jeered" by the Bolsheviks as "the latest product off the capitalist assembly line, shabby delusions glossed in Wilsonian rhetoric to fool the workers."

During the three years of war between the Bolsheviks and the Soviet Constituent Assembly forces under Aleksander Kolchak, Wilson might have led in some form of American intervention. But, Gardner concludes, in Russia as in South America, Wilson opposed counterrevolutions on the grounds that they were the work of "special interests," frustrating the spontaneous progressivism of the people. In the end, where Wilson was concerned, the ultimate consequences of revolution in Russia, as they so frequently had been in South America, were antithetical to the philosophy and methods of his ideals.

Bolshevism was the ultimate negation of the traditional forms and values by which the Western world had lived. Its menacing fire, fueled by the exhaustion and disillusionment that fell upon many in the months just after the war, arose here and there across Europe. Monday, January 9, was a critical day in the history of Germany. "What Monday witnessed . . . was perhaps the greatest proletarian demonstration that History has ever seen," declared the communist newspaper *Red Flag*. "We do not believe that in Russia such an exhibition could have taken place. From Roland to Victoria the proletarians stood head to head. Far into the Tiergarten they stood. They had brought their weapons with them; they let their red banners stream. They were ready to do anything, to give everything, life itself. An army of 200,000 men such as no Ludendorff had ever seen." The day passed, cold and fog enshrouded; the proletarians stood their ground. Here and there throughout Berlin their leaders were debating and parleying. But there were no decisions, and when evening came, those who might have made a revolution went home.

By nightfall the pendulum had begun its reverse swing. At 3:00 on the following afternoon the government of the Majority Socialists began assembling arms and men in the suburb of Dahlem. Gustav Noske took charge. That evening soldiers marched into Berlin and the next morning laid siege to the building where the communist Spartacists had gathered. After four days all resistance had been overcome. On January 15 the two Spartacist leaders, Karl Liebknecht and Rosa Luxemburg, were found and arrested. The next day they were questioned at the Eden Hotel, used at the time as the headquarters of the Berlin military. Following the interrogation they were ordered to prison, but en route both were murdered by their military escort. Rosa Luxemburg was clubbed at the hotel entrance as she was being led to a car; Liebknecht was clubbed and then shot to death on the way to prison.

The *New York Times* carried the story of their deaths on January 18, adding an editorial on the subject: "Regrettable as is the manner of the death, the work of private violence, not the law, that came to Dr. Liebknecht and Rosa Luxemburg, it was to be expected, and does a summary, if irregular, justice to the fomenters of robbery, murder, and anarchy." The editors thought that much could be excused if Germany were prevented from following the path that Russia had taken.

At 3:00 P.M., on January 18, the peace conference opened at Paris. Now, at last, the reconstruction of Europe and the world could begin. Germany was spent, lacerating itself. But the vision of peace, of a new order and a new brotherhood—the vision of a new world, described in phrases that rolled so easily from the tongues and pens of patriots who cried for every sacrifice and heroism to achieve it—seemed more remote than ever. Now, in 1919, what the Allied managers of history wanted was to restore as quickly as possible the civility of the world they had known. They had been through nearly five years of agony, and each was convinced beyond all doubt that his own country had not transgressed but had been transgressed upon. As they saw it, they had every right to demand that what had been destroyed by war be restored to them, and that conditions be set up to ensure that they would not again be forced to fight.

The League of Nations? The Fourteen Points? No one would disavow the ideal, but as David Lloyd George, the British prime minister, later said, the Fourteen Points "were in places phrased in the language of vague idealism which, in the absence of practical application, made them capable of more than one interpretation." Britain would want its own "exegesis of the sacred text." In *The Truth about the Peace Treaties,* Lloyd George said he was convinced that "at first the idealistic President regarded himself as a missionary whose function it was to rescue the poor European heathen from their age-long worship of false and fiery gods." Woodrow Wilson had preached to his Allied associates "about right being more important than might, justice more eternal than force."

Winston Churchill, then a member of the British Cabinet, was Wilson's most acidulous critic. "If Mr. Wilson had been either simply an idealist or a caucus politician, he might have succeeded. His attempt to run the two in double harness was the cause of his undoing. The spacious philanthropy which he exhaled upon Europe stopped quite sharply at the coasts of his own country." Wilson had come to Europe, Churchill said, seeing himself "for a prolonged period at the summit of the world, chastening the Allies, chastening the Germans and generally giving laws to mankind. He believed himself capable of appealing to peoples and parliaments over the heads of their governments. . . . In the Peace Conference . . . President Wilson sought to play a part out of all proportion to any stake which his country had contributed or intended to contribute to European affairs." What the president should have done, in Churchill's view, was to permit himself to be directed by the calmer, wiser, more experienced leadership of Lloyd George and Georges Clemenceau. But he did not; and as a result, he "consumed his own strength and theirs in conflicts in which he was always worsted."

Churchill's pronouncements aside, there still was something about Wilson, perhaps a core of self-righteousness, that no one, with whatever logic or force, could change. Was this his Calvinism, a position at ease in the Enlightenment universe of law, where the covenant idea added the dimension of sacred commitment to uphold the laws of nature?

Wilson could seek advice and take advice, but anything or anybody that challenged the formal arrangement of his universe would not get a hearing, only a sermon. And what idealist in that day, after reading or hearing Wilson's polished and exalted rhetoric, could not but feel its force? Persons who were close to him—Colonel E.M. House and Joseph Tumulty are conspicuous examples—never questioned the magisterial aura of moral and intellectual infallibility that he wore. When anyone in his circle gave evidence of doubting this infallibility, the skeptic was cut adrift. House's relationship with Wilson shows that he understood this. House was little more than an extension of the president, and while he conferred, advised, and reported, he advised and reported as he knew he must. He was a man on the end of a string. In the crucial days of the peace conference, when he essayed an independent judgment on the course of affairs that seemed to affront Wilson's position, he was cast loose. In the end, so was Tumulty, who was never anything but loyal to Wilson and Wilson's "idea."

Although the president must have been aware of the opinions of him held by the Allied leaders, he did not respond to them. Edith Wilson, at least by the time of the publication of *My Memoir* in 1937, knew of them and made her own answer. She saw her husband as the one who had stood on the front line, carrying the battle for peace and justice against those who would settle cheaply for what the war had cost. Who were these persons whose vision never rose above a pedestrian national self-interest? They were "M. Clemenceau, an avowed cynic, distrustful of humanity's ability to rise to unselfish heights; . . . Mr. Lloyd George, a political weather vane shifting with every wind that blew across the Channel lest it affect his personal fortunes; . . . Signor Orlando, whose ear was ever to the ground for fear Italy should not get all she hungered for." Among those bending reeds, her husband "stood practically alone— with some very lukewarm support from some of his own commission, such as [Secretary of State Robert] Lansing."

Mrs. Wilson's attitude toward Lansing may have been justified. The very soul of unyielding self-righteousness on the issues that separated America and Germany in the years of America's neutrality, Lansing took a rather mute and recessive role at the peace conference. Ray Stannard Baker, in *Woodrow Wilson and World Settlement*, reports that Lansing said, "The more I think about the President's declaration as to the right of 'self-determination,' the more confirmed I am of the danger of putting such ideas into the minds of certain races." When the secretary of state returned from Europe on July 22, he declined to make any comment on the League of Nations being "completely out of touch with affairs because the wireless aboard the ship was not capable of sending or receiving messages over long distances." Later, on August 6, when he appeared before the Senate Foreign Relations Committee, where it was presumed that he would defend the League, he again pleaded "unfamiliarity with many details of the peace negotiations and the treaty," which had been "negotiated largely by the President, who alone of the American delegation would be able to reveal details of the discussion."

When Wilson began work on the war settlement in Paris, his hope was to get the substance of the peace plan in a definitive form before Congress adjourned on March 4. But such was the inertia and confusion at Paris that the president concentrated his efforts on preparation of a draft of the League covenant, with the idea of incorporating the League into the body of the treaty. In his view, the League came first. Whatever inequities were written into the treaty, wherever wobbling joints were to be found in the world of politics—all could in time be made right through the League. The League of Nations was the Holy Grail, and Woodrow Wilson was the knighted one, commissioned to pursue its light through all darkness.

The president worked unremittingly, eighteen hours a day, says Edith Wilson, who watched him "growing grimmer and graver, day by day." Once, as a result of pressure from the French, he visited Rheims and Soissons, desolated by the war. Mrs. Wilson remembered a gray Saturday afternoon, standing before the cathedral at Rheims. She and her husband were met by a priest, "his small figure outlined against the vast interior. . . . He was very frail-looking, and wore a black cassock, and one of the flat black plush hats of his order." He had on gloves of red silk that were much too large. Years later Mrs. Wilson recalled the light snow that "drifted silently down through the great holes in the roof which had been made by the bombshells."

In those days Wilson liked to identify himself with the American soldiers who, in his view, had borne all. Once he and Mrs. Wilson had an afternoon tea for those detailed to the Murat Palace, where the Wilsons lived. The president relaxed in the soldiers' company; they called him "the Old Man" and gathered around the piano and sang; they ate sandwiches and ice cream.

On February 14, Wilson read the draft of the League covenant to a plenary session of the peace conference, which provisionally adopted it. The meeting was in the Room of the Clock in the French Ministry of Foreign Affairs. After it was over, Mrs. Wilson, who had managed to get herself and Dr. Grayson admitted to the proceedings as onlookers, met the president outside. As he slumped in his seat in the presidential car she asked, "Are you so weary?" "Yes," he said, "I suppose I am, but how little one man means when such vital things are at stake." It would be "sweet" to go home, he thought, "even for a few days, with the feeling that I have kept the faith with the people, particularly with these boys, God bless them."

That evening the Wilsons entrained for Brest to board the *George Washington,* scheduled to sail the next day. The president would take three weeks away from the conference to go home and explain to the nation, and especially to Senator Lodge and the Foreign Relations Committee, what he had done. A White House dinner was planned for committee members on February 26. On February 4, after nearly running aground in a dense fog off Newfoundland, the *George Washington* landed at Boston. All was sunny and serene. On the whole, wrote Mrs. Wilson, it had been a good trip, especially because of the "very delightful" companionship of Assistant Secretary of the Navy and Mrs. Franklin D. Roosevelt. Greeting Wilson at the docks was the Massachusetts governor, Calvin Coolidge, who escorted the president to Mechanics Hall. There, Wilson spoke of what he had accomplished at Paris.

Already the hounds were baying. On the day that Wilson left Paris, Senator William K. Borah of Idaho assailed the idea of a League of Nations, insisting that there would be peacetime conscription. "Would the citizens of the United States volunteer to enter the army for the purpose of settling difficulties in the Balkans?" he wondered. Nicholas Murray Butler, president of Columbia University, criticized the former president of Princeton for his composition: "The draft itself is as clumsy a bit of workmanship as the history of international agreements affords. . . . It lacks to an extraordinary degree orderly arrangement, precision of language and conciseness. Prolixity and diffuseness as well as bad arrangement make it hard to read and difficult to understand."

On February 22, Senator James A. Reed of Missouri argued that the League ran contrary to the U.S. Constitution because it put into the hands of foreign delegates, "most of whom could not speak the English language," the foreign policies of our government. The *New York Times* noted that "after the Senator's peroration an unusual demonstration occurred." For five minutes the Senate chamber resounded with a storm of applause. "Not even the outburst that followed the declaration of war . . . could be compared with it."

In the meantime, Senator Borah announced that he would not attend Wilson's dinner, and Senator Albert B. Fall released a telegram saying that he, too, was declining. When the dinner was held, bonhomie was not spontaneous. Afterward, there were cigars and careful questions but no rallying around the president. Nine days later, on March 4, at 12:02 A.M., Senator Lodge offered a resolution in the Senate that the League draft, as it stood, should be rejected, and he urged the delegates to the peace conference to expedite the signing of a treaty before taking up the League issue. Thirty-nine Republican senators signed the resolution, which meant that the League, at that point, did not have the support of the requisite two-thirds of the Senate.

That night, after the Lodge "Round Robin," as it was called, Wilson spoke to an audience at the Metropolitan Opera House. The former president William Howard Taft was there to introduce him and to register his approval of the League. As Wilson prepared to speak, the band struck up "Over There." Wilson said that, indeed, he would not come back until it was over, "Over There," and that when he did bring back a treaty, the League covenant would be a part of it. As he and Mrs. Wilson prepared to leave, one more matter intruded to claim his attention. A delegation of Irish-Americans had come to present a petition. The president agreed to see them, but they would have to deposit their leader somewhere else, since he had been loud in his opposition to the war. The leaderless committee went backstage and briefly made its representations in the interest of Irish freedom from British repression. An impatient Wilson then left for the docks, to board the *George Washington*, which was scheduled for a midnight sailing.

As the fluming trail of the ship's propellers tracked eastward, Wilson's spirits rose. But behind him there was no mounting, rolling wave of support from the American people. The *New Republic* was distressed by the muted enthusiasm for the president. It said that the thirty-nine senators who had voted that the League was unacceptable were "blinded by their bitter personal animosity to Mr. Wilson. . . . If they persist in this . . . they will endanger the peace of the world." The fundamental issue was a moral one. Why had America gone to war? What had all the shouting, the intolerance, the suffering and death been about except to raise the world to a new level of law and to have a new institutional form to see to it that the law was obeyed? According to the *New Republic,* "American public opinion should not allow itself to be deluded as to the sinister meaning and incalculable results of the position which these Republican senators have assumed."

Back in Paris, the climate in which Wilson worked was not appreciably better than the one he had found in Washington. In peace making the president kept his vision on the Kingdom he had foretold, but his associates wanted reparations and buffer zones around their boundaries so that the Germans could not get to them again. Near exhaustion and shadowed by failing health, Wilson nonetheless worked doggedly to rebuild a world community according to the principles outlined by his Fourteen Points. But how did they apply in every particular the world around, where boundaries were contested, claims made, national sensibilities bruised, people starved, and the fires of revolution bursting into flame? Desperately, the world needed a settlement. Desperately, to save his League, Wilson compromised and traded. In the end the League was preserved, but the idealism that had billowed about him and sustained him before the Paris venture had, in many instances, turned to bitterness.

On July 8, President Wilson returned to America. An escort of forty-five naval vessels met the *George Washington* at Sandy Hook and escorted it to its pier at Hoboken, docking at 4:25 P.M. From there the president motored between lines of cheering schoolchildren to board a special ferry that took his party to the Manhattan ferry slip at Twenty-third Street. Then, moving slowly, the motorcade turned north on Fifth Avenue and headed for Carnegie Hall. Thousands of people, leaving work, stood on the sidewalks.

At 5:37 P.M. he appeared on the stage at Carnegie Hall. A police band started playing "Over There," and the audience stood and cheered. Cleveland H. Dodge, a longtime friend of Wilson's, leaped to the front of the stage and, raising his cane, called for cheers for the president. The uproar continued for several minutes, during which Wilson smiled and bowed. Then the band played the national anthem, after which the president was introduced to two British flying officers. There were more cheers, which were ended by a police glee club singing "For He's a Jolly Good Fellow."

Wilson's speech was brief and subdued. He spoke of America's mission to heal the world. "I am afraid some people, some persons, do not understand this vision. They did not see it. They have looked too much upon the ground." He had "never had a doubt as to where the heart and purpose of this people lay." America would "not disappoint any high hope that had been formed of her. Least of all will she in this day of new born liberty all over the world fail to extend her hand of support and assistance to those who have been made free."

Afterward, the president and his party boarded a train at Pennsylvania Station for the three-hour trip to Washington. It was nearly 10:00 when he arrived, but a crowd had gathered to welcome him. One person, sitting in a car parked at the edge of the throng, had come to witness the homecoming out of a malice-saturated curiosity. Alice Roosevelt Longworth watched as Wilson left the station; then she sped to the White House to see how many would be there to greet him. When she got there, she stood on the curbstone so as to be near him as he passed through the gate. When he did, she crossed her fingers and cast a spell upon him.

On the afternoon of July 10, Wilson reviewed for the senate the peace treaty, which included the establishment of his League of Nations. It took twenty-seven minutes to read the text. When he finished, he turned to the Republicans present and directed at them a solemn, professorial summing up of the meaning of the events of the two previous years. "The stage is set, the destiny disclosed. It has come about by no plan of our conceiving, but by the grace of God, who led us late this way. America shall in truth show the way. The light streams upon the path ahead and nowhere else."

Wilson's star-sprinkled rhetoric had been heavily sifted over the world, and wherever there were people who longed to establish their own community, unfettered by the necessity of bending to another's will, they had come to believe that his words were absolute. Now they seemed like meteors that blazed over the vaulted darkness of the night, only to fade and die before touching earth. Yes, the Fourteen Points had served as the basis for giving a national identity to millions of subject people, but was this why millions had died? Who could say that by cutting off the head of one monster ten had not appeared? What new pollution had been poured into history's process that somewhere along the line of time would produce a disease more horrible than that which the war was supposed to cure?

When Wilson came home for the last time he was spent. At Paris he had fought doggedly and used unsparingly the reserves of his strength to bring his ideal world into existence. But amid the clamor for "rights," "just retribution," "guarantees," and territorial adjustments, he could only retreat. Where Germany was concerned, his Fourteen Points became a shattered structure. His words had died. Tumulty quotes Newton D. Baker as saying: "More than once, there in Paris, going up in the evening to see the President, I found him utterly worn out, exhausted, often one side of his face twitching with nervousness. . . . Day after day in these months we saw him growing grayer and grayer, grimmer and grimmer, with the fighting lines deepening in his face."

On May 30, still showing signs of the illness that had kept him bedridden for several weeks, Wilson went to the American military cemetery at Suresnes to make a Memorial Day speech. It was a beautiful day, with nature abloom, and in the softly stirring air American flags fluttered gently over graves marked by lines of white wooden crosses. Mrs. Wilson described the scene: "In the centre of the cemetery on a small platform stood the President, his head bared—and how white the hair had grown these last few months—his tall, slight form tense with emotion, as he spoke to the living and for the dead in a passionate plea to end all wars and never again make such a sacrifice necessary." Edith

Wilson said that her husband had had to struggle against waves of rising emotion in order to finish his talk, and that when it was over many were weeping.

The peace treaty was signed by thirty-two nations on the afternoon of June 28, in the Hall of Mirrors at Versailles. Herbert Hoover was there but, as he said, he had difficulty keeping his mind on what was going on. He kept thinking of "the fearful consequences of many of the paragraphs which these men are signing with such pomp, and then going back to the high hopes with which I had landed in Europe eight months before. I did not come away exultant."

One-half hour after the cannons had announced the conclusion of the treaty-signing ceremonies at Versailles, newspapers appeared on the streets of Coblenz, Germany, where American troops were stationed. A squadron of American military planes took forty thousand copies of the papers aloft to scatter them over the city. One plane crashed, and the pilot was killed.

The German populace took no notice of the occasion, but at a Rhine beer garden, owned by one Herr Mayer, a young German began singing patriotic songs. An American M.P. told him to cease. The young man paused, then said he had no fear of the American soldier and would continue to sing for Germany. He started again, but the M.P. seized him and pushed him out the door. "Here he fell to the pavement shouting 'Deutschland uber Alles.' Eight men were required to hold him as he raved."

Nine days after Wilson placed the treaty before the U.S. Senate, the great spokesman for the convictions of settled and conservative middle-class America, the *Saturday Evening Post,* editorially ruminated on the events of the recent past and offered a program for the future. The world, it said, was "fed up with doctrines. . . . More or less we Americans hitched our wagon to a star and found it had run into a stump." There were "always ten men who can show you how to hitch your wagon to a star for one who can show you how to get the stump out of the road." What Americans now needed was "a stump-pulling Administration at Washington; one that is mightily concerned with getting the best service out of the railroads, the most wheat to the acre . . . not by star gazing but by experienced and practical-minded application to the immediate concrete problems. . . . We want that sort of wisdom that can deal best with the immediate concrete situation—the business man's sort of ability, if you please."

SOURCES

The account of the revolutionary demonstration in Berlin is from Elmer Luehr, *The New German Republic: The Reich in Transition* (New York, 1929). Secretary of State Robert Lansing's muted comments about his work in Paris and his view of the League are from the *New York Times* (July 23 and August 7, 1919). Nicholas Murray Butler's prolix statement is from the same source, February 16, 1919. A good and concise statement of Wilson's labors in Paris is found in Walter Lafeber's "Victors without Peace," *The American Age: United States Foreign Policy at Home and Abroad Since 1750* (New York, 1989). The account of Alice Roosevelt Longworth's spooky work, where Wilson was concerned, is from her *Crowded Hours* (New York, 1933). The story about the disconsolate German youth's reaction to the Treaty of Versailles is from the *New York Times* (July 1, 1919).

FURTHER READING

Professor Arthur Link's works on Wilson highlight the latter's career as a Progressive. Foreign policy, however, is treated in *Wilson the Diplomatist: A Look at His Major Foreign Policies* (Baltimore, 1957). Lloyd C. Gardner, *Safe for Democracy: Anglo-American Response to Revolution, 1913–1923* (New York, 1984), provides the corrective of actuality in revolutionary situations to the professions of democratic idealism. Thomas A. Bailey, who redeemed the textbook rendition of American diplomatic history from the lugubrious phrasing of Samuel Flagg Bemis, has what is still a very useful essay of sources in an appendix, "Negotiating the Treaty of Versailles," in *A Diplomatic History of the American People* (New York, 1969).

9

The Marvelous Machines

IN MANY WAYS WORLD WAR I was different. There was a new sound and force about it. Energy broke in waves over the land and was made audible in the sound of engines: in the drone of an airplane motor, throbbing unseen in the high haze of an August afternoon; in the excitement of planes roaring low over the ground and then, in a mighty crescendo of sound, passing overhead and as quickly out of sight; in the slow beat of a tugboat engine, borne by a new northern wind into the silence of a September night; in the washing of ship's propellers; and in the far whistle of a train, coming, it almost seemed, with ghostly voice from beyond the bounds of time.

The sound of engines was the chrism of energy's promise. It was the sign of the new servant of precisioned steel that handed to people what they had come to believe in as the all-redemptive character of energy. In World War I the sound of engines pierced the sky and rolled over the land and sea, its pulsing signifying that all of the holy causes of war and the rush to Armageddon had been given the grace of a new power.

In the spring of 1919, as Woodrow Wilson worked to rebuild the world, machines came to life in bedazzling new forms. Among the nations that had been at war, a new and sweet air began to move. The future beckoned, promising ease and sense delight. The old ways began to slip into the shadows.

For Americans, especially, the automobile brought them into this new world. Before the war there had been some five million cars in the United States, a number that suggests this new instrument of mobility had already met with widespread appreciation. Some 924,383 cars were built in 1918, about one-half the number produced in 1917. By the beginning of 1919, most automakers were manufacturing cars again and were looking forward to increasing production.

On February 1, the *New York Times* announced the opening of the city's annual automobile show at Madison Square Garden and at the Sixty-ninth Regiment Armory, an event that had begun in 1900. Hours before the doors opened for the show at 8:00 P.M., Madison Avenue, in front of the Garden, was crowded the entire width of the sidewalk for several blocks. The *Times* observed that "never has a motor car exhibit in the city had a larger attendance on the first night, and it was easy to see that the majority of the visitors were genuine seekers for the latest improvements in design and mechanism." One of the most eye-catching displays at the show was a new Buick, a "bridal blue roadster, just roomy enough for two . . . sentimentally decorated with white ribbon bows." Two other roadsters that attracted attention, both "a snappy bright red," were a trim little Maxwell and a long Stutz speedster.

Among the cars on display was the new Jordan, whose paneling and moldings were of "Circassian walnut marquetry," whose upholstery was of the finest worsteds fitted over Marshall cushion springs, whose body was all aluminum. "Picture the new European wide-opening doors," one ad read, "—the rectangular mouldings—the smart French angle at the dash—the cocky seat cowl—the perfectly straight flat top edge—the distinctively different fenders—the tall hood with twenty-nine louvres—the slanting sport-type windshield—the gunmetal instrument board—the artistic hardware—the floor rugs of velvet texture."

The Jordan was decidedly a car for the young. According to the ad: "The road skims beneath you, winds before you, and unless a man is bloodless he cannot but surrender himself to that fine intoxication that comes of such motion in the open air. It begins in a sort of breathless sensation and ends with that pleasuring drowsiness—and silence in which two people need exchange no words to understand." Ad-makers knew where to aim their shaft—at the young men who sought the caresses of those petulant and powdered creatures with cupid-bowed lips who were not loath to sway to time's embrace—the Daisys and Glorias and Rosalinds that F. Scott Fitzgerald would soon write about.

There were other cars on display, most of them no longer known, having been eliminated by the scourging work of the Great Depression. There was the Dort, a small car that aspired to capture some of the Ford market, powered by a Lycoming engine and distinctive for having the clutch and brake on the same pedal. There was the Elgin, a basic medium-sized car; the sporty Kissel; the Liberty, a light car; and the Velie, a heavy one. There was the Franklin, which saw its last year of production in 1934, but which in the thirty-three years of its history was powered by the world's most successful air-cooled engine before the advent of the Volkswagen. The Franklin was unique for its wooden frame and aluminum body, features used to reduce weight and increase gas mileage.

The Hudson Motor Car Company introduced its Essex in the 1919 automobile show. The Essex, which survived until 1932, could, with its four-cylinder engine, reach a top speed of sixty miles per hour. The characteristic feature of the Essex over the years was its distinctive high whine at any speed over thirty. An automobile of advanced engineering was the Owen Magnetic, an all-aluminum car with an automatic transmission. Then there were the cars whose names have long since been forgotten: the Templar ("The Superfine Small Car"), the Wescott ("The Car with a Longer Life"), the Grant Six ("The Epitome of Smartness"), and the Oakland "Sensible Six."

Bright with excitement and anticipation, the crowd moved from one to another of the marvels that American industry had produced. Among the throng on that opening Saturday night was Captain Eddie Rickenbacker, in New York for the banquet to be held in his honor on the coming Monday. Perhaps Rickenbacker was even then thinking of the car that in the twenties would bear his name.

Thursday, February 6, was "Society Day" at the automobile show. For that crowd the Cadillac was a popular exhibit, what with its luxuriousness and its being "credited with having been the first to cross the Rhine." Yet being first across the Rhine was not everything, for Packard, perhaps the best-known name in American motoring at the time, had taken the lead in designing and building the wartime Liberty aircraft engine. The most prestigious of Packard's production was its "Twin-Six," a V-12 engine that had first been introduced to the motoring world in June 1913. Production of this car was resumed in 1919 and on September 2, the twenty-four-thousandth Packard Twin-Six was delivered to the showroom. Other well-known quality cars were the Nash valve-in-head "Six", and the Studebaker "Big Six," equipped with shock absorbers, "genuine hand-buffed leather upholstery," and a silver-faced, jeweled, eight-day clock.

The most expensive car at the show was the Pierce Arrow Brougham, which sold for $7,800. For years, Pierce Arrow's highly distinguishing mark was the way in which its headlights came trumpeting out of its front fenders. The cheapest car, of course, was Henry Ford's Model T runabout, a two-seater with a folding top whose twenty horse-power engine would run it up to nearly forty miles per hour. The Model T, which sold for around $500, was introduced in 1909 and steadfastly retained its essential character until 1927. If, for example, one needed an engine valve for a 1927 Model T, the Sears Roebuck catalog of that year indicated that the valve would also fit all models for the preceeding eighteen years.

Altogether, there were fifty-eight makes of cars at the show. Most of them were "assembled," in that the wheels, engines, and running gear came from standard manufacturers. The Moon, for example, used a Continental Red Seal engine, a Fedders radiator, a Rayfield carburetor, a Borg and Beck clutch, a Brown-Lipe transmission, a Spicer drive shaft, Gemner steering parts, and Timken brakes.

Yet some of the cars had unique engineering features. Apart from the Owen Magnetic and the Franklin, the Willys-Knight had an engine that was "knockless" and that was supposed to improve with age. The quietness of the engine was achieved by dispensing with ordinary valves and using a cylindrical sleeve that moved up and down within the cylinder wall, exposing and closing ports as it moved. The self-starter was in general use in 1919, available even on the Model T. Some of the larger enclosed sedans had an interior roominess and elegance (curtains that could be drawn and flower vases on doorposts) that has not been equaled since streamlining began to force rear-seat passengers into compartments that suggested they were being readied for a moon shot.

By 1919 there was no question that the horse-and-buggy days were over. Something of neighborliness and serenity would be lost, and the ends of existence had begun to move toward the sensate, but for the moment the air was fresh and no clouds darkened the sky. As the makers of the Standard Eight, boasting its eighty-three horsepower, said in one of their advertisements, "Who Denies that Power Gives Pleasure?" The roads of the newly marked federal highway system wound to places never before beheld.

What wonder, running at forty miles an hour in an open Hupmobile through the gray mists that hovered at first light over the pine flats of north Florida and then, with the sun up, crossing into Georgia over the St. Mary's River on a bridge that rattled noisily as the car passed, stopping on the other side at an old shed where cars were repaired and gasoline was dispensed from a Standard Oil pump, or seeing in the pine woods of south Georgia a sawmill and a mountain of sawdust, where an old-fashioned train engine, with a flaring, high smokestack hauled lumber. Rounding a curve to confront a large billboard depicting an open book, the pages of which marked "the way to places of unusual interest" and pointed out that United States tires were "the short, straight road to tire satisfaction." Turning west at Waycross, Georgia, and behold-ing the roads made of red clay, where detours took the car over a bridge so terrifying in its rickety underpinning and thin rail tracks that the captain of the ship ordered women and children to dismount as he took the vessel across. Driving north on U.S. 41, the road newly asphalted and pools of water appearing in the distance in the bright glare of the hot afternoon sun, only to vanish when approached. Then finally, as the sun began to lower, beholding in the distance the dome of the courthouse at Ashburn, Georgia, the town of our destination.

Still and all, no machine bespoke the enchanting force of this new world like the airplane. An aeronautical exposition followed the automobile show at Madison Square Garden and the Sixty-ninth Regiment Armory. If the seeds had already been sown that in the future would make the honeymoon a quaint institution of bygone times, the air show was not aware of it. Just as the automobile show had featured a cozy little Buick for honeymooners, the Dayton-Wright Aircraft Corporation showed its DeHaviland A rigged out for newlyweds. "Luxuriously upholstered," the forward cockpit was for the "sky chauffeur," while the enclosed rear compartment was equipped with a buffet board, thermos bottle, and sandwich box. For the bride there was a vanity case, locker, and mirror set; for the groom, a smoking outfit and luggage compartment. Of the many foreign planes at the armory, the two that captured the most attention were the British Handley-Page bomber, with a wingspread of 103 feet, and the Italian Caproni triplane, a behemoth with a 130-foot wingspread.

The exposition clearly showed that, under the impetus of war, the airplane had metamorphosed. It was no longer a flimsy kite, rising and descending in pastures, but a sophisticated machine that made people think in terms of a performance potential that six years before had been unthinkable. In a speech to the Manufacturers' Aircraft Association on January 8, Colonel Billy Bishop, the Canadian ace, had said that aviators would "have to show some enterprise or zeppelins will sail into an Atlantic harbor first." Bishop had in mind that the 670-foot-long British dirigible, the R-33, was at the moment being readied for a trial flight and that an Atlantic crossing was in prospect. But he need not have been concerned about the want of enterprising pilots. All they needed was a faint hope that their machines could make it and they would be off. Besides, there was the $50,000 prize being offered by the *London Daily Mail.*

"Atlantic Flight May Come Soon," declared a *New York Times* headline on March 19. Within two weeks the front pages of American newspapers were giving their prime space to what was emerging as the big transatlantic air derby. On March 29, Harry G. Hawker, a test pilot for the Sopwith company, and Lieutenant Commander Mackensie Grieve, a navigator, arrived at St. John's, Newfoundland, with their Sopwith biplane and began preparations for a flight across the north Atlantic. Their assumption was that they would be ready in two weeks and would then try to leave by the light of a full moon on April 15. On April 11, Captains F. P. Raynham and C. W. F. Morgan of Canada arrived in St. John's with their Martinsyde F4 biplane, a lighter but faster machine than the Sopwith.

During the first weeks of April, newspapers gave a day-by-day recital of the testing and preparation going on in St. John's. Yet the predictions of imminent departures were always followed by cancellations due to weather or the discovery of some mechanical trouble. April passed. The *New York Times* became restless. On May 8, an editorial addressed the situation: "For more than five weeks the British aviators who came over with the redoubtable Sopwith machine have been tuning up and waiting for acceptable take-off conditions. . . . It is admitted that they have missed more than one propitious day." People in St. John's were wondering "whether the British aviators will ever take a sporting chance." Well, then, if those English aviators "who are coveting a substantial money prize . . . do not mean business, perhaps the Americans, who will fly for glory, do."

Fly for glory? Why, the Americans were already on their way! On May 8, as the morning sun rose over the marshland of what today is New York's Kennedy Airport, its glancing shafts touched the bright yellow wings of three huge seaplanes resting on their carriages at the Rockaway Beach Naval Air Station. At 9:30 A.M., Commander John Towers, the captain of the fleet, announced that the planes would take off at 10:00 A.M. One by one, the twelve 400-horsepower Liberty engines were started and run up to full throttle, providing such a raging sound and furious lashing of the air that spectators were awed into adoring submission to the potency of these wonderful machines. At 9:30 A.M., Towers, in his leather and furs, lightly vaulted the iron railing that held back the crowd, climbed into the front cockpit in the hull of the NC-3, and gave the sign to be off. Taxiing to takeoff position over the idly swelling waters of Jamaica Bay, the NC-3, then the NC-1, and finally the NC-4, with the glorious sound of thundering engines echoing over the bay, headed for Halifax, Nova Scotia, the first leg of their journey.

In the front cockpit of the NC-3, riding with Towers, was Lieutenant Richard E. Byrd. He was testing navigational instruments and would go as far as Newfoundland. In the twenties, Byrd became one of the fabled heroes of the new air age. Of himself and the other American pioneers of the air, he would write: "In us America . . . dramatized that superb world-conquering fire which is American spirit. For the moment we seemed to have caught up the banner of American progress. For the moment we appeared to typify . . . the spirit of America."

The NC flying boats were products of the war. In 1914, with the financial backing of the department store magnate Rodman Wanamaker, Glenn Curtiss built a flying boat, the *America,* designed to fly the Atlantic in quest of the *Daily Mail*'s prize. The *America* did not fly the Atlantic but was sold to Britain and used for submarine patrol work.

When the United States entered the war, Admiral David W. Taylor, a navy planner, called Curtiss to Washington and told him to present plans for a new flying boat that could cross the Atlantic. The relative simplicity with which technology proliferated during this era enabled Curtiss to return in three days with two plans: one for a three-engined craft and the other for a craft featuring five engines. The navy planners, of course, liked the five-engine proposal, but an airframe capable of sustaining the weight and stress of five engines would have to be so huge that the operation of the controls for such a plane would tax the strength of more than one pilot. On the other hand, the availability of the "new U.S. motor," as the navy plan called it, with more than three times the horsepower of the old Curtiss OX engine, made possible the proposed three-engined craft. So plans were made for a three-engined plane, officially designated "NC," which stood for "Navy-Curtiss."

The new U.S. motor was raised in official statements and in the press to the level of an authentic American technological miracle, one worthy of public veneration. "The story of the production of this engine is a remarkable one," said Secretary of War Newton D. Baker. "Probably the war has produced no greater single achievement." An article in the *Saturday Evening Post* cited a wartime official who claimed that actually there was "nothing wonderful or strange" about the new engine. "It's merely the perfect motor."

That perfect motor was the Liberty engine, designed by Major Vincent of the Packard Motor Company and Major Hall of the Hall-Scott Company, two men who were regarded as the nation's best engine designers. Both men, brought to Washington on June 3 and charged with producing an "all-American" engine, were, according to Secretary Baker, "figuratively locked in a room in a Washington hotel. For five days neither man left the suite of rooms engaged for them." Each man worked alternating twenty-four-hour shifts. It was, said Baker, an "inspiring" spectacle of "motor manufacturers who gave up their trade secrets under the emergency of war needs."

And so it was that after five days "a remarkable American engine was actually produced three weeks before any model could have been brought from Europe." Twenty-eight days after the drawings were begun, the first "miracle" engine was assembled in Detroit by the Packard Motor Company. Draped with the American flag, with four men standing constant guard, it was transported to Washington in a special car and run on July 4 at the Bureau of Standards. It was, eventually, a twelve-cylinder, 400-horsepower model of the Liberty engine that powered the NC planes.

Work began on the production of four NCs in December 1917 at the Curtiss Aeroplane and Motor Company at Buffalo; in January 1918 production was transferred to the Curtiss Engineering Company in Garden City, on Long Island. With much subcontracting, the Garden City company was able to deliver the NC-1 to the naval facility at Rockaway Beach during the last days of September 1918. At noon on Friday, October 4, the plane was towed from its hangar. With its 126-foot wingspan, it was larger than anything in Europe or America; in fact, its wingspan exceeded that of the World War II B-17 by more than 22 feet. The two wings of the NC-1 were 12 feet wide and 14 feet apart at the center. The boat was 44 feet, 9 inches long, separated into five compartments. Unlike previous flying boats, the tail rigging was not placed on a rear extension of the hull but was carried high above the water on an outrigger.

The NC-1 was nonetheless a machine of the Wright brothers era, a mammoth kite of spars, cloth, glue, and wire rigging. It was given a brief trial flight by Lieutenant Commander Holden C. Richardson, and then, three days later, Richardson, with a full crew, took it for an extended flight to the Washington naval yard. On November 28, a world's record was achieved when the NC-1 rose thirty-five feet above the water carrying fifty-one persons, including one stowaway.

The NC-2 was completed in January 1919. Unlike the NC-1, the NC-2 had four engines, arranged in tandem pairs, that is, two tractor engines backed by two pushers. At the suggestion of Lieutenant Commander Marc Mitscher, the configuration was changed; a tandem pair was placed in the center of the wing with a tractor on either side. This gave the plane more maneuverability and stability. The engines of the NC-1 were also changed to this configuration, and since it seemed to work well, the system was used in the NC-3 and the NC-4.

As the summer of 1918 came to a close and an Allied victory seemed assured, Commander John H. Towers, a thirty-six-year-old Georgian who had been head of the Naval Air Station at Pensacola, wrote to the chief of naval operations suggesting that he, Towers, command an ocean flight in the spring of 1919, "war or no war." Towers was actively supported in his proposal by Assistant Secretary of the Navy Franklin D. Roosevelt, and on February 4 the navy secretary, Josephus Daniels, gave the project his approval.

Towers thus found himself in the midst of what was heating up to be the first transatlantic air derby, fueled, of course, by the *Daily Mail* prize, but more powerfully impelled by all those young Richard Byrd types and would-be heroes who, under the mantle of the Union Jack or the Stars and Stripes, would gladly entrust their lives to the Rolls-Royce engine, the Liberty engine, or one of the various brands of engines made in their country—who would dare all for glory, that transcendent moment that comes with the performance of a deed of valor.

In mid-April a British crew, flying a Short torpedo plane, the *Shamrock*, began a transatlantic flight in England, intending to land in Ireland and then fly to Newfoundland. On April 18 engine failure forced the plane down in the Irish Sea. On that same day a Handley Page Vimy bomber was in the process of being freighted across the Atlantic, headed for Newfoundland to join Hawker and Grieve, the Sopwith crew, and Raynham and Morgan, ready to fly their Martinsyde. There were also three other transatlantic projects in the early stages of planning.

The U.S. Navy's effort, however, was considerably different from those whose crews were feverishly tuning and rigging their machines. Towers and his men had the entire U.S. Navy behind them, and they were not competing for the *Daily Mail* prize. Nonetheless, the fever of being first across ran high in April as the testing of the NC-1, NC-2, and NC-3 continued and as the NC-4 neared completion. Serious and nearly fatal delays were confronted. On March 27 a gale destroyed one side of the lower wing of the NC-1 and the NC-2 was vandalized to restore the wing. On May 2 the appointed takeoff day, a fire ruined the other wing of the NC-1 and the NC-2 was stripped of its remaining wing; the NC-2's designated commander, Marc Mitscher, was assigned to pilot the NC-1. Towers, as head of the entire flight, took the NC-3 as his ship; the NC-1 was captained by Lieutenant Commander Patrick N. Bellinger and the NC-4 by Commander Albert C. Read.

These were names that would figure prominently in the naval operations of World War II. Bellinger is remembered for his cryptic message from Ford Island three minutes after the first Japanese bomb fell on Pearl Harbor: "Air raid, Pearl Harbor—this is no drill." Towers was commander of the air force in the Pacific, and Read headed the Pensacola Naval Air Station. Marc Mitscher was captain of the *Hornet* and participated in the crucial battle of Midway on June 4–6, 1942. In the latter part of the war, he headed a carrier task force that was active around the Mariana Islands.

The NC-1, NC-3, and NC-4 were formally commissioned on Saturday, May 3, 1919. Towers and his crew stood at attention, the bugler sounded "to the colors," and the American flag was attached to the stern of each plane. For the next four days bad weather along the Canadian coast kept the planes on the ramp. Then clearing weather prompted Towers to decide to go.

The departure could not have been delayed much longer under any circumstances. The route had been conceived as a wartime measure for the rapid transportation of planes to Europe. It consisted of a 335-mile flight to Halifax, Nova Scotia; 474 miles to Trepassey Harbor, Newfoundland; a long flight of 1,206 miles to Ponta Delgada, Azores; 768 miles to Lisbon, Portugal; and 860 miles to Plymouth, England. Now, with the flight about to begin, the navy had stationed along the way, at 50-mile intervals, vessels whose function was to provide a continual visual reference for navigation and to maintain radio contact with the planes. At night the ships would loft star shells to keep the squadron on course. No wonder that Harry Hawker, the Sopwith pilot, would later say that the American venture was not one in which the "sporting chance" had figured large. "If you put a ship every fifty miles, it shows you have no faith in your motor," he was quoted as saying.

The first day of flight, May 9, went well enough except for the NC-4. One of its engines began freezing up and it had to land at sea in the afternoon. With its good motors it taxied fourteen hours to the Chatham, Massachusetts naval air base, where the work of installing a new engine commenced immediately. Meanwhile, in the last light of day, the NC-1 and NC-3 landed at Halifax. An entranced reporter for the *New York Times* described the arrival of the NC-3 over the town: "The machine glittering with lights against the greenish pallor of the evening sky seemed like a magic constellation of stars traveling a cyclonic orbit." When "the roaring of the mighty engines" was heard, "wondering watchers" went into the streets and on the rooftops to "gaze at the sky long after silence had stolen away the throbbing of the machinery." It was, he declared, a "vision to be long remembered."

The next morning, as the NC-1 and NC-3 were made ready for the six-hour flight to Trepassey Harbor, cracks were discovered in the propellers of the NC-3. Byrd, riding as far as Trepassey, remembered a store of propellers at a small naval supply base he had established at Halifax during the war. By noon the repairs had been made and the plane was on its way, reaching Trepassey that evening at 8:00. The NC-1 was already there, moored to the navy supply ship, *Aroostook.* Both planes had been forced to make perilous cross-wind landings on the narrow sliver of water that was Trepassey Harbor.

For the next two days the question was, would the NC-4 make it to Trepassey in time to join the NC-1 and NC-3 on the long trip to the

Azores? On May 14 the *New York Times* reported that Towers would "not keep the two gallant craft . . . from starting on their great adventure on account of the non-arrival of the NC-4." The next day the newspaper reported that the NC-4 had finally left the Chatham base and had reached Halifax, "traveling at the high speed of 98 miles per hour." But would it reach Trepassey in time?

As the NC-4 sped northward, a side drama was precipitously unfolding. A new navy dirigible, the C-5, was tracking the same course, except that at Newfoundland the C-5 planned to head directly across the Atlantic and perhaps be the first across. The ship was a nonrigid dirigible, 198 feet long, and according to calculations hastily made by its commander, Emory W. Coil, was capable of crossing the Atlantic. On the morning of May 15, Coil and his crew of five lost their way. Through a thick early-dawn mist they spied beneath them a railroad track which they followed into St. John's. Descending, they were taken to the navy cruiser *Chicago,* tied up at the St. John's docks. As they refreshed themselves, disaster struck. Just three hours after landing, the dirigible was whipped around so violently by a sudden wind that it broke from its moorings, forcing the maintenance crew to jump for their lives. Racing along with the gale, the unmanned ship disappeared over the Atlantic and was never recovered. Three years later, Emory Coil was sent to England as a member of a team that would take delivery on a British dirigible, the R-38, which the Americans would fly home. In a trial flight on August 24, 1921, the big ship buckled in the air and crashed. Sixteen Americans died in the wreck, among them Coil.

Two hours after the C-5 had disappeared over the Atlantic, Commander Towers in the NC-3 cast off from the *Aroostook,* followed immediately by the NC-1. Plowing through the wind-chopped waves, both planes made takeoff runs but neither could rise. The NC-4 arrived just as they were hurtling full blast down the narrow cut of Trepassey Harbor. Towers called off the departure until the next day, declaring that the three planes would go together. That night the NC-4 had another engine change. Towers, Bellinger, and Read tried to figure out how they could lighten their loads for the next day's takeoff.

The following afternoon Captains Towers, Bellinger, and Read gathered on the afterdeck of the *Aroostook* to work out the last details of their departure. Then they climbed into their ships. The *New York Times* described the great moment: "Towers, seated in the navigator's forward cockpit of the NC-3, waved his hand as a signal to Bellinger and Read in the NC-1 and NC-4, respectively, and set the great undertaking in motion with a phrase that perhaps in time may rank with the other treasured utterances of naval commanders. 'Let's go,' he said." But having thus been spoken, the immortal words drew no response. The NC-4 was again having trouble with the bothersome center-forward engine. It simply would not start, even with its new electric starter. Towers pulled back the cuff of his flying jacket and, looking pointedly at his wristwatch, called out, "How much longer?" "Fifteen minutes, sir," Read responded.

Finally, the engine started and the three planes headed for the wind-indicated takeoff position. But the wind that day was blowing crosswise to the ideal takeoff track and it was decided that the attempt would have to be made over the narrow breadth of the waterway. Towers tried and failed. Would the daring Americans have to postpone the takeoff again? No, the *New York Times* reported, because the American spirit, disdaining shackling conventions, moved to the fore in the person of Lieutenant B. F. Stone, pilot of the NC-4, who, "in violation of all theory and more than likely of all orders, headed directly into the Narrows and took off successfully in the cross-wind, though any seaplane pilot can demonstrate by the hour that that was almost suicide and next to impossible." The newspaper asked, "What lies ahead of the three gallant crews?" Americans would know with the next day's edition.

For the moment, ahead lay twenty-two destroyers marking the route between Newfoundland and the Azores. As the NCs flew through the night, all went well. Following the star shells and searchlights of the destroyers made navigation relatively simple. The main problem was one of flying in formation. The NC-1, with its borrowed wings, could not keep up, and eventually the formation was broken and each plane flew its own course.

At dawn, all three were flying. But a light mist gradually turned into a dense fog, and with all navigational orientations failing, Bellinger had pilot Mitscher put the NC-1 down at sea, where, it was hoped, with engines off, a clear radio contact could be made with one of the destroyers. The NC-1 would fly no more, however, as the plunging and yawing of the plane in the heavy seas began a process of attrition that seemed to portend its eventual breakup. The anxiety of Bellinger and his crew on this score was brief; they were shortly picked up by a Greek freighter and the NC-1 was put in tow. Later, contact was made with an American destroyer, which took over the work of towing. But whatever hope there may have been of continuing the flight was lost when the battered plane turned over and sank.

Within twenty minutes of the descent of the NC-1, the NC-3 also alighted, hoping likewise to get a bearing on its position. The sea-battering began, but by using the engines to taxi, Towers and his crew were able, after two days, to bring their craft into the harbor of Ponta

Delgada. The NC-4 was even luckier. It was able to outrun the fog, perhaps because of its superior speed and better radio communications. Read had Stone bring the plane down at Horta, on the island of Fayal. That evening, May 17, New Yorkers heard of the plane's successful landing. At a meeting of the Pan American Aeronautical Convention, banqueting representatives from seven countries listened to President Alan R. Hawley read a message announcing the successful flight of the NC-4. "The guests arose as a unit in tribute to the daring crew . . . and burst out in enthusiastic cheers." The flight had vindicated the Liberty motor, Hawley said.

Back at Newfoundland, on May 18, as the NC-1 was sinking, the two British crews decided their day had come and they still might beat the Americans across. At St. John's Cochran House, the crews of both the Sopwith and the Martinsyde arose to a cloudless day and reports of a high-pressure system spreading over the north Atlantic. Proceeding to their respective fields, they spent the day making final preparations for takeoff. At 5:51 P.M., Hawker opened the throttle of his Rolls-Royce Eagle engine and began his takeoff run. Struggling into the air, the plane headed directly for the sea and was last seen crossing a line of white hills that formed the seacoast. At that point Hawker pulled the trap that released the plane's undercarriage and spectators watched it tumble to the ground. Hawker and his navigator, Grieve, were on their way. An hour later, Raynham and Morgan began their run, but at the point where the Raymor was about to rise, a sudden cross-wind violently buffeted the plane and its undercarriage collapsed. Raynham and Morgan were out of the race.

It was presumed that Hawker and Grieve would arrive at London's Brooklands Airport on Monday, May 19 around noon. Although it was an overcast, threatening day, several thousand people gathered at the airport, straining to catch the sound of the Rolls-Royce engine that would signal glory for Britain. But there was no sound forthcoming. "Hawker and Grieve . . . Missing," said the *New York Times* headline on May 20. Another declared, "NC-4 Starts at 3 A.M. Today for Lisbon"; and another, "Towers Tells How He Saved the NC-3." Americans moved into a high state of excitement.

For the next five days on both sides of the Atlantic people anxiously waited for news of the fate of Hawker and Grieve. No word came, and the sad and inevitable conclusion was that they had gone down at sea. King George sent a telegram of condolence to Mrs. Hawker. Then, on May 26, the public learned that Hawker and Grieve had been forced down by an overheated engine and were picked up by an old Danish freighter, the *Mary.* The *Mary* had no radio to report the recovery of the two men. In Europe and America there was profound rejoicing, like the glad relief that comes to a family when a member miraculously survives a pronouncement of death. "A feeling like this is worth many years of life," the *New York Times* editorialized on May 26. There was also something instructive in the flyers' having been saved by an old tramp steamer. Indeed, so moved was the editorial writer that his feelings flowered into poetry:

> T'was Danish Mary picked them up;
> Out of the air and sea;
> A shoddy trudging lollypop
> A traipsing slatternly.

On May 20 the NC-4 was in the air again, making the short trip from Horta to Ponta Delgada, where Towers and his crew were recuperating from their difficult experience. Read had assumed that the NC-3 was still flyable and that Towers and his plane would join him for the remainder of the trip. But he found Towers a captain without a ship and resignedly accepted the probability that he would have to surrender his plane to Towers. However, Navy Secretary Josephus Daniels ruled that Read was to continue.

Because of bad weather, it was not until May 27 that the NC-4 left Ponta Delgada for Lisbon. Again, destroyers, fourteen of them, marked the route. That night at 8:00 the plane approached Lisbon over the Tagus River. The journalist Walter Duranty, standing on the deck of the cruiser *Rochester,* watched the NC-4 approach. "Far away in the western sky there appeared a tiny speck, clearly visible against the gorgeous panorama of the sunset, with its rosy wisps of mare's tail clouds—'like a Belasco setting,' " Duranty quoted someone near him as saying. Floating down out of this colorful backdrop, the plane landed in the center of the river and was moored to a buoy. Then a launch from the *Rochester* picked up Read and his crew and took them to the ship. As the men walked up the gangway, they were greeted with a great cheer from the ship's crew. On the deck, John Towers came forward to shake Read's hand.

Dead silence followed as a band began "The Star-Spangled Banner." It was, wrote Duranty, "a wonderful picture. In the foreground was the little group who had done what no man had ever done before, standing stiffly at salute in the dazzling brightness of a searchlight. Beyond them were rows of naval and military officers in uniform, and a dark mass of civilians.... On the left was the witchery of colored lights gleaming amid the bright-hued flags, and in the center and on the right background were sailors' faces—brave and reverent in homage to their country's

national hymn—rising tier upon tier until lost in the darkness overhead."

Later, a reporter asked Read, "How did you feel when you sighted
land?" The reply "was typical in its simplicity." "Well, we felt pretty
good," said Read. More deathless words? Or was it merely that Read was
not the kind to elaborate on a subject?

The NC-4 landed at Plymouth, England, on May 31, a Saturday, in
the afternoon. There to meet the plane was the *Aroostook,* the supply
ship from which the three planes had taken their leave at St. John's
more than two weeks previous. The next day headlines all over America
proclaimed that the NC-4 was the first plane to cross the Atlantic.

The crew of the NC-4 said the plane had made it because of the
sterling qualities of the Liberty motor. Certain elements of America's
free business system advertised their contribution. One ad bragged that
of "the 15 American men who flew on the NC-1, NC-3, and NC-4 . . .
twelve chose Fatimas [cigarettes] to keep them company on the long,
lonely, daring flight." Why Fatimas? "Just enough Turkish." Another
large advertisement declared that "the NC-4 is varnished with valspar.
. . . Take a tip from the Navy and use valspar whenever you varnish
anything anywhere."

Back home, the NC crews got their heroes' welcome on July 10,
arranged by Glenn Curtiss. He rented a hall at New York's Commodore
Hotel and entertained the flyers and assorted notable guests at a banquet.
The room was decorated as a cabin of a giant seaplane crossing the
Atlantic. "When the guests were inside the searchlights played outside,
while the land, sky and ocean unrolled before the cabin windows." A
periodic buzzing sound in the background created the illusion of a
wireless sending out messages.

When the NC-4 came home, it was placed on exhibition in New
York's Central Park. Then, in the fall, it made a 3,000-mile navy
recruiting tour that took it down the Atlantic Coast, around Florida to
the Gulf Coast, and up the Mississippi to the Great Lakes. Subsequently,
it was stored and almost forgotten at the Norfolk Navy Yard. After World
War II it was taken to the Smithsonian, where it was restored and
exhibited on the Washington Mall in May 1969, the plane's fiftieth
anniversary. Today it is on exhibition in the main hall of the Pensacola
Naval Air Museum.

Two weeks after the NC-4 had landed at Plymouth, two Englishmen,
John Alcock, a Rolls-Royce engineer, and Arthur W. Brown, successfully flew the north Atlantic route in a Vickers Vimy twin-engined
bomber in sixteen hours and twelve minutes. Although the two flyers
landed in a peat bog in Ireland, they won the *Daily Mail* prize and

stirred the *New York Times* again to lift its voice in verse, the last three lines of which ran, "Laurel, your crown / Glorious pilots / Alcock and Brown."

SOURCES

All of the material on the new automobiles of 1919 is from advertisements in newspapers and magazines and from the *New York Times* reports on the automobile show. Information on the transatlantic flights of the NC planes is mainly from the *New York Times.* Also used was Richard K. Smith, *First Across: The U.S. Navy's Transatlantic Flight of 1919* (Annapolis, Md., 1986); C. R. Roseberry, *Glenn Curtiss, Pioneer of Flight* (New York, 1972); and Richard E. Byrd, *Skyward* (New York, 1928). The segment on the Liberty engine is from Elizabeth Frazer, "America in the Air," *Saturday Evening Post* (January 4, 1919).

FURTHER READING

Three interesting nostalgia pieces on the automobile are Joseph F. Clymer, *Those Wonderful Old Automobiles, 1919–1939* (New York, 1953); Stephen W. Sears, *The American Heritage History of the Automobile in America* (New York, 1977); and Ken W. Purty, *Motorcars of the Golden Past: One Hundred Rare and Exciting Vehicles from Harrahs' Automobile Collection* (Boston 1966). The advent of the automobile, where American life and manners are concerned, is well presented in one chapter of a now-vintage work: Preston W. Slosson, *The Great Crusade and After, 1914–1928* (New York, 1930). On airplanes of the past, see Harold Blaine Miller, *Navy Wings* (New York, 1937); and Cecil R. Rosebury, *The Challenging Skies: The Colorful Story of Aviation's Most Exciting Years, 1919–1939* (New York, 1966).

10

"I'm Forever Blowing Bubbles"

IF, IN 1919, THERE WERE dark fumings in the subterranean chambers of history's process, only a few brooding souls were affected. What better indicator is there of the spirit at work in the character of an era than its popular music? For a while after the war—a decade, almost—there were lingering signs of respect and even nostalgia for the old ways, as they were represented in the songs that people wanted to hear. In 1919 many American schoolchildren were singing from *The Golden Book of Favorite Songs,* a yellow paperbound classic that contained the traditional American music sung by previous generations. Stephen Foster melodies, patriotic airs, and those sad reminders of time's remorseless course—"The Old Oaken Bucket," "When You and I Were Young, Maggie," "Darling Nelly Gray," "Old Black Joe," "Old Dog Tray"—filled the book, most of them sung in glad uncaring chorus by children in the bright morning of life, children across whose path no existence-clouded shadows had begun to fall.

Although time would soon have its way, there was still romance, lying like a shimmering mesh over history's harsh determinism, with soft touches that told of beauty and eternity. In music it was operetta that still spoke of romance—princes and lovely maids who were faithful and pure were brought together at last through the temptations of flesh and gold to love everlasting. In 1919 the beautiful Fritzi Scheff was past her prime, but the spell she cast over America and operetta still remained. In 1905 she had premiered in Victor Herbert's *Mlle. Modiste* at New York's Knickerbocker Theater, and when she sang "Kiss Me Again," the male part of the audience was reduced to prayerful adoration. In March 1919, Victor brought out Mabel Garrison singing Herbert's heartthrobbing piece on a popular Black Seal record. Herbert's operettas, as well as those of Sigmund Romberg and Rudolph Friml, provided sufficient fare for stage vocalists and household singing for two more decades.

The popular new songs of 1919, show tunes for the most part, tell of an untroubled world of romance and dreaming. From the show *Irene* came "Alice Blue Gown"; and *The Passing Show of 1918* still had people singing "I'm Forever Blowing Bubbles," a song that speaks of a world of blue-laundered, perfumed innocence, one from which, in the end, all of the passion, turmoil, and grand designs of men would pass. The hit of Ziegfeld's *Follies* of 1919 was "A Pretty Girl Is Like a Melody," and the show *East Is West* featured "Chinese Lullaby." Three other favorites of that year were "The World Is Waiting for the Sunrise," "Let the Rest of the World Go By," and "Love Sends a Little Gift of Roses."

For the young, the advanced spirit of the time was found in the foxtrot—dance music with a catchy, accelerated tempo. In 1919 the favorites in this category were "Dardanella" and "Hindustan," the latter suggesting the mystery and silken opulence of India.

New York was, of course, the center and source of America's popular musical fare, served up mainly in musicals, with their potpourri of acts hung together with lavish dance productions and female stars who, dancing and singing, had attained an aura of the ultimate in feminine allure. In 1919 Ziegfeld's *Follies* opened at the New Amsterdam Theater, and Schubert's *Passing Show of 1919* opened at the Winter Garden. A new show, *Scandals of 1919,* produced by George White, opened at the Liberty Theater and featured Ann Pennington, hitherto one of Ziegfeld's stars.

The annual show that had come to be regarded as setting the standard in the way of beautiful girls and spectacular staging was Ziegfeld's *Follies,* and 1919 was one of its best production years. First, there were five hit songs, although two ordinarily was the norm for a successful production. In addition to "A Pretty Girl Is Like a Melody," by Irving Berlin there was "Mandy," "Tulip Time," and "My Baby's Arms." Then Eddie Cantor, playing an osteopath in a scene with George LeMaire, sang the song with which he would ever after be identified, "You'd Be Surprised!"

Cantor, born Izzy Iskowitch on Hester Street on New York's East Side, made his professional debut in 1907 at the old Clinton Music Hall. His next stand was at a Coney Island saloon, where he ogled, danced, pantomined, and sang with the help of a young pianist named Jimmy Durante. Cantor was heard in 1912 by impressario Gus Edwards, who gave him a job in a vaudeville production called *Kid Kabaret.* The show included others who would also become well known: Eddie Buzell,

George Prince, Lila Lee, Gregory Kelly, Walter Winchell, and George Jessel.

In 1916 Cantor joined the *Follies,* the same year W. C. Fields came in with his juggling act and the year before Will Rogers was brought into the show. After the 1919 *Follies,* Cantor moved to the Shubert Theater, and Fields left too. But Rogers, doing his rope tricks and delivering his homey commentary on the times as he performed, stayed with Ziegfeld until 1926, by which time he had become an American institution. Offstage he was as he appeared on, a shrewd observer and a kindly man whose personal values were in order and who never fell into the gaudy roles that show life seemed to make attractive and plausible. Perhaps at first some of the women of the show thought him a rube, but in time they came to respect him immensely because he treated them as people rather than as sex objects. "They were beautiful, they were desirable, but he had a wife and he loved her alone," wrote Marjorie Farnsworth in her history of the *Follies.* In an age of soap drama, a Rogers marital constancy would appear amusingly archaic, but to his admirers then, and through the twenties, it was a part of his person that made him "ring true" when he delivered his rustic homilies.

The *Follies* moved around its lovely women, and Florenz Ziegfeld (Rogers always called him "Mr. Zieg-*field*") came to be regarded as the ultimate arbiter of scantily clad female beauty—"The Glorifier" of American womanhood, as he was called. In 1919 the "glorified" woman, beyond all others, was Marilyn Miller. She was born Mary Ellen Reynolds in Evansville, Indiana. Her family included mostly vaudeville people, and she followed them onto the stage about as soon as she could walk. As Marilyn Miller (Miller being the name of her promoter-stepfather), she was "discovered" by Lee Shubert in a London night club in 1913, and for the next four years she danced in Shubert's *Passing Show.* Ziegfeld first saw her in 1915, dancing down the Winter Garden's long runway that ran from the stage to the rear of the orchestra seats.

Miller first appeared in the *Follies* in 1918, where, as Billie Burke recalled, she walked down "those long, glorious stairs in mock minstrel costume displaying legs that I believe have never been matched for sheer, slim, provocative beauty. Miss Pennington was famed for pretty knees and Mistinguette had wonderful ankles, but Marilyn—I think Marilyn had everything." Her stage character clearly struck a harmonic note with some basic wave of excitement that was beginning to roll in life—the throat-tightening sense of youth, of a new time at its dawn, of George Gershwin's music, of skyscrapers, airplanes, and automobiles, of the petulant and lovely women that F. Scott Fitzgerald would write about. One biographical sketch of Miller acutely senses this quality:

"Five three, slender, perfectly formed, with bright, blue eyes, and a sunny smile, she was a golden-haired wonder girl of a newly gilded age. Her grace, youth, talent, and charm made her seem a glimpse of joy everlasting to audiences mesmerized by the freshness, extravagance and glamour of the stage she skipped across."

In 1920, Marilyn Miller left the *Follies* for musicals. Success was immediate and overwhelming, first in *Sally*, which ran for three years. The big hit song of that show was "Look for the Silver Lining," and when Miller sang it the Broadway musical achieved its brightest moment. Next came *Sunny*, with another three-year run. Jerome Kern wrote the hit of the show, "Who?" Back with Ziegfeld for *Rosalie*, Miller opened on February 2, 1927, in the new Ziegfeld Theater. Then came *Smiles* in 1930 and *As Thousands Cheer* in 1933.

Miller's personal life was somewhat unsettled. She married Frank Carter in 1920, but soon after, he was killed in an accident in his new Packard, the door of which carried the monogram "M.M. and F.C." After his death she became a "party girl." In 1922 she married Jack Pickford, brother of Mary Pickford, at Pickfair, the fabulous Beverly Hills home of Mary and Douglas Fairbanks. Marilyn and Jack Pickford were divorced in 1927. On April 7, 1936, at the age of thirty-seven, Miller died suddenly and, where the public was concerned, unexpectedly. But it was not unexpected to her. One cold day in mid-March, just as she was about to go into a hospital to have a chronic sinus infection treated, she stopped before the window of a Fifth Avenue dress shop, looked at a blue silk dress, and told her companion she wanted it. "To leave the hospital in?" she was asked. "Yes," she said, "when I leave. I want to be buried in it. I am certain I won't leave the hospital alive."

Flo Ziegfeld, between 1916 and the mid-1920s, was the great producer of shows that had featured women like Marilyn Miller. He had an imagination for extravagant stage layouts and the ability to enlist the financial support with which to put them into effect. Born into a family of distinguished musicians (his father had organized the Chicago Musical College), Ziegfeld took leave of the family tradition when he exhibited Sandow the Strong Man at the Chicago Columbian Exposition in 1893. It was no cheap tent performance he put on, but one staged in a drawing room atmosphere where the well-to-do would be invited to ogle Sandow and even feel his biceps before he performed his amazing feats of strength.

Had it not been for Ziegfeld, the name of Anna Held would have long since rested in obscurity, for she was little more than a European music hall performer of no distinguished talent. But Ziegfeld brought the well-proportioned young woman to America from Paris, married her, and made her the feature attraction in his 1907 *Follies* — the first. When the show seemed to lag, Ziegfeld concocted the "milk bath" hoax, claiming that Held got her fulsome curves by bathing in milk. Journalists seized on the story, and the public was enthralled.

Ziegfeld was a restless and inconstant husband; his wife, as it turned out, had a practical mind that made a little quiet and security seem more appealing than living up to her image as a high-voltage sex figure. So Ziegfeld left her and in time they were divorced. She died in 1918, still in love with him, it was said.

Ziegfeld's greatest passion was Lillian Lorraine, introduced to the *Follies* in 1910 when she sang her famous "Swing Song." As they used to say, she became "the darling of cafe society," a dazzling creature whose life moved in an aura of ermine and diamonds. She laughed a lot, had a mania for fast cars and parties, and felt for Ziegfeld no exclusive passion. On New Year's Eve 1913, Ziegfeld went alone to a party at a private club, the capricious Miss Lorraine having sought excitement in another's company. Overcome by his desire for her, and brought to a point of emotional overflow in the reflection that she was likely in the arms of another, Ziegfeld went to an empty room and gave himself over to tears. There he was found by his friend Gene Buck, who urged him to seek solace in the party.

As the two men returned to the stairs that led to the ballroom, the great Ziegfeld stopped. On the landing stood Billie Burke, one of Charles Frohman's leading stars. As Ziegfeld and Buck ascended, they encountered Burke and her escort, and Ziegfeld had Buck introduce them. Soon the music began and Ziegfeld, who was reputed to be one of the great waltzers of his time, whirled Burke into the crowd and finally (if one has the script right) onto the patio, where, hand in hand, they looked at the moon-drenched towers of Gotham. They were married on Saturday, April 11, 1914, and although Ziegfeld's wandering impulses returned, Billie Burke remained his wife until the end.

A debt-ridden Ziegfeld died in Hollywood on June 27, 1932. Burke, to a large extent concerned with paying off her husband's debts, developed a career in the movies, playing an almost standard role as a somewhat fey middle-aged woman. The year after his death, the Ziegfeld Theater reopened as a Loew's moviehouse. Among the Ziegfeld girls introduced from the floor was Lillian Lorraine. Gus Edwards, sitting at the piano on the stage, asked her if she would come up and sing her old song, "By the Light of the Silvery Moon." She went up, but she could not sing. Sobs shook her so that she had to be led back to her seat. She died in 1955 at the age of sixty-three.

During the spring of 1919 at the Winter Garden Theater on Broadway and Thirtieth Street, Al Jolson, another East Sider who had worked his way uptown, was playing in *Sinbad*, which had opened on February 14, 1918. *Sinbad* was a two-act extravaganza of singing, clowning, and dancing in which Jolson played the lead. The Winter Garden, with its runway out over the audience, was the theater that enabled Jolson to demonstrate his talent. "It was supposed to be used by the chorus girls as they paraded up and down it. But the moment I saw it I knew it gave me a big chance. I used to get confidential with the audience by running up and down on this platform, stopping for a chat with people, and by kidding the audience and performers in general."

Jolson's voice was like a rasp, which ordinarily would have driven into the streets anyone with sensitive ears, but he combined with his singing such emotion that the audience believed it liked what it was hearing. He sang two songs in *Sinbad* that became very popular and for him an indelible part of his label for the rest of his years. The first was "Mammy"; the second, "Swanee." When Jolson sang the latter there was usually shouting approval from the audience.

"Swanee" had its inception in a conversation between twenty-one-year-old George Gershwin and lyricist Irving Caesar. Lunching at Dinty Moore's restaurant, they talked about their work and came up with the idea of writing another lively one-step like "Hindustan," then currently popular. Gershwin added that the song ought to have an American theme, "something like Stephen Foster's 'Suwanee River.'" With musical phrases running through their minds, they took a bus to the Gershwin family's apartment in Washington Heights. Making their way around a card table where brother Ira Gershwin and some of his cronies were playing poker, they went to a piano and in fifteen minutes turned out "Swanee." It was immediately taken by Ned Wayburn, who was producing a revue at the Capital Theater. There it was sung by Muriel DeForest to the accompaniment of Arthur Pryor's band, while sixty showgirls, with electric lights in the toes of their dancing shoes, twinkled out the song in a darkened theater. Jolson heard "Swanee" at a party one night shortly thereafterward and added it to *Sinbad*.

George Gershwin, as Americans came to know, was far more than a writer of popular tunes for musicals to which his brother, Ira, contributed sophisticated lyrics. His musical ideas, which ranged from formal compositions to songs for Hollywood musicals, were not confined to established musical traditions, either classical or popular. They came from the soul of that new spirit that was breaking over America and the Western world after World War I. One hears this in Gershwin's music, but something else too—that over the bursting rays of light and the daring and exciting rush of sound that floods the senses, there is a sense of diffusely brooding death.

In 1936 George and Ira Gershwin went to Hollywood to write songs for the lavish musicals that were filmed in that era. Their last assignment was for a Fred Astaire–Ginger Rogers movie, *Shall We Dance.* One of the songs from the movie, "Love Is Here to Stay," was Gershwin's last composition. He died of a brain tumor on July 11, 1937.

At the same time that Al Jolson was singing "Mammy" and Dixie melodies, something more authentic than an East Side reading of southern themes was moving out of the South into the New York area. On March 10, 1919, the *New York Times* noted something new in the air where music was concerned: "Two companies of negro singers and players of instruments, including the strange devices known as 'jazz' music, were heard last evening." The event was a program of black music at the Forty-fourth Street Theater. W. C. Handy, the saloon piano player from Memphis's Beale Street, was there to play and to lead an orchestra in "Memphis Blues." The part of the program that the newspaper thought to be of "most value" was that given over to "old negro melodies and songs of religious fervor."

To persons of cultured sensibilities, accustomed to finding in their music intimations of order in the universe and the implicit melodic promise that in the end all would be well, jazz was like releasing demons from hell into the area of musical expression. It was sense music, a pulsing plunge into an orgiastic mood whose focus was the sex act. And that it was, music from the New Orleans Tenderloin, from Beale Street in Memphis, that had made its way up the Mississippi to Chicago and quickly to New York—a pestilential fog, the purists thought, that should be halted at any cost. But the compulsion for humans to express themselves in the symbols of art is constant and universal, and has to be done out of the materials at hand. Black musicians, playing in bordellos, took the conditions of their life and fashioned an art. And in art, one may believe, lies a way to freedom.

In 1919, eighteen-year-old Louis Armstrong started playing a jazz cornet in Kid Orey's band, a twelve-piece group that played at the Peter Laias Cabaret on Iberville and Maris streets in New Orleans. In November of that year Armstrong went with "Fate" Marable to play on an excursion steamer, the *Dixie Belle.* "She had her berth at the foot of Canal Street," Armstrong remembered. "The orchestra would start playing at eight o'clock, while she was at the wharf, to attract people, and then she would shove out into the river at eight-thirty every night with a big crowd on board and cruise slowly around until about eleven o'clock when she would come back in."

In the spring of 1920, Armstrong traveled up the Mississippi on the *Dixie Belle* to Chicago, where jazz first broke through into the awareness of white America. "It was a warm spring day and the river was high with water," he recalled. "After a while, when we had had our last look at New Orleans, I found myself a nice corner up on the top deck right under the pilot house and settled down with my trumpet and polishing rag. I had bought myself a fine new instrument just before starting out, but even that wasn't shiny enough for *this* trip." Armstrong remembered, "I put her to my mouth and tried out a few blasts. She sounded strong and sweet, with a good pure tone. I swung a little tune and saw we were going to get along fine together."

In 1919 Paul Whiteman, the director of a salon orchestra, left San Francisco to work in Atlantic City. The next year, having played at the Palais Royale in New York, he made two records that were immensely popular: "Whispering" and "Japanese Sandman." With those songs Whiteman began to establish the place he held for two decades as the sophisticated, big-orchestra interpreter of what was occurring in the new areas of new creation in American musical life. Well known by 1924, on the evening of February 12 of that year he presented a jazz concert at Aeolian Hall, customarily a place where classical music was played. That year, too, Whiteman introduced to the public George Gershwin's "Rhapsody in Blue."

On the night of Whiteman's concert, Marshall Stearns wrote in *The Story of Jazz*, "Louis Armstrong was probably playing close to his all-time best a few blocks away at the Roseland Ballroom on Broadway." Armstrong, playing with Fletcher Henderson, had made it to the big city after three years in Chicago with King Oliver, the trumpeter whose place Armstrong had taken in 1919 in New Orleans with the Kid Orey Band at the time of Oliver's departure for Chicago.

In the mid-thirties jazz was molded into a sophisticated form called "swing," a form that held through the years of World War II. Nonetheless, with all of the "swinging" that marked popular music, there was still a point of return for musicians after they had taken their instrumental meanders through the musical byways. But such has been the acceleration in the process of cultural change that Benny Goodman was probably much closer to Mozart than rock is to swing.

SOURCES

Much of the material in this chapter is from show advertising in the *New York Times*. The biographies used are: Michael Freedland, *Jolson* (New York, 1972); Robert Kimball and Alfred Simon, *The Gershwins*

(New York, 1973); and Eddie Cantor and David Freedman *Ziegfeld the Great Glorifier* (New York, 1934). Biographical information on Marilyn Miller is from Edward T. James, ed., *Notable American Women, 1607–1950,* vol. 2 (Cambridge, Mass., 1971); Marjorie Farnsworth, *The Ziegfeld Follies* (New York, 1973); and Billie Burke, *With a Feather on My Nose* (New York, 1949). Farnsworth's and Burke's books also contain much of the biographical information used on Will Rogers and W. C. Fields. The segment on music is from Louis Armstrong, *Swing That Music* (New York, 1936); and Marshall W. Stearns, *The Story of Jazz* (New York, 1956). An article in *The American Magazine* (December 1919), by Florenz Ziegfeld, Jr., entitled "Picking Out Pretty Girls for the Stage," includes material on Marilyn Miller.

FURTHER READING

Reminiscences and biographies are the best sources for these show business lives. See: Eddie Cantor, *As I Remember Them* (New York, 1963); W. C. Fields, *Fields for President* (New York, 1971) and *W. C. Fields by Himself* (Englewood Cliffs, N.J., 1973). Also, Charles Higham, *Ziegfeld* (Chicago, 1972). George Gershwin's work and life is detailed in Edward Jablonski, *George Gershwin* (New York, 1962); and in Robert Rushmore, *The Life of George Gershwin* (New York, 1966). Louis Armstrong and jazz are described in Max Jones, *Louis: The Louis Armstrong Story* (Boston, 1971); Sydney Walter Finklestein, *Jazz: A People's Music* (New York, 1948); and Richard Hadlock, *Jazz Masters of the Twenties* (New York, 1965).

11

Caruso and Galli-Curci

BY 1919, THE PHONOGRAPH had become an almost necessary fixture in the American home. That year the price of a Victor machine ranged from $12 for a simple table model to $950 for an ornately styled grand. All of the machines had essentially the same mechanism: a windup spring motor that supplied enough power to play two or three records and a steel needle pickup that transmitted vibrations to a disk diaphragm that carried those vibrations through a hollow arm to an amplifying sound box. Volume was regulated by opening or closing shutters in front of the sound chamber. Victor machines also had the familiar label showing a dog crouching in front of an acoustical horn— "His Master's Voice," which, like the Packard automobile's "Ask the Man Who Owns One," suggested distinction and quality.

The musical tastes of Americans who liked semiclassical and classical music is indicated by what they listened to. Those who owned the large machines—the Victrola or the Grafonola—and those who kept their Columbia, Edison, or Victor Red Seal records catalogued and sheathed in manila folders usually held record collections dominated by performances by leading concert artists. Victor was the big publisher of classical music, and in the mid-1919 announcement of new records it offered violinist Mischa Elman playing "Nocturne in D Flat," the famous Flonzaley Quartet performing Beethoven's "Quartet in C Major," and violinist Efrem Zimbalist playing Franz Drdla's "Souvenir." Vocalists were also very popular, and by World War I any American who knew anything about music certainly believed that Enrico Caruso was the greatest tenor of all time. If one had nothing else from his recorded repertoire it was necessary to have

"La Donna e Mobile" from *Rigoletto* and "Vesti la Guibba" from *Pagliacci.*

In 1919 Caruso was a unique American institution. Already famous in Europe, he had come to New York on November 11, 1903, to sing at the Metropolitan Opera House, where he would perform for the remainder of his operatic career. Warm-hearted and expansive, he lived joyously and ate copiously in the company of as many friends as he could gather around him at his favorite Italian restaurant. Delighted to be living in America, he appeared to want to become the country's premier patriot. Everywhere he went during the war he was called upon to sing George Cohan's "Over There," which he did with such great verve that listeners were swelled with patriotic emotion, similar to that caused by the sight of the flag in front of a marching column of men. Caruso was, in fact, the George M. Cohan of the Metropolitan. Guileless and simple, he sought only to sing to the best of his ability—to move people—and this he could do because his voice was incomparably great.

The year 1919 was one of Caruso's most active. The opera season of 1918–19 still bore the mark of wartime hysteria in that German works were excluded. On the other hand, a long stand of "one hundred nights" was given over to Italian composers, mainly Verdi and Puccini. These composers had written arias that the public would have no one but Caruso sing.

Caruso was also widely sought for concert appearances. In early March, in Ann Arbor for a concert, he received a telegram from Otto Kahn, chairman of the Metropolitan Opera Company, telling him to return to New York for a League of Nations concert. Caruso readily complied, and it was at this point that Giulio Gatti-Casazza, just completing his eleventh year as musical director at the Met, had an idea. Gatti-Casazza was aware that on Saturday, March 22, Caruso would complete his 550th appearance at the opera house, as well as a quarter century in opera. The evening would be celebrated as Caruso's silver jubilee.

It was a grand affair. New York's governor, Alfred E. Smith, attended and shared two boxes with New York mayor John Hylan, heading the city's delegation. Major Benjamin O'Ryan was in box 3 and the Italian consul's party was in box 4. Mrs. Caruso, the former Dorothy Benjamin and the tenor's bride of one year, sat in the Astor box with Mr. and Mrs. Park Benjamin, Jr., and Mr. and Mrs. Seton Henry. Across the house, opera stars Mary Garden, Geraldine Farrar, and John McCormick made up another box party. Caruso and the opera company and the orchestra presented segments from three operas. There were speeches lauding Caruso, and after they were over Geraldine Farrar brought the affair to a close by kissing Caruso on the cheek and calling for "three cheers for Caruso." Caruso, smiling happily, called for "three cheers for America."

The affair had its element of unpleasantness, nonetheless. James Beck, a New York city political figure, had been asked to be one of the principal speakers. Just before the curtain rose on the final round of speeches, Mayor Hylan sent his functionary, Grover Whalen, to the Met management with a notice that Beck must not appear on the program. If he did, the city delegation would leave. Beck, it seemed, had given a muted and conditional endorsement of the war and to the proposition of Germany's exclusive guilt in starting it. Not wishing to embarrass anyone, Beck withdrew, saying that the colossal tragedy of the war should incline persons toward reconciliation rather than perpetuating wartime animosity.

Caruso closed the season on the evening of Thursday, April 17, as Radames in *Aida*. Three days before, he had sung Don Jose in *Carmen*. "Both were of a lyric sweetness beyond compare," wrote James Gibbon Huneker for the *New York Times*. But Caruso would have only one more year with the Met. As he began the season of 1920–21, his health began to fail. The summer of 1920 had been one of strenuous concertizing, including a trip to Cuba. His biographer, Stanley Jackson, remarked that "towards the end of October he arrived back in New York weary in body and spirit." He had picked up a cough which seemed impervious to the normal modes of treatment. On December 4, while driving in Central Park with his wife, he was seized with a shuddering chill. Nevertheless, four days later he was determined to sing *Pagliacci*. A heavy smoker, he had his customary cigarette before going onstage. He was singing "Vesti la Guibba," the one aria that Americans knew beyond all others, and the one they singularly identified with Caruso, when his voice broke. Staggering into the wings, he lay for a while on a cot, racked with intense pain. "Intercostal neuralgia," pronounced the doctor, who proceeded to tape up Caruso's ribs and then let him go out for the second act.

On December 11, at an operatic performance in Brooklyn, Caruso hemorrhaged profusely but continued to sing, mopping the blood from his mouth as he sang. A physician, summoned to the dressing room, diagnosed the problem as "a small burst vein at the tip of the tongue." Plagued by pain, Caruso continued to sing until Friday evening, December 24, when he gave his 607th Metropolitan performance. Thereafter, he steadily declined, and he lapsed into a coma in mid-February. He was given last rites by the church and then, rallying, asked to say good-bye to his friends. Antonio Scotti, a baritone and friend since the early years at La Scala, was sent for, as were the sopranos Lucrezia Bori and Rosa Ponselle. Thousands jammed the churches of New York to pray for

Caruso, and more brought medals and holy cards to the hospital. Then he began to rally. By the end of April he was taking daily drives in Central Park, though he remained gaunt and gray. At last he decided to go to Italy, where, he thought, the sun would restore his health. Dropping by the Metropolitan to say goodbye to Gatti-Casazza and others there, he was assured by all that they would be looking for him in the fall season. In Sorrento, his health indeed seemed to improve. Sun bathing masked his gray pallor, and he professed to be feeling better. But by the end of July he was again in agonizing pain. An "abscess" had been found near his kidney, but an operation was thought inadvisable. Caruso died in Rome on Tuesday morning, August 2.

Stanley Jackson described the almost universal grief that accompanied the singer's death: "On the day of the funeral the flags of New York flew at half mast. The facade of the Metropolitan would be draped in black throughout that month. . . . In Naples every shop had closed in mourning. The tenor's coffin . . . was . . . drawn by six black horses. The procession moved slowly along Santa Lucia with 100,000 people lining the route." In England, on Brighton Pier, a bandmaster stopped his concert to play a record of "Vesti la Guibba," while the holiday crowd stood with heads bared. Many wept.

There would be great tenors after Caruso—Beniamino Gilli, Jussi Bjorling, Giovanni Martinelli, and the Mozart singer John Brownlee, but none could sing Italian opera with such emotional sweep and purity, or reach a high C with such marvelously rich tones, as had this son of a mechanic, born in the slums of Naples. Never again would Americans feel so close to a great artist as they had felt to Caruso. No doubt many of them, not yet brought to the levels of brittle sophistication that in a later day would make "Vesti la Guibba" sound overwrought and emotional, played that piece on their parlor gramaphones and mourned, along with the rest of the world, the loss of a great artist.

In 1919 Victor Records brought another voice into American homes, one that had grown in popularity during the war years. That year Amelita Galli-Curci, a Milanese, recorded "Caro Nome" from *Rigoletto,* which, along with her recording of the "Bell Song" from *Lakmé,* rivaled Caruso's records in popularity. In writing of the concert year of 1918, James Gibbon Huneker observed that "the winning of New York by Galli-Curci forms the most interesting incident of the present musical and operatic season . . . for she has stepped at once into the front ranks of artists, a triumph matched since 1900 by only Farrar and Caruso." On February 15, 1918, between seven and ten thousand people tried to get into the Metropolitan to hear her sing the role of Violetta in *La Traviata,* which includes two of the most famous soprano arias in operatic literature: "Ah, fors' e lui," and its companion, "Sempre libera." Standees began lining the sidewalk at nine o'clock in the morning, and when evening came, the streets were blocked solid with automobiles from Park Avenue to Third Avenue.

When the performance ended, there were forty curtain calls. As midnight approached the crowd went wild, swarming down to the footlights to demand that Galli-Curci sing "Home, Sweet Home." This song, with which the soprano had closed her concerts in the war years, had touched something in peoples' hearts, as it had in the Civil War years, that spoke of home and peace. So at a quarter to midnight a piano was rolled out between the velvet draperies and Galli-Curci, accompanying herself on the piano, sang the old song. The next year her concerts at the Hippodrome sold out six times in a row.

Galli-Curci sang at the Met for the last time on January 24, 1930, in *The Barber of Seville.* Her career was cut short by a throat ailment, though she lived to the age of eighty-one, dying at La Jolla, California, on November 26, 1963. To the elderly Huneker, she was a great singer, but one who did not "make the most of her vocal resources. . . . She is not brilliant in the sense that Luisa Tettrazzini was brilliant. She had a sympathetic delivery yet she lacks variety in tone color."

By what authority did Huneker make such statements? By that of Madam Frida Ashforth, who "inclines to the belief expressed above." And who was Madam Ashforth? In February 1919 when Huneker made his pronouncements about Galli-Curci in the *New York Times,* Ashforth was in her eighties. She had been a well-known singer in the years after the Civil War and had turned to teaching voice. For half a century she had reigned as New York's teacher of great singers, a teacher of teachers. Huneker knew that she would remember the "voices of yesteryear . . . Patti, Melba, Eames, Calvé, Lehmann, Tarnina, Sembrich . . . names to conjure with."

Through 1919 and the following year, Huneker contributed his lofty reflections on the arts, and even philosophy, to the *New York Times.* Readers must have sometimes been bemused by what he was saying, but since his ideas sounded obscure and he could cite European thinkers who were even more obscure, many probably decided that his ideas must be right. Catching a glimpse of the proportions of the intellectual changes occuring in the late nineteenth century, Huneker seemed to think of himself as a kind of filter through which the cultural light of Europe would be shed upon young Americans who wanted a new vision. He tried to bring the sound and flavor of Europe to America; he liked European words and names, which he appeared to use with great familiarity. But the end impression of reading his pieces in the *Times* is that he floundered in his words; he was unable to conceptualize what was going on in the world of ideas with sufficient coherence to assist readers toward intellectual clarification.

In the Sunday *New York Times* of September 7, 1919, Huneker wrote his personal philosophy, which, as a hodgepodge of undigested ideas and heavy-breathing phrases, was no philosophy but was clearly Huneker. His was "not a philosophy of iron certitudes. I have never been an agnostic. I have always believed in something, somewhere, as Emerson would say; in fact I believe in everything. I am a Yes-Sayer to life. . . . The vicar of hell is he who teaches the negation of things."

Having affirmed life, Huneker then disavowed it. It was all an illusion. "Nothing endures but mobility, changeless change. Yet we dare speak of stability, personal immortality, the absolute when nature abhors an absolute. Relativity rules. . . . Hope of Future life is the aura of the young, healthy cellular tissue. The sap mounts . . . the call of the cells . . . love is cell-hunger. . . . As Cabanis, the materialistic philosopher, puts it: man is a digestive tube pierced at both ends."

Perhaps the war—its monstrous carnage and irrationality—had destroyed an optimistic view of progress that Huneker may once have had. Dispirited, he died on February 9, 1921. His funeral service was held in the auditorium of the New Town Hall, where a quartet of strings played Mozart's *Ave Verum Corpus,* music that speaks of the eternal so directly and clearly that one wonders how Huneker, the music critic, failed to hear it in his lifetime.

When America entered the war, music, no matter how free and truthful it might be in its essential character, was affixed with national labels and was judged worth hearing or condemning according to those labels. The banning of Mozart from opera and concert stage for two years was of itself an action that should have forced a questioning of the whole apparatus of war justification. But amid muted misgivings here and there, Mozart was banned, Wagner was banned, Beethoven was banned—and how many others, whose names had a slightly Teutonic sound, were left off programs because of pressure from ravening patriots?

In March 1919, hoping that sanity had returned, the Rudolph Christians Producing Company planned a German opera at New York City's Lexington Avenue Theater. A "report" went out that soldiers and sailors in the city would wreck the theater. The Italian Chamber of Commerce asked Mayor John Hylan to stop the "anti-patriotic" performance. Speaking "on behalf of the citizens of Italian blood," the group begged "to register a most emphatic protest." To put on the opera would be a "public defiance of American patriotism and public decency, tending to create a false impression of sympathy for Germany in that very language which is known in Northern Italy, Belgium, Northern France, Poland, and Serbia only through abominable curses from German military monsters, devastating property, killing innocent people, and perpetrating most infamous crimes upon women and children" (*New York Times*, March 9, 1919).

Two days later, Dr. Max Winter, speaking for the opera company, announced an "indefinite postponement" as requested by Mayor Hylan and the ubiquitous Grover Whalen. Nevertheless, that evening five hundred sailors and soldiers formed in front of the Navy Club and marched to the Lexington Avenue Theater. They were greeted by Police Captain W. W. Duggan of the East Fifty-first Street Station, who told them that they had won a victory over German-language opera— whereupon the men saluted, cheered, and broke ranks. "They're a fine bunch of lads," Captain Duggan said later.

In any case, it seems that Captain Duggan need not have been concerned. William G. McRae, secretary of the For America League, said in a talk to three hundred wounded soldiers that, unbeknownst to the police, "there were two machine guns mounted on the roofs adjoining the opera house on that night." McRae linked the malevolence of the Hun with that of the Bolsheviks, adding that "fully 75 per cent of the labor organizations of this country are filled with Bolshevist ideas and German propaganda." It was the intention of the For America League to "wipe this stuff out entirely" by organizing all returning veterans "so that they could take the work to their home towns when they were discharged" (*New York Times*, March 16, 1919).

Apparently no one at the time who was prominent in musical life openly deplored this irrational behavior. Elenora de Cisneros, a mezzo-soprano who had sung Wagner at the Met, did her dramatic best to contribute to the hysteria. She declared that she could not sing Wagner anytime soon because she had had a vision: "I saw the Somme! I saw a place in 'No Man's Land.' " Then, she said, the Somme vanished "and I was listening to a superb rendition of the 'Prelude' of *Tristan und Isolde*, the first Wagner . . . I had heard since 1916." Around her were "hundreds of Americans" and the music was discordant and tragic. "I would as soon have applauded as I would have laughed at a procession of the weeping, violated women and children of France and Belgium!" If there was still a person in America who listened to German music, then that person was "either a German, a neutral, or a pacifist" (*New York Times*, May 20, 1919).

German music was heard on April 12, although it was not hospitably received. "Teuton Syllables Echo in New York Halls Patronized by People Who Don't Like American Language," read the headline in the

New York Times on April 13. A group called The Madrigal Quartet, made up of Germans who had been with the Met, sang selections from the classics and ended with a group of German folksongs. "There was an appreciable stir in every seat. Everybody bent forward in close interest." The first words heard were "Nach der Heimat Mocht Ich Wieder." Out of the darkness of the audience "a sob arose, then other sobs. Song after song was revived, and each time there was sobbing."

SOURCES

James Gibbon Huneker's concert reviews and his random musings on the New York music scene are the principal sources for this chapter. The books that were most helpful in preparing this chapter are Dorothy Caruso, *Enrico Caruso, His Life and Death* (New York, 1945); Richard Aldrich, *Concert Life in New York* (New York, 1941); and Irving Kolodin, *The Metropolitan Opera* (New York, 1966).

FURTHER READING

A strongly suggested supplementary activity for one wishing to hear, muffled as they are, some of the vocal and instrumental sounds of the war years and just after is to listen to the recordings of the time. Caruso's Victor recording of "Over There" remains, as Huneker would have put it, a musical experience "to conjure with." For corroborating judgments on Huneker's writings, see Waldo Frank, *Our America* (1919), pp. 188–89; also Daniel Aaron, *Writers on the Left* (1961), p. 9.

12

Summer Diversions

In JUNE 1919 THE NEW YORK theatrical world was disrupted when a large number of show people decided to strike, having recently organized themselves into the Actors' Equity Association, an affiliate of the American Federation of Labor. The opposite of this new organization was the Producing Managers' Association, "a national association of vaudeville, burlesque, and motion picture producers." On June 7 most of New York's theaters were dark—all except the Cohan and Harris Theater, where *The Royal Vagabond* was playing.

George M. Cohan was one of America's top showmen in 1919. Not yet forty, he was a playwright, producer, manager, actor, song writer, and dance man. Cohan, accompanied by his good friend Steve Reardon, heard about the strike while in New Haven, Connecticut, on what was to have been a leisurely automobile trip to Chicago. In half an hour he and Reardon were on their way back to New York, and shortly he and some commandeered associates filled the vacancies in the cast of *The Royal Vagabond*. The *New York Times* said that Cohan knew "about one line in ten," but that he managed to get away with it.

Aside from his writing and performing talents, Cohan was a hard-headed businessman—a "rugged individualist." The idea of performers joining together in common cause against producers seemed almost sinful to him, as did, for that matter, an organization of producers. Operating in a loose way, he got together an Actors' Fidelity League, which was made up of actors *and* producers. As the head of the league he worked out an agreement with the actors that granted every demand of the Actors' Equity Association except that of recognition as the official arbiter for actors. At a meeting at the Biltmore Hotel on August

27, Cohan read his settlement proposal to an audience of show people. Concluding his recitation of terms, he leaned far out over the speaker's podium and shouted, "I don't want to pin any bouquets on myself, but don't let anyone tell you that the Actors' Equity Association is responsible for this! I'm responsible for this."

Cohan's proposal satisfied almost everyone except the chorus girls at the Hippodrome. Their main complaint, about which they were most emphatic, centered on the person of Charles B. Dillingham. It was said that Dillingham's presence in the Producing Managers' Association was the cause of the strike in the first place. When Dillingham resigned on August 29, the strike was over. In addition to getting rid of Dillingham, the chorus girls got a raise from twenty-four to thirty-five dollars per week.

Visitors to New York in 1919 who were looking for entertainment had available two shows with Oriental themes, both enjoying long runs. *Chu Chin Chow* originated in London in 1916 and was in its third season in New York at the Century Theater. Another long-running production was *East Is West*, playing at the Astor Theater, featuring Fay Bainter. At the Henry Miller Theater, Ruth Chatterton starred in *Moonlight and Honeysuckle*.

Gaities of 1919, another popular show, included a comedy routine by Ed Wynn, who, as the *New York Times* observed, had "come to the front" as "one of the best low comedians of the year." Wynn had been a vaudevillian, and like Fred Allen and Jack Benny, he would go on to star in radio during the thirties. In 1919, though, he was at the point where old-time vaudeville, such as had come from the stage of the Jefferson Theater on Fourteenth Street, had, through the showmanship of Ziegfeld and White, taken on an uptown style.

Fred Allen, reminiscing about vaudeville at the Jefferson, described acts that had been "combed from the jungles, the four corners of the world," appealing alike to "the intelligentsia and the subnormal." There were acts featuring "an endless, incongruous swarm of performing lions, bears, tigers, leopards, boxing kangaroos, horses, ponies, mules, dogs, cats, rats, seals, and monkeys in their wake." There were others in which people "rode bicycles, did acrobatic and contortion tricks, walked wires, exhibited sharpshooting skills, played violins, trombones, cornets, pianos, concertinas, zylophones, harmonicas, and any other known instrument. There were hypnotists, iron-jawed ladies, one-legged dancers, one-armed cornetists, mind readers, female impersonators, male impersonators, Irish comedians, Jewish comedians, dramatic actors, Hindu conjurors, ventriloquists, bag punchers, singers and dancers of every description, clay modelers, and educated geese—all traveling from hamlet to town to city."

Allen remembered one vaudeville act that must have been the world's most unique. It featured Orville Stamm, billed as the "Strongest Boy in the World." To demonstrate his enormous strength, Orville played the violin with an enormous English bulldog suspended from the elbow of his bow arm. "The bulldog made graceful arcs in the air as Orville pizzicatoed and manipulated his bow." To conclude his act, he lay flat on the stage and arched his back, a position called "bending the crab." With abdomen high, he suffered an upright piano to be placed on a platform set on his stomach while a musician stood on his thigh and played and sang "Ireland Must Be Heaven, Because My Mother Came from There."

What with the wonder of an act like Orville Stamm's, and especially with its references to Ireland, Heaven, and mother, there were some who would condemn vaudeville out of hand. One was the Reverend William Burgess of the Illinois Vigilance Association. In an address on June 4, 1919, to an Atlantic City Conference on Social Work, he declared that "the modern stage is set for hell." Except for "a few worthy and notable exceptions of legitimate drama, the stage reeks with moral filth and sensual exhibits which might make the devil blush. . . . No hug step or wriggling monstrosity is too strong for the stage of so called burlesque and vaudeville."

Speaking before a large Atlantic City audience could be heady business, and it may have carried the Reverend Burgess into an excess of generalization. Fred Allen recalled that the Kieth vaudeville circuit allowed "no profanity, no suggestive allusions, *double-entendres,* or off-color monkey business" in its acts. Behind the stage in every Kieth theater was a "Notice to Performers" that, among other admonitions, included, "Don't say 'slob' or 'son-of-a-gun' or 'hully gee' on this stage unless you want to be cancelled peremptorily. . . . If you are in doubt as to the character of your act, consult the local manager before you go on the stage, for if you are guilty of uttering anything sacrilegious or even suggestive, you will be immediately closed." What were examples of material that could not be used at a Kieth theater? A performer could not say "hell" or use old wheezes like "Lord Epson, Secretary of the Interior," or "an old maid taking a tramp through the woods."

Movies were rapidly replacing vaudeville acts as the chief source of entertainment for most people. Taking the place of the Orville Stamms were rugged and handsome actors and beautiful actresses. On their faces the camera could linger, savoring all the subtleties of their emoting; of special interest was the shadowed and suffering countenance of the heroine, who, from her stronghold of impregnable virtue, made her way around the pitfalls that had been set for her. In the end, of course, the true and the good won out, and the token of triumph was the long-denied kiss, chastely given as sweeping dark lashes lowered over glistening eyes to shut out the distractions of the world.

Still, the theme of the "fallen" woman, so prominent in song and prose at the turn of the century—"She had quaffed to the lips the unholy chalice of sin; she had waded in the wine vats and crushed to a pulp under her feet the purpling grapes of desire," wrote "Colonel" Michael W. Connelly in the Memphis *Commercial Appeal* on October 2, 1898—was alive and its tragic character almost universally affirmed. It could also be put to the use of profit, at least where one movie of 1919 was concerned. Evelyn Nesbit, ex-showgirl, whose husband, the play-boy Harry K. Thaw, had murdered another man because he had pre-sumably shared her favors, starred in a film called *Her Mistake*. It was "the story of a radiantly beautiful girl of a back woods village, married and betrayed by a man from the civilized world, who sacrificed her happiness to satisfy his lustful desire."

Her Mistake was not one of the classics, but then neither were any of the others that year. Producers ceased to feature the villainous, monocled Hun and turned instead to the West and the felicities of a simple American life. D. W. Griffith's Artcraft production of *A Romance of Happy Valley* was a picture of this kind. It was about "John L. Logan, Jr.," who wanted to leave "Happy Valley," his sweetheart, and his home to go to New York City. John's father sternly advises him to stay home and hoe the corn; John's mother takes him to church where the parson offers his recommendations; and the sweetheart gets a new dress and tries to hold John with feminine allure. But John goes anyway and for several years spends much of his time resisting temptations of the flesh. Finally, he invents a mechanical frog that can swim and returns to Happy Valley with ten thousand dollars—just in time to prevent a mortgage foreclosure and to save his sweetheart from becoming an "old maid." That was how the *New York Times* described the story on January 27, 1919. Many felt, however, that Griffith, who had produced *The Birth of a Nation* in 1915, with its blatant racist theme, was now apparently providing moviegoers with an allegory, the deeper meaning of which seemed to have escaped everyone.

The most widely advertised picture of the year was the Goldwyn studio release of Rex Beach's *Girl from Outside*, described in these terms: "Five crooks loved a girl! When alone and friendless, she came into frozen Alaska to mould her destiny among men who knew no law save that of their own making." What followed was "one of the most powerful and absorbing trains of events that the screen has ever seen."

The summer of 1919 had its moments of soaring excitement, a welling hope for the future, and the conviction that the invincible

American spirit could overcome every obstacle in life. One sign was the rise of a tough young boxer from the West, Jack Dempsey. Born into a family whose characterizing marks were instability and poverty, Dempsey grew up a wanderer, taking odd jobs and moving up from a barroom fighter to pugilist status, who could make ten to twenty dollars fighting a match in some edge-of-town warehouse. His qualities as a boxer came from his marvelous quickness and something lethal in his punches when he found an opening in his opponent's defense. When Dempsey fought, the match, which might appear to be going to his opponent, would frequently end so suddenly that his opponent was down and out before anyone realized what had happened. The only apparent touch of grace in Dempsey's young life came from his brief marriage to a prostitute.

By 1919 Dempsey had won enough fights and put on enough weight to be considered a heavyweight contender. In February it was announced that he would meet the reigning champion, Jess Willard, at Toledo on July 4. Tex Rickard, known for his soaring promotional imagination, arranged the fight. At a conference on February 4, Jack Kearns, Dempsey's manager, agreed that $27,500 would be an acceptable remuneration for the challenger.

By mid-June the upcoming fight began to attract increasing amounts of attention from sportswriters. Comparisons were made and so impressed were the writers with Dempsey that one week before the fight the odds had shifted in his favor. On July 1 the *New York Times* described Dempsey's workout as "a four-round flash of continuous speed. He ducked and danced and side-stepped around like a featherweight. It is doubtful if there has ever been seen a heavyweight boxer who could move around as quickly as the challenger." As for Willard, it was noticed that he was breathing through his mouth, which led observers "to believe that the champion's wind is short."

Several days before the fight the odds shifted back to Willard—after all, he had beaten Jack Johnson in Havana, Cuba, just four years earlier. (Johnson, a black heavyweight, had been a continuing affront to the sharply honed racial sensibilities of white boxing fans, especially since it was known that he kept company with a white woman.) Willard was therefore given his due. And, as some of the analysts began to note, Willard weighed 241 pounds to Dempsey's 189. The challenger was hardly a heavyweight.

In Toledo things began to boom. Fans started to pour into the city on July 1; moviehouses stayed open all night; and tents were set up around the city when hotels became full. The spectacle, when it finally began on July 4 at 3:30 P.M., did not last long. Within one minute Dempsey had sent a punch to the champion's jaw that, traveling no more than fifteen inches, spun Willard around and knocked him to the floor. Willard struggled to a standing position and, covering up, held on until the round ended. Two more rounds, "amid scenes of wildest excitement," followed. Dempsey pursued Willard with a complete disdain for anything the champion could do to him. Six times in the bout Willard was knocked down, but gasping and bleeding he always managed to struggle to his feet. In the third round the champion lost six teeth and his face was battered beyond recognition. When the bell sounded for round four he could not go out.

The next day Willard said he was through with fighting; he thought he had enough money to keep his family comfortable and his ranch in good repair. That was all he wanted. He praised Dempsey for his abilities as a fighter. Dempsey, for his part, assured the press that he would indeed draw the color line. He would "pay no attention to negro challengers" (like Jack Johnson) but would "defend his title against any white heavyweight."

Most summer sports fans took their pleasure from baseball. According to the *New York Times,* the summer of 1919 was a great baseball season, "one of the greatest in the history of the game." In August the principal excitement centered around a six-game series between the Cincinnati Reds and the New York Giants, which, according to the usual development of things, would probably forecast the winner of the National League pennant. On Friday, August 15, more than thirty-eight thousand people pressed their way into the Polo Grounds and ten thousand more stood outside, howling to get to the ticket windows. At one entrance the crowd rushed the closed gates and poured into the stands, descending with such force against the railing on the runway that led to the upper tier that the barrier gave way and a number of people fell to the concrete floor below. Five of them had to be taken to the hospital.

This demonstration of devotion to John McGraw's men did not lead to victory on the field. The Giants lost two games that afternoon, and the next day they lost two more. For certain, Cincinnati had the National League pennant.

The *New York Times* thought the Reds' sweep so significant that an editorial was composed to mark the event. For Cincinnati, the season had been a cosmic event: the "brilliant campaign made this year by the . . . Reds . . . is not a race for a pennant; it is the liberation of an oppressed nationality. For fifty years Cincinnati has been the jest of the baseball world. Its citizenry have drunk each year the bitter draught of hope deferred. The notable turning of this . . . worm is something to be marveled at by the entire country. . . . It is the vindication of a moral order in the universe." Who could have predicted that the heroic Reds, with no blemish on their honor, would in the end, after a World Series with the Chicago White Sox, find that they had been cynically used by a few White Sox players?

For those sophisticates who liked to entertain themselves with amused discussions of the vagaries of the prominent, the summer's principal news item was Henry Ford's suit against the *Chicago Tribune* for having referred to him as an "anarchist." An anarchist, in the minds of most Americans, had something to do with beards and bombs and the denial of God and the flag. So Ford had taken exception to the statement and had brought suit against the *Tribune.* In early July the trial began. Since the *Tribune's* attorneys could not prove that Ford was an anarchist, their defense consisted of showing that he had a sinister record where public matters were concerned and had therefore behaved like an anarchist.

First and foremost, Ford had been a pacifist. In December 1915, overcome with horror at the massive killing on the Western Front, the motor magnate had financed what newspapers made to appear to be the ludicrous voyage of the peace ship *Oscar.* Laden with a cargo of well-known peace advocates, the *Oscar* made its way to Sweden, where it was hoped an international conference could be held that would end the war. In America there had been much tittering over Ford's "naive" performance, and in Europe the Ford idea scarcely cleared the third desk of the embassies. When the United States entered the war, Ford seemed a likely candidate to wear the label of "pro-Germanism." For all too many, so delightful was the thrill of the chase where this subject was concerned, there was almost a rejoicing when anyone could be found to be tagged with the label.

Reviving this issue was the work of the *Tribune's* counsel. One Ford employee, E. F. Clemett, testified for the defense that he had been one of four hundred members of the American Protective League in the employ of Ford and that what might be called the Ford section of the league had made it its business to ferret out pro-Germanism among Ford workers. There had been as many as five of them, Clemett said. One employee, Carl Emde, chief draftsman in the tool-making department, was particularly suspect. Clemett explained to the jury that "Emde had opportunity to get practically complete drawings of the Liberty motor, and that once he was said to have passed an imperfect drawing for a motor part." When he, as the league's directing agent at the Ford Company, had refused to give Emde an alien permit to work, Ford overruled him, Clemett said.

Defense testimony suggested, too, that Ford's stature as a patriot suffered on another score: his supposed refusal to do war work at his plant. This talk was based on a newspaper report of a speech in which the speaker (whoever he was) declared that he had interviewed Ford on the subject of doing war work at his plant, and while Ford said that he would do it, he "would not do the work for a profit." This, some of the jurors may have felt, was about as un-American as a person could get.

As for Ford's "anarchist" tendencies, the *Tribune's* counsel declared that pacifism and anarchism were manifestations of the same disease and therefore, like the QED in algebra, one part of the equation equaled the other. In four hours of "merciless crossfire of questions by Elliott G. Stevenson, senior counsel for the defendant," Ford said that he had been a pacifist but that he ceased to be one when he saw the war was aimed at establishing a "universal peace for good." Even if the League of Nations should fail, and it could be proven that another great war would bring a universal and final peace, he would favor that war, too. Nonetheless, he still thought that soldiers were "murderers."

Ford was then accused of wanting a world citizenship, a disposition that one Professor Reeves held as anarchistic. Of several "selected expressions attributed to Mr. Ford" one had him saying: "World citizenship—that is the thing we want to glorify. That sort of teaching will do more for the world than all the religious teaching has ever done." Bishop Charles D. Williams of the Episcopal Diocese of Michigan backed Ford, saying that such a sentiment was not anarchistic but in accord with Bible teaching.

After ten hours of pondering, the jury found for Ford but awarded him only six cents for his pain. That did not matter, said Ford's supporters. It was the principle of the thing. Besides, what could six cents matter to Henry Ford—or to millions of other Americans? And, further, was not Ford, in wanting "to glorify" the ideal of world citizenship, especially in the face of the tragic madness of the war, affirming an ideal whose nobility had been exalted by great minds and spirits of the past? Sadly, from the standpoint of a latter-day judgment of Ford, his internationalist idealism has been overshadowed by less edifying aspects of his social philosophy, principally his critical attitude toward Jews, which arose from an insensitivity to the richness and meaning of their culture.

For New Yorkers, there was a marvelous spectacle that summer in the form of another miracle of the new age of technology. In March, news came from England that a British dirigible, the R-33, was making its trial flights. Weeks later, the R-34, a slightly larger ship, took to the air, and an announcement was made that it would fly to America and back. The dirigible, many thought, was the answer to long-distance mass air transportation. With the American NC flying boats claiming world attention in May, England would have its turn in July.

On July 2 the R-34 left Edinburgh at 1:48 A.M., wallowing westward at forty miles per hour into a headwind. The next day it radioed a report that it was sailing smoothly at two thousand feet but was in a thick fog and still meeting headwinds that were causing the use of more gasoline than had been expected. On July 4 the ship passed over St. John's, Newfoundland. There, a Handley-Page bomber, which once had been scheduled to fly the Atlantic, was ordered to fly down the coast and rendezvous with the R-34 at Atlantic City. The Handley-Page never made it. Lost in fog, it landed on a field at Nova Scotia, turned over, and was wrecked to the point of requiring a protracted period of reconstitution.

In the meantime, Major G. H. Scott, commander of the R-34, realizing that his fuel would not permit him to reach Atlantic City, put down at Roosevelt Field, on Long Island, on the morning of July 6. With the blight of Prohibition about to descend upon American life, the first question that greeted the ship's crew was, had she brought over any liquor? Two days later a weary Woodrow Wilson came to New York on the *George Washington,* and that evening at Carnegie Hall officers of the R-34 met briefly with the president as he prepared to launch his fight to save the League of Nations.

The excitement in New York that week, however, did not come from Wilson's presence. It was the wonder of the R-34 that took up space in the columns of the *New York Times* and gave reporters a subject on which to expend their superlatives. The R-34 was "the dreadnaught of the air," it was a "mammoth vessel"; its captain "must be rated one of the leading air navigators of the world." All true, perhaps, and all of it like a benignant sign of new forces in the world—a sign of truth, an object of worship that caused people to soar above the splintering forces of the new time and find community as adorers of this overwhelming spectacle that moved through the skies.

The late-night crowd in New York was provided a vision on July 10, for at midnight the ship ascended from Roosevelt Field to the sound of the blaring horns of a great multitude of automobiles. An hour before the departure, a *New York Times* reporter asked the R-34's captain if he would fly over the Times Building before heading out over the Atlantic. "Fly to the Times Building?" asked Major Scott. Why sure, he could do that. "That's the tall building at Forty-second Street and Broadway where the lights dazzled me the other evening?" Yes, that was it.

Immediately the news was telephoned downtown and announced in all the restaurants and theaters. All of the lights in the Times Building were turned on and a bulletin at the northern end of the building announced the imminence of the spectacle. It was 1:06 A.M. when the ship, over two football fields in length, passed over Times Square. At that moment the large searchlight on the Times Building darted up the Square and brought the whole underbody of the vessel into a silver radiance against the blackness of the sky. "Cheer after cheer rose, hats were tossed, the early edition of the newspapers were torn to tatters, and an effort was made to toss them up in the air." The following day an advertisement in the *Times* declared that "Adams California Fruit Gum Shares in the Conquest of the Air. . . . The R-34 sails home with an increased supply of Adams California Fruit Chewing Gum . . . the thinking man's, the fighting man's nerve ration."

There was another wonderful occurrence that summer, when Professor R. L. Garner of the Smithsonian returned from Africa with four tons of "specimens" and important news for the world of science. " 'Twas far up the Congo," said Garner, that he had run into an animal that appeared to be a cross between a gorilla and a chimpanzee. To his amazement, he found that the animal could talk in a limited way to natives of the French Congo. In fact, when he approached the animal, he was greeted with a hearty "waa-hoo."

"Ahoo-ahoo," replied Garner.

It took a while, but finally the professor was able to translate what the animal was saying: "Where are you?"

Garner's answer to this love call had been, "Here I am." It was almost like a Jeanette McDonald–Nelson Eddy duet. In reporting the matter on June 6, the *Times* said that Garner had "spent weeks perfecting himself in imitating the call of the female."

SOURCES

Most of the information in this chapter is from the entertainment section and show advertisements of the *New York Times*. Fred Allen's reminiscences about vaudeville at the Jefferson Theater are from *Much Ado about Me* (New York, 1956).

FURTHER READING

There are several good sources on vaudeville, including Anthony Slide, *The Vaudevillians: A Dictionary of Vaudeville Performers* (New York, 1981). Jack Dempsey has narrated his life story through the writing of Bob Considine and Bill Slocum in *Dempsey: By the Man Himself* (New York, 1960). Nathaniel Fleischer's *Jack Dempsey* (New York, 1972) is a short biography.

Old-time movies are treated in John T. Weaver, *Twenty Years of Silents* (Metuchen, N.J., 1971). The background of Henry Ford's legal involvements can be found in Barbara Kraft, *The Peace Ship: Henry Ford's Pacifist Adventure in the First World War* (New York, 1978).

13

Summer Fever

THE FELICITIES OF SUMMER, light and carefree as tradition has them, were paralleled by what appeared to be a dramatic menace to the character of American life. As midnight approached on the evening of June 2, bombs exploded in buildings in eight cities. In New York, the front part of the four-storied brownstone residence of Judge Charles Nott at 151 East Sixty-first Street was heavily damaged. Judge Nott was out of the city and Mrs. Nott, sleeping in a bedroom at the rear of the house, was unhurt. Two persons, unidentified, were blown to pieces.

In Boston, the house of Justice Albert F. Hayden of the Roxbury Municipal Court was bombed. Hayden was not injured. The *New York Times* added what was presumably enlightening information about Hayden: he was "widely known as a foe of Bolshevism and is the judicial officer who a few weeks ago sentenced William James Sidis, known as the 'Harvard Prodigy,' to six months . . . and to an additional year in the same prison for assaulting a police officer during a radical celebration in Roxbury." "Prodigy" Sidis had earned his title by graduating from Harvard at age fifteen.

In Philadelphia, a Catholic rectory was bombed; in Pittsburgh, a house was damaged; and in Cleveland, the mayor's house was attacked. But the most dramatic assault was made on the home of the U.S. attorney general, A. Mitchell Palmer, who resided at 2132 R Street in Washington, D.C. Again, the front part of the house was blown out, but the Palmers, who were in the rear, were uninjured. Across the street all the windows of the home of Assistant Secretary of the Navy Franklin D. Roosevelt were blown out. "That the attempt was made by anarchists or Bolsheviki," noted the *New York Times*, "was evident from the fact that anarchist literature and leaflets were scattered around the street." There was a touch of the macabre in the bombing of the Palmer home, for the bomber, whoever he was, had been practically atomized by the blast.

It was assumed that the bombings were the work of radicals. Newspaper headlines suggested who they may have been: "European Reds May Have Set bombs"; "French Wallet Found at Palmer's Home." One news item had it that the man blown up at Palmer's house was "an Italian and a member of an anarchist group." The country was in a general state of alarm. If some people wondered—as surely some did—what President Wilson was doing in Europe while the dreaded Bolsheviki was attacking at home, they were reassured by the way in which the attorney general moved into the breach to give the appearance of forceful leadership. The "Red Plotters" would be "Run . . . to the Earth at all Costs" said Palmer, whose "courage was praised at every hand." Soon after the bombings, Palmer got a half-million dollar appropriation from Congress to expand the Justice Department's antiradical effectiveness, and young J. Edgar Hoover was appointed the head of a new division for gathering and coordinating intelligence on radicals.

Palmer was a sincere Quaker, highly intelligent and able. Against the background of revolution in Europe and the criminal acts of violence of May and June, surely committed by simple-minded zealots who thought that the tide of revolution would soon roll them to a position of power over those they chose to regard as their oppressors, the actions taken by Palmer through the remainder of 1919 and into 1920 do not seem repressive or irresponsible. If anything, to a number of legislatures, businessmen's clubs, and patriotic organizations, it seemed that the Justice Department was doing little except gathering information. These groups wanted dramatic arrests, mass deportations, and even sanguinary confrontations.

Deportations there would be—during the approaching fall—but never in sufficient numbers to quiet the clamor for drastic action by those who yearned for some heartening sign of middle-class unity and invincibility against demented types who presumably lived in ghettos. Three days after the bombings the great nationwide "dragnet for Reds" produced the following: an Italian suspect in New Jersey and a report by Department of Justice agents in Pittsburgh that they had "accumulated sufficient evidence to indicate that emissaries of the Bolshevik leader, Lenin, had framed the bomb explosions" and that an "Irishman" was thought to have made the bombs.

So it was that even before Wilson had concluded his work in Paris, a new crusade was in the making. On June 5, Columbia University's president, Nicholas Murray Butler, gave the university's Victory Commencement Address. Butler, who appeared to regard himself as the nation's high counselor, did not mention Wilson and the unfinished business of war. Rather, he spoke of the necessity of creating a self-disciplined nation, of "training its youth through discipline to self-discipline" so as to build "on a sure foundation not only for prosperity, but for that progress, that usefulness and that satisfaction which gives to prosperity its real significance." Whatever Butler meant, it sounded stern and forward-looking—building a disciplined nation of disciplined persons where no looseness would admit of such things as midnight bombings and an international commitment that would permit suppurating wounds of Europe to ooze into the stream of American life.

By mid-June the issues of the war seemed remote; it was Bolshevism that mattered. In the state of New York the Boy Scouts of America were recorded as "Foes of Bolshevism," which brought from the state's attorney general the statement that he could see in "the expansion of Boy Scout activities a deterrent to the growing unrest which we have come to call Bolshevism." He thought that "movements of this character" were very important, "designed to instill in the new generation a respect for orderly government and love of flag and country." Seeking to be as American as any, the Knights of Columbus announced that they would begin a campaign against Bolshevism. In July the National Security League, a volunteer vigilante group that had arisen during the war, formed an Americanization Advisory Service to combat "Bolshevists, anarchists, and International Socialists." The plan was to supply information and suggestions to teachers, women's clubs, and civic societies to combat "un-American doctrine."

Suburban America thus gave signs that it was marching off to a new battle. The signs were similar to those that had given such exciting color to the great national effort two years previous—lurid and hate-provoking delineations of the enemy with a call for an undifferentiated unity by those who proclaimed that they were the truth. And who better to exploit such possibilities than the Reverend Thomas Dixon, America's foremost literary figure on the subject of confrontation? In the theater section of the Sunday *New York Times* of July 20, it was stated that "probably the first offering in August will be Thomas Dixon's drama, 'The Red Dawn,' described by the author 'as the first serious play on socialism to be produced on the American stage.'"

Dixon, born in North Carolina in 1864, had graduated from Wake Forest College, and then, in the early eighties, dabbled briefly in the study of history at Johns Hopkins University, at about the time Woodrow

Wilson was a student there. But Dixon soon chose the Baptist ministry over the academic life and shortly thereafter became pastor at one of New York City's larger churches. It is said that he was a popular preacher, mainly because of his thunderous denunciations of persons and views that to him symbolized the erosion of his fundamentalist universe. The noted atheist orator of the period, Colonel Bob Ingersoll, was one such object of hate.

By the 1890s Dixon had given up pulpiteering for writing, and in 1902 his first big success, *The Leopard's Spots,* was published. Its lurid racist theme produced a responsive reaction from at least a hundred thousand Americans who bought his book in its first year of publication. *The One Woman,* published in 1903, was republished in 1905 as *The Clansman,* which in turn appeared as a movie in 1915, *The Birth of a Nation.* One of the early colossal cinematic successes, it served no cause of art; and how much of its ugly theme filtered out as a lynching statistic no one could know. Dixon's long life ended in 1946. Whatever the sunnier elements that brightened the days of his closing years, they were not enough to preclude the intrusion of bitter thoughts on Eleanor Roosevelt—because she had goaded the nation's conscience on its shameful treatment of its black citizens.

The Red Dawn was first presented at the Thirty-ninth Street Theater on Wednesday evening, August 6, 1919. The story involved "a wealthy young dreamer" who had founded a colony on an island off the coast of California to prove the workability of socialist theories. Into this young idealist's world came an evil-looking representative of "The Central Soviet of Northern Russia" who wanted to use this innocent experiment in socialism as a base for making the revolution universal. Where would the money come from? Five billion counterfeit dollars would pay the bill. From what sources would the revolutionary fighters be recruited? Their ranks would be filled by all those who were taking bitter exception to the contemplated era of prohibition; they would be filled by one million ex-convicts and ten million blacks. The blacks were especially to be feared because some of them had been in France and had been taught to use the bayonet. If anyone had the stomach to stick around to see the mess through, they would find General Pershing in the second act and eventually America would be saved.

The review that appeared the following day in the *New York Times* said it was indeed true that the play had been written "in deadly earnestness," but that it was so "hopelessly clumsy and preposterous that the . . . audience . . . [gave] way to helpless and honest merriment." Yet it was probably true that among the many admirers of Dixon throughout the country, some of whom would invest him with the status of prophet, *The Red Dawn* did not seem so farfetched, especially the part where Dixon made ten million blacks supporters of revolutionary action. There were signs that the presumed universal docility of blacks was giving way to a disposition on the part of an educated few to ask direct questions about their status in American society, especially in terms of those expansive ideals involving human rights which during the war had been so loudly trumpeted about the world.

Seemingly very few of those who had supported the war on the grounds that it would bring a new era of equity and justice for the world's oppressed—or who recognized the hellishness of racism in terms of its dehumanizing consequences on all life; or stood aghast at the gross insult to the value of personhood that was implicit in segregation—appeared to have been overly concerned with the ghastly spectacle of lynchings. Yet it would appear that to many the trumpet calls, resounding over the land in 1917 and 1918, were not just calls to do battle with the Hun but also to hold in force all the sacred canons of racism. At the war's end, one can well imagine that those who had been the loudest in their denunciation of the Hun were now promoting an image of the returning Negro veteran, not as the hero who had helped deliver America from the Hun, but as one who had learned to bayonet white men and, worse, had consorted with those decadent females with which France was so bountifully supplied and who now would seek to defile American white women.

As the summer of 1919 fell upon the world, American newspapers from time to time reported, on an inside page and with a modest use of space, that a lynching had occurred. On June 26, for example, there was one at Ellisville, Mississippi, reported the next day in the *New York Times* as having been carried out in an "orderly" manner. Those in authority in the state had "refused to interfere." For most white Americans it was a self-deception of the most fatuous kind to presume that informed blacks would fail to observe the tragic discrepancy between their lot at home and the idealistic aims some four hundred thousand of their race had gone to Europe to achieve.

One highly educated and literate black who had been pointing out the discrepancy between the ideals that had given life to America and the status of the Negro in that life was W. E. B. Du Bois. In 1910, when the National Association for the Advancement of Colored People was founded, Du Bois, its sole black officer, began editing *The Crisis,* a journal that voiced black concerns and aspirations. During the war years, a new and what at the time was regarded as a radical black press emerged in Harlem. Among the magazines and newspapers that were published were *The Challenge, The Voice, The Crusader, The Emancipator, The Negro World,* and *The Messenger.*

One of the most radical and influential of these publications, *The Messenger,* was founded in 1917 by A. Philip Randolph and Chandler Owen. Randolph, from the miserable black ghetto of Jacksonville, Florida, had come to Harlem in 1911, where he introduced himself to the community as a street-corner agitator, pleading the cause of labor unionism and socialism. When the war came, *The Messenger* opposed it, saying that it would cause an increase in violence toward blacks.

The Messenger took exception to Du Bois's support of the war. In an editorial in *The Crisis* in July 1918, Du Bois had counseled blacks to "forget our special grievances and close our ranks" while the war lasted. To this star-spangled declaration *The Messenger* responded that "we would rather make Georgia safe for the Negro than to follow Du Bois' prescription of going abroad to pursue through a welter of blood the illusory goal of making the world safe for democracy." Accordingly, around *The Messenger* collected "The *Messenger* radicals," or the "New Negro Crowd," as they were called in contradistinction to the "Old Crowd Negroes" who were of the Booker T. Washington point of view, largely content for blacks to be segregated, to be menials, and asking only that the white community give them a measure of peace.

What did the New Negro Crowd want? They wanted a clear recognition of the black person as fully human—an objective that, in terms of immediate objectives, meant an end to segregation and all legal and political inequities. But more than this, they wanted to share in a sense of national community. *The Challenge,* a monthly published in New York by William Bridges, made "Six Demands" relative to this concern. "We demand first, that instead of being re-Americanized into accepting sterner patriotic obligations we be thoroughly informed why we should be loyal to any Government that does not protect our lives and property the same as it protects those of other people with less claim to protection." Further, the magazine asked, why should blacks be asked to detest Germans when "no matter how diminished the respect of white Americans for them may be, it still transcends that which white Americans have for us." So far as *The Challenge* knew, Germany had no history of lynch mobs. The magazine wanted lynching to be made an active federal concern, adding that if federal officers could with zeal hunt down "illicit whiskey makers all over the South," why could they not also "hunt out every white devil that lynches?"

For the new black radicals the watchword of the time was "Resist!" The mood had been set by the black poet Claude McKay, whose "If We Must Die" was first published in 1917 in Waldo Frank's *Lively Arts:* "If we must die, let it not be like hogs / Hunted and penned in an inglorious spot / While 'round us bark the mad and hungry dogs / . . . / Pressed to the wall, dying, but fighting back!" In 1919 the poem was frequently carried in black publications, serving as a literary model for other young blacks who wanted somehow to express their indignation and their resolution to resist.

As for Claude McKay, for a time in the early twenties he worked as a kind of token editor of *The Liberator.* His Marxist enthusiasm took him to Russia, but once there it waned and he returned to the United States. In the course of the depression years, seemingly through a contact with Dorothy Day, the great Catholic pacifist revolutionary, McKay became a Catholic. In 1945, when the noted communist Louis Budenz became a Catholic, Day wrote in the *Catholic Worker* that she hoped Budenz would not take to the lecture circuit to denounce his old faith. Writing to Day, McKay said that he was "a little bewildered" by her remarks, suggesting that she was all but "soft" on communism.

In the summer of 1919 an increase in the aggressive spirit among elements of the white population, coupled, no doubt, with a growing disposition among blacks to resist, erupted in violence. On July 20, in Washington, rioting occurred in the area around Seventh Street and Pennsylvania Avenue. The *New York Times* reported that roaming bands of soldiers, sailors, and marines had attacked blacks "in retaliation for attacks on white women in Washington during the past month." The next day the paper said that roving bands of blacks were shooting back at whites.

A week later a riot broke out in Chicago after trouble developed at a Chicago beach. Roving mobs, mostly white, burned and pillaged the black section of the city for two weeks. When it was over, twenty-three blacks and fifteen whites were dead—to say nothing of the thousands who were left homeless. Through the summer it went on: Knoxville, Omaha, and Blaine, Arkansas—hellish mobs of hate, contorted visages, jeers, the cry for blood, and the insane jibberish of those seeking the ecstasy of hate's madness in the lynch mob. By the end of the year there had been some twenty-five riots where hundreds, mostly blacks, had died and a hundred more, all black, had been lynched in that ultimate ritual of hate.

What had caused this bloody summer? The *New York Times* of July 28 had an explanation for it that white America probably endorsed. Perhaps, the *Times* said, "Bolshevik agitation had been extended among negroes, especially those in the South. . . . We stand at present amid the outburst of social forces of which we know little. How far the original

German propaganda among the negroes may have been utilized subsequently by the I.W.W. we do not know."

On August 3 the *Times* added a further reflection, this time on the riot in Chicago. The city's mayor, William Hale Thompson, "widely known as a pro-German," had made Chicago's black community a part of the base on which his political power was built. "So openly did the Thompson crowd treat with the negroes that somebody dubbed the City Hall 'Uncle Tom's Cabin.'" It was this "bestowal of political preferment, and the license under which 'everything went' in the Black Belt" that was "the inflammable part of the tinder which finally set the city ablaze." But that was not all that ailed Chicago, said the *Times*. There had been too much interracial socializing: "All night cabarets were jammed with whites and blacks until the morning sun streaked the sky over Lake Michigan.... Jazz bands filled the air with syncopated sound, while in the cabarets whites and blacks intermingled in carousal."

Representative James F. Byrnes of South Carolina, who later would be Harry Truman's secretary of state, blamed black journalists for the country's race troubles. "A fair illustration of this type of negro leader is W. E. B. Du Bois, editor of the Crisis Magazine," said Byrnes. He wanted Du Bois investigated by the attorney general for violation of the Espionage Act. Byrnes also wondered about Randolph's and Owen's *Messenger*, which was printed on "fine quality paper and does not carry half a dozen advertisements other than its own." It was evident that it was supported by contributions from "some source," one that was probably "antagonistic to the United States. It appeals for the establishment in this country of a Soviet Government."

In November the Department of Justice published *Radicalism and Sedition among the Negroes as Reflected in Their Publications*. Some sixty pages long, it was a patchwork of editorials from the new black press, offered as documentation to the charges that black leaders were counseling retaliation and that they were advocates of Bolshevism and social equality. Among the many examples it cited was an editorial from the October *Messenger*, "A Reply to Congressman James F. Byrnes, of South Carolina." "As for social equality," responded *The Messenger*, "there are about 5,000,000 mulattoes in the United States. This is the product of semisocial equality. It shows that social equality galore exists after dark, and we warn you that we expect to have social equality in the day as well as after dark." The Department of Justice report said this comment showed "a spirit of insolent bravado" that was the mark of the radical black press.

The *New York Times* on November 23 graced the Justice Department's report on blacks with the dignity of a solemn review on its editorial page. It said that "among the more salient points to be noted in the present attitude of the negro leaders" were, first, the "ill-governed reaction toward race rioting"; second, "the threat of retaliatory measures in connection with lynching"; third, an "openly expressed demand for social equality, in which demand the sex problem is not infrequently included"; and fourth, "the identification of the negro with such radical organizations as the I.W.W. and an outspoken advocacy of the Bolsheviki . . . doctrines." Perhaps, the *Times* suggested, blacks had had too much freedom in France.

If this was the view of the enlightened and judicious *New York Times,* what must it have been in the minds of those who fed on such humid fumings to moisten the dark recesses of their being where the seeds of violence grew? One "militant" black journalist, John Edward Bruce, wrote to the *New York Herald* of his conviction that it was "wicked . . . to spread the report throughout this country and the world that . . . the Bolsheviki and I.W.W. are inflaming the Negroes and encouraging race riots. You would be nearer the truth if you could muster the moral courage to state that what is inflaming the Negroes of this country, especially those who have fought its battles, is the unjust and unfair and devilish treatment shown to those who bared their breasts to German bullets." The *Herald* returned the letter to Bruce, unpublished for "want of space."

Bruce might well have fired a broader shot at the American press, which generally depicted blacks as a sub-species of humanity, not worthy of the dignity accorded to whites. One of the widely read books of 1919 was Albert Payson Terhune's *Lad, a Dog,* published by Dutton. Lad was a collie that went through a number of adventures, playing his role in life as if he knew all twelve of the Boy Scout laws and would abide by them no matter what. With this nobility he combined an inherent sense of racial ordering, instinctively sensing the villainous character of persons with German names and otherwise sharing what one occasionally finds in rural regions as the mange-consumed yellow mongrel's taught antipathy for blacks. When "the Master," with pistol and flashlight in hand, runs downstairs to find out what the fuss is about, he finds a confusion of blood and smashed furniture, while outside the window was "the Negro sprawled senseless upon his back. Above him was Lad, his searing teeth at last having found their coveted throat-hold. Steadily, the great dog was grinding his way through toward the jugular."

Finding any considerable body of vocal opinion in America in 1919 that opposed lynching would have been difficult. Or was there anywhere an occasion on which some wretched black, fleeing the horror of the mob, was succored by a white person and saved? Perhaps there was—no doubt there was—but whoever this person was, he or she consigned that deed to oblivion for safety's sake. What did white America do, the part that professed to abhor violence? Mostly it looked on and scarcely commented. Comment, such as it was, came from the town sports, who on the day following a lynching would importantly detail the more grisly aspects of the affair for the delectation of the curious.

Still, there were some who objected to the inhumanity and horror of a lynching. One notable instance was the Reverend Will Alexander, Methodist minister of Tennessee, who in the course of the year organized the Commission for Interracial Cooperation. Through the work of the commission a number of interracial councils were organized throughout the South. Usually, they were made up of thoughtful members of the white clergy and their counterparts from the black community. Whether these councils ever penetrated the essential pathology of the problem is a question that cannot be answered, at least for those who like their conclusions supported by "objective" data. Who knows where the spirit of goodwill, when brought into the substance of life, will settle out as a datum? Or, for that matter, who can predict the ultimate humanizing effect of a national ideal, such as the Declaration of Independence, in shaping a nation's history?

SOURCES

The sources for the main body of this chapter are the periodicals named herein. See also James Weldon Johnson, *Black Manhattan* (New York, 1946); and Jervis Anderson, *A. Philip Randolph: A Biographical Portrait* (New York, 1972). The U.S. government document entitled "Radicalism and Sedition among the Negroes as Reflected in Their Publications," *Investigation Activities of the Department of Justice* (U.S. Senate Document No. 153, 66th Congress, 1st Session, 1919), contains fact and opinion on black publications during and after the war.

FURTHER READING

See Eugene Levy, *James Weldon Johnson: Black Leader, Black Voice* (Chicago, 1973); and Harold W. Felton, *James Weldon Johnson* (New York, 1971). Two notable contributors to the history of black America, John Hope Franklin and August Meier, have together produced a useful reference work, *Black Leaders of the Twentieth Century* (Urbana, Ill., 1982). See also August Meier, *Black History and the Historical Profession, 1915–1980* (Urbana, Ill., 1986). Herbert Aptheker's compilation of *Selections from* The Crisis (Millwood, N.J., 1983) is a useful work for apprehending the mind and sense of black leadership after World War I.

CHAPTER

14

The Beginnings of Drought

WHEN THE UNITED STATES went to war against Germany, one of the marvels of this venture was how quickly and effectively the nation was able to marshal its might against the enemy. But when it came to using its power to prevent the nearly two hundred lynchings during the war period, it could do nothing. The Supreme Court, in the years following the Civil War, had said that for the most part civil rights were derived from state and not federal citizenship. No federal law could be passed against lynching without a constitutional amendment, and such was the dedication of southern politicians to the principle of resisting federal intervention into the internal affairs of the states concerning human rights that no amendment could be had.

On another matter, however, the constitutional amending process was being used to attain what many regarded as a far more exalted objective—one that, when reached, some insisted, would remove the root cause of evil in the world. On Friday, January 17, 1919, newspapers announced that Nebraska had become the thirty-sixth state to ratify the Eighteenth Amendment to the Constitution, thus providing the necessary two-thirds majority. Section 1 of the amendment stipulated that after one year all liquor traffic would be banned; the second section directed Congress to pass enforcement legislation.

The seeds of the national amendment, in its late nineteenth-/early twentieth-century phase, seemed to have germinated in the disposition of a sizable segment of American Protestantism to register what it would regard as its spiritual vitality in massive effects—filled halls, rousing hymn singing, and fiery exhortation, all culminating in the call to commitment. In Memphis, for example, Mary H. Armor, national vice president of the Women's Christian Temperance Union after fervid and continued flailing of strong drink, led her audience into the singing of "Tennessee's Going Dry," to the tune of "Bringing in the Sheaves." The *Commercial Appeal* noted the next day that the Central Baptist Church was "trembling."

Frances Willard had founded the Christian Temperance Union in 1874 to advance the proposition that the prime sign of the Evil One was fermented beverages. For a number of persons, many women included, who longed for a cause, who wanted the experience of a heartwarming togetherness such as occurs in a crusade, a frontal assault on liquor seemed irresistibly attractive.

All over the South and West, but especially in the South, people rallied to the cause of rural Protestantism. Perhaps somewhere at the source of the feeling that led so many to troop to the standard of prohibition was the feeling that rural people may have had against the wealth, economic imperialism, and presumed "godlessness" of the industrial-age city. It was a way of imposing their own conditions on the lives of those who thought of themselves as more sophisticated, cultured, and wise.

For southerners, Prohibition was closely involved with the race issue. At times, when the crusade against drink reached ecstatic heights, orators would invoke the spectacle of alcohol's ultimate horror, the "gin-drinking nigger," in whose blood coursed satanic juices that gin in particular would excite to an eruption of rape and violence.

For the South and the West, too, there was also the issue of the Catholic church, whose adherents, in increasing numbers, were crowding into the cities of the East and the Midwest. It was not just that Catholics appeared indifferent to the presumed menace of alcohol but that their life-styles in some ways celebrated it; rather than admit that alcohol was evil by nature, they affirmed it as a humanizing force that, when rightly used, made for community. For example, in Milwaukee, Wisconsin, where the consumption of beer per person was far greater than in any other American city, the murder rate was the lowest in the country.

How the image of the tavern as the locale of neighborhood sociability had changed—an image celebrated in the novels of Sir Walter Scott and others as the haven of safety at the end of the day's journey, where the roaring fire and tankard of ale provided the impulse for good talk and a welling up of the spirit of community! Why this picture gave way later in the American scene to the evil saloon has never been entirely explained. But the disposition of the prohibitionist crusaders to blame the manifest evils of a certain aspect of saloon culture on alcohol itself was off the mark. To a certain extent the image change from tavern to saloon arose from altered circumstances. The openness of American life—the frontier—which freed the desperate and unscrupulous from the bonds of civility, had something to do with the change.

The war gave its own particular impetus to the movement for prohibition. America was marching to Zion, and in the process the prohibitionists were able to cast off their rural trappings and make themselves synonymous with the attainment of the heavenly city. Away with the Fourteen Points, trailing their wispy vapors into the outer haze of creation, where they would have as much effect on the true evil of the world as would a pale star in lighting the path of a midnight traveler during a storm. How, for that matter, could the League of Nations conceivably be used as the subject for a hymn suitable for congregational singing? On the other hand, the saloon was right here, harboring idlers, the besotted, and the lecherous. A booze-free nation was the true substance of the great moral leap forward occasioned by the war—not a misdirected international wandering.

The war-bred millennial mood that supported the cause of prohibition was underwritten by what many understood to be the direct complicity of the Hun in laying upon America the burden of alcohol. Out of St. Louis, Cincinnati, and Milwaukee flowed the golden brew, produced by companies bearing Hunnish names like Pabst, Schlitz, Anheuser Busch, and Miller. The brewing industry, it was said by some, was guilty of pro-German sentiment and even pro-German activity—if for no other reason than it was perceived as blunting the edge of stern determination required by the times, with those periods of relaxing conviviality that beer produces.

On January 28, *The Literary Digest* did a roundup of press comment on the adoption of the prohibition amendment to the Constitution. New York's Baptist *Watchman Examiner* was so elated by the adoption that it evoked "a vision of the 'saints in glory' tendering an 'impromptu reaction' to Neal Dow and Frances Willard." The comment the *Digest* took from New York's *Catholic News* indicated that the *News* was in no mood to congratulate the prohibitionists, who were said to "believe that . . . they will cure intemperance in the use of spiritous liquor. Now, if some one could devise a scheme to put a curb on intemperance in speech by prohibitionists the public would regard him as a benefactor." The *News* was disturbed by a recent verbal assault made by the state superintendent of the New York Anti-Saloon League on James Cardinal Gibbons. It was "an illustration of the lengths to which fanaticism leads the ordinary type of prohibitionist."

Fanaticism there was. An unusual demonstration of it occurred on

May 3, when the "superdreadnaught" *Tennessee* was launched. That the ship had been christened with champagne brought a protest from Governor A. H. Roberts of the dry state of Tennessee. *The Literary Digest* wondered at the "almost intemperate speed" with which Prohibition had come and quoted the *New York Tribune* as saying it was "a sailing ship on a windless ocean propelled by some invisible force." The brewers of New York State made a bitter but nonetheless prophetic statement: "National prohibition will instantaneously make hundreds of thousands of violators and evaders of the law and as many more hypocrites. . . . prohibition violates the laws of nature. We certainly have gone made if we actually understand and approve the extreme tyranny possible under the national prohibition amendment."

The most frequently heard lament from the antiprohibitionists was over the economic impact of a dry law. The amendment, it was said, would wipe out at one stroke 236 distilleries, 992 breweries, and more than 300,000 saloons and liquor stores. There would also be significant losses to the federal and state treasuries. Absolutely not, said the prohibitionist press. The February 1 issue of *The Literary Digest* quoted the *Philadelphia North American* as hailing the Eighteenth Amendment as "the most important measure of social and economic legislation adopted since the Republic was formed." Rather than producing depressing economic effects, it would mean "a conservation of national wealth which within ten years will equal the colossal costs of the war." Prohibition ended a "wasted expenditure of two billion a year," an amount that now could be diverted "to satisfying demands for necessaries and comforts of life, creating incomparably the greatest new market any legislation could open to American industry." It would conserve "vast stores of foodstuffs, . . . ease the strain upon transportation, end a tremendous waste of fuel, and release scores of thousands of workers for productive employment."

This was only the beginning. The outlines of the heavenly city were starting to show clearly through the noxious alcoholic haze that had clouded history. Incomparable social changes were at hand. Prohibition would "immeasurably reduce the evils of vice, crime, illiteracy, insanity, preventable disease, and poverty." It would drastically lower the tax rate because public almshouses and asylums would no longer be needed. It would "do more than any other one thing to eradicate the slum from the cities and rural districts." Politics would be cleansed, "especially in the large cities, where the saloon and the liquor vote have been the mainstays of machine despotism and corruption." And, finally, "beyond all these things," there would be an immeasurable spiritual gain, a new life for "faculties which have been benumbed by the crushing weight of this evil and the hopeless struggle against it."

This was, of course, old-time prohibitionist romance, the kind of stuff one heard from circuit-riding zealots who, likely as not, would embroider their vision of the glories to come with a recitation of their own personal struggle with alcohol and the depths to which they had fallen. An up-to-date explanation for Prohibition's arrival came in the July issue of *McClure's Magazine,* when Dr. Frank Crane, an analyst-journalist, tersely stated: "Booze got in the way of Business. That is why it had to go. Long ago, Business discovered that alcohol spelt inefficiency. And Business directly or indirectly controls this people. In this decision, Business was backed up by science. Alcohol may have its place as a medicine ... but as a food, it has no standing whatever."

The prohibition amendment provided a year in which the brewing and distilling industries might make their final arrangements. But even that period of grace was intruded upon by a congressional enactment, the Wartime Prohibition Act, scheduled to go into effect on July 1, 1919. The legislation had arisen from the argument that the grain used for producing alcoholic beverages should be put to direct wartime purposes. As the date for the enforcement of the wartime prohibition approached, few except the liquor dealers paid much attention to it. They, with tongue in cheek and an eye narrowed on profit, announced in large newspaper ads that the end was at hand but one could still buy extensively from their well-stocked shelves. "Do you know that in a few days no wines or liquors can be sold?" asked the Park and Tilford Company. Few were alarmed.

Still, a time was ending, and the saloon, an honorable institution, was itself being lynched by a people who knew not what troubled their spirit. Within its shaded and moist interior, filled with the aroma of malt, spiced sausage, and sweat, men could drink beer and find themselves moved above the morbidities of body and spirit to a higher plane where they sensed the unity of creation, where community lay. In places like Milwaukee's Schlitz Palm Garden there was a special and authentic vision of the heavenly city. For the Milwaukee male who took delight in the feminine mystique, what more could be added to the healing qualities of a sparkling, golden draught than the presence of the ultimate touch of God's creation—a lovely woman who became even lovelier and more bewitching when seen through the amber glass?

SOURCES

The sources for most of the material in this chapter are named in the text. Two books helped to provide reference positions that support some of the generalizations of this chapter: Jack S. Blocker, *Retreat from Reform: The Prohibition Movement in the United States, 1890–1913* (Westport, Conn., 1976); and Norman H. Clark, *The Dry Years: Prohibition and Social Change in Washington* (Menasha, Wisc., 1965). William D. Miller, *Memphis during the Progressive Era* (Madison, Wisc., 1957), was the source of the material on Memphis. Facts on murder rates are from Andrew A. Bruce and Thomas S. Fitzgerald, "A Study of Crime in the City of Memphis, Tennessee," *Journal of the American Institute of Criminal Law and Criminology* 19, no. 2, part 2 (August 1928). Information on the number of saloons in particular cities is from the U.S. Bureau of the Census, *Statistics of Cities, 1902–1903,* Bulletin 20 (1905).

FURTHER READING

There are several older works on Prohibition that have substance and a point of view that make them very worthwhile for anyone interested in pursuing the subject: Charles Merz, *The Dry Decade* (New York, 1931); Herbert Asbury, *The Great Illusion* (New York, 1950); and Andrew Sinclair, *Era of Excess: A Social History of the Prohibition Movement* (New York, 1962). For a larger view of the movement by American blacks to receive their human due, see John Hope Franklin, *From Slavery to Freedom* (2d ed.; New York, 1956).

CHAPTER

15

At the White House

AS THE SUMMER DOLDROMS settled over the country, the sentiment for the League of Nations, as far as any heated, concerted public
action was concerned, shimmered away in the summer haze. On July
10, two days after his return from France, President Wilson put the
Versailles treaty before the Senate. Included in the treaty, as Wilson had
steadfastly insisted, was the League Covenant.

In telling of this time, Mrs. Wilson related that the conferences went
on "day after day, week after week" and that "nothing seemed to result
except increased fatigue for the President." She added that anyone "who
knows the heat of Washington in July and August can picture the way
energy is sapped, with no strain needed to add to that of the weather.
The increasing demands on my husband's brain and body exacted a toll
which pyramided." After his toil in Paris, the ideal summer for Wilson
should have been carefree, his attention directed only to the lemonade
pitcher, the cooling evening automobile rides that he enjoyed so much,
and the bright laughter and warm endearments of his wife.

But no, the cry to level the edifice he had struggled to raise was
already being heard across the country. As the weather warmed, so did
the oratory of the anti-League stalwarts. The debate in the Senate
opened on May 23, over the issue of having the State Department
furnish the Foreign Relations Committee with a complete text of the
treaty with Germany. A resolution to this end was offered by Hiram
Johnson, an anti-League bitter-ender. Nothing came of the three-hour
debate except some florid oratory from Senator Lawrence Sherman of
Illinois. The next day the *New York Times* reported the debate and
featured the Senator's performance. Sherman had professed indignation

that the League "must be accepted as it flashes from the summit where dwells the incarnate wisdom it has become political blasphemy to question and treason to try to understand." He had declared that five members of the Cabinet were "tainted with Socialism. A vast swarm of Wilson's appointees are known to be open and avowed Socialists." Furthermore, the administration was "a hybrid between the French Revolution and an oriental despotism. History would forget Caligula in the excesses and follies of the American Government operated under the League of Nations interpreted by President Wilson and Colonel House."

In the first week of June, two weeks before the Versailles treaty signing, Lodge made what was purportedly a sensational revelation of administration perfidy to the American public by announcing that the treaty text was already in New York and was being circulated by "Wilson's followers." Lodge said that a copy had been offered to him but he refused to accept it unless he could make it available to the American people. Senator William E. Borah, a no-League zealot, told the Senate he had heard that several copies of the treaty text were in the hands of "special interests in New York." Certain "financial interests in Wall Street . . . had obtained copies," he said, and "were using them to advance their own projects abroad."

In Paris, the American delegation to the peace conference said that it would not authorize publication of the unsigned treaty and that it knew nothing of New York bankers having a copy. Nonetheless, the treaty was out, for the *New York Times* published the text on June 9. As the *Times* reported three days later, Lodge had obtained his copy from Elihu Root, former senator and secretary of state, and, somewhere or somehow, copies had proliferated.

In the midst of this treaty text issue, the former president William Howard Taft, now Kent Professor of Law at Yale University, admonished his fellow Republicans to keep the debate at a responsible level. Otherwise, he said, they would block the peace. But Taft had little standing with Lodge and those who, like Lodge, galled at the mention of Wilson's name.

To the question of what the war had been about, most of the anti-League senators would have replied that it was fought to defeat Germany and now the business of ending the war was largely a matter of getting the United States out of Europe. But this was not at all in accord with what Wilson had told the world were the contractual conditions under which America had gone to war, and one anti-League Republican senator, Philander Knox of Pennsylvania, tried to produce something more positive than simple anti-League negativism. On June 10, Knox presented a five-part resolution to the Foreign Relations Committee that, in effect, separated the League issue from the treaty, saying that no country would be required to join the League as a condition of making peace with Germany and that whatever time was necessary could be taken in reaching a decision. The fifth section disavowed isolationism, stating that it would be the "declared policy" of the United States, when the peace of Europe was threatened, to "consult with the other powers affected with a view to devising means for the removal of such menace" and do what was necessary "with complete accord and cooperation with our chief cobelligerents for the defense of civilization."

What Knox had in mind was to shelve Wilson's League, which seemed to be picking up too many encumbrances, and replace it with his own idea of a league of victors. However, those isolationist senators who professed an objection to Wilson's League primarily on the basis of its Article X, which would have committed the United States to joint action against an aggressor nation, liked Knox's concept even less. "I am an American first," said Senator Johnson during the discussion on the Knox resolution. "I confess a profound interest, of course, in Lithuania, Hedjas and other remote states. But my interest is chiefly in my own country."

In the long run, the resolution would have fractured the Republican opposition to Wilson's League and for this reason, probably, Lodge never pushed it for a vote in the Foreign Relations Committee. Presumably, he felt that the focus should be kept on the president.

For Senator Sherman, the complexities of the Knox resolution were too much to comprehend. Nevertheless, the front page was his on June 21 as he expatiated on a danger from the League as yet unperceived, one about which a continued silence would render him "derelict" in his duty. He had observed "from an early age" that "the occupants of the Vatican have believed and still believe in the inherent right of papal authority to administer civil government." It was "with the utmost regret" that Sherman failed "to find recorded in the course of papal claims of later days any renunciation or disavowal of that doctrine." Of the twenty-eight Christian nations that would make up the League, "seventeen are Catholic nations" and, no doubt, "the seventeen . . . will be represented in the League in all human probability by Catholic delegates."

Since the appeal of demagoguery is difficult to overestimate, it is likely that Sherman's revelation provided further substance for a growing hard-line anti-League position. Yet, as Sherman certainly knew, his position was endorsed by many Catholics. On July 10, seventeen thousand "Friends of Irish Freedom" rallied at Madison Square Garden to hear the Irish patriot and political leader Eamon De Valera declare that the war had been fought for the right of self-determination by small nations and yet, where the League idea was concerned, the claims of Ireland had been ignored. When Wilson's name was mentioned, the crowd hissed and booed. To be sure, "The Star-Spangled Banner" was sung, but the *New York Times* noticed that the tenor John J. Flanagan, of St. Patrick's Cathedral, used a version of the anthem that was "the old one in which England was criticized."

The publication of the Treaty of Versailles brought the intellectual leadership of the liberal and the Marxist points of view into the chorus that voiced its dislike of Wilson. John Dewey of the *New Republic* regretfully concluded that the Wilsonian idealism that had led him to endorse the war had been dashed to smithereens by the terms of the treaty. There, in that document, in its greed and its misreading of the forces that had brought on the great war, lay a major defeat to his hope that the conflict could be the instrument of raising the minds of humankind to new heights of generosity and understanding. The "experience" nonetheless led Dewey to a new position: he became a pacifist.

For those who professed to think that Marx had provided the ultimate ideal toward which the world was moving, Wilson and his League were subjects unworthy of printed space. Max Eastman's *Liberator* found the subject hardly worth mentioning, but when the person of Wilson intruded itself into the news, as it did after the publication of the treaty, he was dealt with contemptuously. In its June 1919 issue *The Liberator* declared that for all of Wilson's "disinterested idealism," the peace terms levied on Germany were exactly those that might have come from a war the object of which was conquest. "So what did his disinterested idealism amount to? It amounted to a heroic determination to surround himself and the general public with a blind vapor of self-righteous emotion all the time the job was being done. That determination he carried out. That is his contribution to history."

Thus did the debate continue throughout the summer. As the president held his conferences and hoped for a rallying to his position, the American people appeared to have grown weary of the subject. According to the *New York Times* of July 12, Secretary of State Lansing returned from the peace conference and, having been strong in his advocacy of war, had nothing to say about the League except to suggest that "the nations are bound together to avert another world catastrophe."

All that summer it seemed that Wilson was fighting his battle without a general staff. Some senators, like Kenneth McKellar of Tennessee, strongly supported the League. In a Senate speech on July 23, McKellar advocated ratification of the treaty, including the League, without reservations. When Senator Borah asked him how he might react to reservations in the treaty, McKellar said that he hoped he would not have to face that question. He said he was going to vote against reservations, but if he had to vote for reservations, they should "be just as innocuous as possible." He therefore hoped that "the Senator from Idaho will not have an opportunity to make them, because they will not be innocuous." Opponents of the League, McKellar insisted, were "reactionaries."

The day after McKellar's speech, the *New York Times* emphasized six clarifying "interpretations" on the League, offered by a former president. William Taft hoped that they would serve as solutions to the principal objections to ratification that had been raised by Lodge and his anti-League supporters. The interpretations dealt with matters like tariffs, immigration, the Monroe Doctrine, and the much-debated Article X of the League Convenant, over which so much oratorical acid had been poured. Under this article, Taft declared, the action of the League Council should be advisory, that is, "each member shall be left free to determine questions of war in its own way, the decision of the United States resting with Congress."

The *New York Times* of July 25 noted that the Taft proposals were a way for Republicans to get out of the trouble "into which cankered minds and blind leadership have brought them"—advice that Lodge passed up. The proposals, in his view, only muddied the water. Even so, a week later several Republican senators said they would support four "mild reservations" to the League Covenant, reservations that were similar to Taft's.

In a two-hour speech on August 12, Lodge derided the League as a "deformed experiment" in which "the inherent interest of the United States" was sacrificed to "a dangerous internationalism." At the end of the speech, an "unusual demonstration of approval broke out in the crowded galleries. Marines, who had been in the attack on Chateau-Thierry and who had squeezed their way into the galleries . . . joined in the wild ovation that was accorded Senator Lodge."

A week later Wilson asked the members of the Foreign Relations Committee to come to the White House for a conference. The president said he would not oppose "interpretative reservations" that would clarify the "understanding of the United States regarding certain features," but he was against any reservations or amendments that would have the effect of recommitting the treaty to the signatory powers.

Clearly, little progress had been made. From the wings, as if he were an end man at a minstrel, insisting on his moment on the stage, came Senator Albert B. Fall of New Mexico. One of the most wooden yet caustic critics of the League, Fall now demanded that Wilson reply to "twenty questions" he had prepared. But Wilson, suffering from "heat prostration," had no intention of dignifying Fall's questions with a response. If Fall had wanted to, he could have asked them at one of the White House conferences Wilson held for senators who wanted clarification on the issue in which the League was involved. But that was not what Fall wanted. Where the League was concerned, he was a camp follower, in the company of those who opposed it; he was, like many others, an obstructionist.

SOURCES

Unless otherwise indicated, the remarks on the treaty made by Senators William E. Borah, Philander Knox, Lawrence Sherman, Kenneth McKellar, and Albert B. Fall are from the *New York Times.* Quotations are also taken from Ralph Stone, *The Irreconcilables: The Fight against the League of Nations* (New York, 1970).

FURTHER READING

Arthur Link's work on Wilson tends to highlight the president's character and accomplishments as a Progressive. Wilsonian diplomacy is treated in Link, *Wilson the Diplomatist: A Look at His Major Foreign Policies* (Baltimore, 1957). Lloyd C. Gardner, *Safe for Democracy: Anglo-American Response to Revolution, 1913–1923* (New York, 1984) is another "look" at the disparity between professions of democratic idealism and their fate in revolutionary situations. Secretary of State Robert Lansing tells his story in *The Peace Negotiations: A Personal Narrative* (New York, 1921). The Senate's rejection of the Wilson-detailed League has been the subject of much historical concern. Ralph A. Stone, *Wilson and the League of Nations: Why America's Rejection?* (New York, 1967), details this episode, one that aside from its merits, produced so much unseemly froth. Two standard but older works are D. F. Fleming, *The United States and the League of Nations, 1918–1920* (New York, 1932); and Thomas A. Bailey, *Woodrow Wilson and the Great Betrayal* (New York, 1945). Bailey's *A Diplomatic History of the American People* (New York, 1969) contains an appendix, "Negotiating the Treaty of Versailles." Except for those studies that have appeared since 1969, Bailey's appendix remains one of the best brief lists of sources on Wilson and the Versailles treaty. The person and politics of Henry Cabot Lodge are closely examined in John A. Garraty, *Henry Cabot Lodge: A Biography* (New York, 1953).

CHAPTER

16

Japan

THE MOST CURIOUS PART of the League debate during July and August was the attention the anti-League element gave to Japan and its claims in the treaty settlement. To this group, Japan became the monster among nations, to be reviled in the opprobrious terms that a year previous had been reserved for Germany. At issue was the Shantung Peninsula; the background of it was this: in 1898 Germany forced China to give it special privileges in Shantung, including the right to lease and manage port areas, to fortify them and to maintain troops there, and to construct and operate railroads there. About two weeks after the outbreak of the war, Japan seized the German interests in Shantung and obtained a secret agreement from the Allies recognizing its claims there. At the peace conference China vehemently protested this arrangement and refused to sign the Versailles treaty.

The star fire of Wilson's idealism began to settle out as the ashes of necessity almost at the very moment peace making began. The Shantung Peninsula matter provided a clear example of the problem. If Wilson stood implacably for an immediate return of the Shantung interests to China, he would force Britain and France to break their pledge to Japan, and this would doubtless keep Japan out of the League. Furthermore, what Wilson (and many others) saw as the preeminent need of the moment was a peace settlement. No one knew how far the virulence of Bolshevism would spread, and the foundation for the beginning of a new and stable Europe had to be laid immediately.

The senatorial band of anti-Leaguers made much of this situation. Senator Sherman declaimed in the Senate on July 17 "that the section [of the Versailles treaty] giving Japan the special lease on the Shantung

Peninsula so taints and poisons the professed altruism with which the League of Nations was heralded as to crown it the superlative treachery in the history of modern times." The Japanese emperor was no better than the German kaiser; Japan would be emboldened to try for a world empire, and so on.

The Shantung Peninsula issue had a popular basis in the existence of a well-established anti-Japanese sentiment in the country, especially in California, where the Japanese immigrants' acquisitive and competitive capabilities were such as to put them in bad repute with the native citizenry. For Americans in general, anti-Japanese sentiment came from something less definable—namely, a legend built over half a century, built on American Protestant missionary activity in China, that the Chinese were, in a special way, brothers or potential brothers in faith. What American pulpit had not had its fund-seeking missionary from China, telling of the quaint customs of that faraway land, exhibiting articles of art and dress, and pointing out how, but for the lack of missionaries, the country would become a great Christian outpost in the Far East?

As for the Japanese, according to the legend, they were imitative and rapacious to the point that when their representatives to Paris in March 1919 asked that the League, as part of its constitution, contain a statement of race equality, Representative James B. Phelan of California called the request "preposterous." "What he asked, "would stop them [the Japanese Americans] from requiring the United States to grant citizenship, the voting privilege, inter-marriage, and the ownership of land?"

In July, after having professed much concern over the Shantung Peninsula issue, Lodge offered a resolution in the Senate requiring that all documents possessed by Wilson concerning the transfer of the German concession in Shantung to Japan be turned over to the Senate. The resolution passed, but Senator John Sharp Williams of Mississippi declared that if the Republican majority persisted in stirring up the matter and making insinuations against the integrity of Japan, there would be a danger of "bringing on a grave rupture" with that country. To this Senator Borah replied that the threat of war with Japan had been held out long enough. If Japan felt that it wanted to challenge the United States for declining to uphold a "bargain that meant the slavery of 40,000,000 Chinese in Shantung," then he, for one, was willing to let the challenge come. The United States could "cringe no longer." If confronting Japan meant war, "the United States could not avoid it."

On August 23 the Lodge Foreign Relations Committee acted to amend the treaty by requiring that the Shantung concessions be surrendered to

China. Five days later the *New York Times* asked the question: Do these rabid men at Washington ever pause even for one instant to inquire what is the controversy in which they are engaged?" It had been said that "they are prompted chiefly by motives of partisanship—the desire to destroy Woodrow Wilson politically." But "in attacking the Peace Treaty these men are seeking to destroy the works of the chief statesmen of the civilized world . . . the world's bulwark against war, the safeguard of its peace. They are doing their utmost to destroy peace, again to deliver the world over to war, and perhaps war not very remote."

The idea of Japan as "the enemy," which sooner or later had to be dealt with, was not the sole possession of some "rabid men at Washington." It was, during the postwar years, one of the themes of America's popular reading, becoming standard fare for some of the pulps of the thirties—like *Flying Aces*, whose villains ceased to be the Hun in a Fokker D–VII carrying an "infernal machine" that could destroy a whole army and became the "Jap," even more villainous but one whose peculiar slanting eyes made it impossible to aim accurately at American pilots. This idea even found its way into a Gene Stratton Porter novel.

Of the writers of popular fiction after the turn of the century, Porter was perhaps the most popular, one estimate being that by the end of World War I her several books had sold over seven and a half million copies. *Freckles,* published in 1904, was her first major success, selling over a million and a half copies. Then came *The Girl of the Limberlost* in 1909, *The Harvester* in 1911, and in 1913 *Laddie,* which was surely her best work, one that effectively spoke of the life and values of midwestern rural life in the period before the war.

Laddie, the story of an Indiana farm family of twelve children, is narrated by Little Sister, the youngest member, whose arrival into the family group was so unexpected as to throw some of the older sisters into mortified consternation. But Laddie, an older brother, who takes over the family farm and who in all things, is brave and true, loves his little sister from the beginning. The main theme of the story is Laddie's wooing of "the Princess," a vibrant black-haired beauty who lives at a neighboring farm and whose father is of English nobility. Unfortunately, the father lives "under a cloud." He believes his own son to be unprincipled, even a thief; as a result he has become a misanthrope and, what is worse, an atheist.

Of course, Little Sister takes a key role in unraveling the problem, and in the end Laddie not only gets the Princess but the thought-to-be wayward son proves that he has scrupulously upheld the honor of the family name and, by the merest coincidence, has met Little Sister's big sister in Chicago and fallen in love with her. Both couples marry, and trembling, acerbic old Mr. Pryor, the "Princess's" father, is reconciled with his son, his neighbors, and God.

The warmth of *Laddie* comes from its feeling for family community. There is creative work for all, and all of their needs from a poultice for croup to a cutter for winter transportation are made by family members and out of family resources. In one part of the book the mother is questioned by Pryor as to how she is able to live so hopefully and effectively in view of the difficult, work-burdened life she leads. Why? Because "shoulder to shoulder, and heart to heart, I've stood beside my man and done what had to be done, to build this home, rear our children, save our property." It was "done by the practice of self-control, study, work, joy of life, satisfaction with what we had, never-ending strife to go higher, and do better." As for Laddie's father, "with all our twelve there never has been one who at nine months of age did not stop crying if its father lifted his finger, or tapped his foot and told it to. From the start we have rigorously guarded our speech and actions before them. From the first tiny baby my husband has taught all of them to read, write and cipher some."

Laddie without the happy ending was autobiographical. In an August 1919 *American Magazine* article, "Why I Always Wear My Rose-colored Glasses," Porter told some of the circumstances of her early life. She was the "Little Sister" of her book, and, as in *Laddie,* the last arrival into an Indiana farm family of twelve. Her mother was forty-six and her father fifty when she was born. Her childhood centered on "a bounding, exultant, unlimited joy in nature; a wild passionate love for the clouds, the sky, the trees, the earth, and all living creatures—a happiness, big, swelling, and inexpressible, found only in the outdoors."

Happiness could only have been the normal state for a healthy child of a large, well-ordered family living in rural Indiana in the 1870s. There, the air, washed and clear, let the bright sunlight beam over nature's array of color and life. What else might a child do but love creation and exult in its beauty?

Still, as with most families, there was suffering and death. "A colt kicked one of my older brothers on a hip joint, which resulted in what was then called 'white swelling,' " Porter reported. This "set the joint supperating, and for months he was bedfast, suffering torture, while I was his chief nurse. I carried him drinks, and cold cloths for his burning brow, made poultices, brought books, took them away, brought a stick to carve, swept up the shavings, pulled down the blinds, put up the blinds, running each day uncounted errands, the result of any fevered fancy." Then, "while my brother slowly crept to his feet, a dearly loved elder sister was hurt in a railway accident, which resulted in an injury almost identical, as even more strenuous nursing began for me, which lasted for nearly three years of indescribable suffering, and ended in her passing."

Of course, there was more. As Gene nursed her sister, a brother "in a distant city" was stricken with typhoid fever. "Mother was away from home a month nursing him, moved him too soon, which brought on a relapse, and his life was saved by the narrowest possible margin." Then the mother nursed two others of the family who had gotten the fever. Finally, she fell ill with it herself, and as she lay in bed, an "adored brother was seized with cramps while swimming ... and was drowned. He, my mother, and my sister were all laid to rest during the same year." The "adored brother" was Leander Stratton, "Laddie."

On August 17, 1919, Gene Porter celebrated her fifty-sixth birthday. It seemed to her that alien forces had taken over the world. "I am desperately tired," she wrote to a friend around this time, "of having high grade literary critics ... give a second ... rating to my literary work because I would not write of complexes and rank materialism, which is merely another name for adultery."

Nevertheless, Porter, breathing a new and supercharged air, was herself swept away from the anchor of nature into new themes. During the latter part of 1919, while living in California, she began the manuscript of *Her Father's Daughter,* which Grosset and Dunlap published in 1921. The characters were not the rural, family-centered types that one found in *Laddie,* but people she doubtless thought of as bespeaking the progressive and open spirit of the twentieth century. The story is about some high school students: the perspicacious, aggressive Linda, who is knowledgeable of the world's "larger" issues, and a somewhat slow-witted Donald, who cannot quite keep up with Linda's racing mind and organizational drive and who wishes that she would slow down long enough to allow him to insert a romantic theme into the conversation. The villainous Oka Sayye, Linda and Donald's classmate, studies too much and is actually quite elderly—but he cleverly hides the fact by putting shoe polish on his graying hair (which Linda, with equal cleverness, detects). There is also the Irish cook, Katy, who seems to have risen beyond any serious involvement with Romanism (as with all of Porter's Irish characters—"Freckles," for example) inasmuch as she sings in the choir of a Protestant church. Katy acts as Linda's effective supporter in the latter's strenuous efforts at "consciousness raising" on the subject of the "yellow peril."

Linda is a "modern" type who stays at the forefront of things. She drives a group of her classmates "over the smooth road from Lilac Valley running south to Los Angeles at a speed that was as near to flying as a non-professional attains. . . . Their eyes were shining, their blood was racing." Thoroughly modern Linda is a character Porter's critics might appreciate. But she also, aside from fast cars, has some old-fashioned ideas; in fact, she sees society falling apart. "If Daddy were living I think he would say we have reached the limit with apartment house homes minus fireplaces, with restaurant dining minus a blessing, with jazz music minus melody, with jazz dancing minus grace, with national progress minus cradles," she says to her clinging-vine type stepsister, Eileen, who, among her other shortcomings, uses rouge.

Perhaps to Linda the past, rather than upholding her with strong, intact traditions, has become quicksand. She must turn to a cause in the objective mode to find a meaning for her existence. She finds it in the menace of the Japanese. It becomes a mania with her, made up of some of the same bitter elements of which others were laying hold. "There are so many of the Japs," she complains. "They all look so much alike, and there's a blood brotherhood between them that will make them protect each other to the death against any white man." There is, she says, "an undercurrent of something deep and subtle going on" in California. "When Japan sends college professors to work in our kitchens and relatives of her greatest statesmen to serve our tables, you can depend on it that she is not doing it for the money that is paid them."

Anguished over California's easygoing ways, Linda exclaims, "We deserve to become their prey if we are so careless." She continues: "We are not going to beat them driving them to Mexico or to Canada, or letting them monopolize China. That is merely temporizing." When "they have got our last secret, constructive or scientific, they will take it, and living in a way that we would not, reproducing in numbers we don't, they will beat us at any game we start, if we don't take warning which we are in the ascendancy, and keep there."

To all of this Donald replies, "Well, there is something to think about . . . " And think he does, for he comes to see the danger as clearly as Linda, and he bends himself to overtaking and surpassing academically his malevolent classmate Oka Sayye, who eventually tries to kill Donald by dropping a boulder on him as he suns himself at the base of a cliff. Thanks to Linda's warning, Donald is able to dodge the boulder. Then, stealthily climbing to where the boulder was dropped, Linda, Donald, and Katy find Oka Sayye and the Irish cook pushes him over the cliff. Oka Sayye catches hold of a bush, but Katy chops at it with the axe she is carrying and Oka Sayye plunges to his death.

When Gene Porter wrote this, her last book, it had been only a year since the Great War, and there should have been produced a foreboding of what lay ahead. There were few forebodings, but somewhere there may have been, for Porter as for others, the memory of the near-ecstasy of community that the war had brought.

SOURCES

The sources for this chapter are mainly the *New York Times* and the two Gene Stratton Porter novels discussed in the text.

FURTHER READING

The subject of Japan has been extensively treated in the body of work called "diplomatic history." This chapter is intended to suggest the presence of something in the feeling and spirit of many Americans for the Japanese that was irrational and noxious and that, perhaps, made its way into the formal level of diplomacy. The most fundamental source of this "pollution" was a legend that circulated as a street-corner conversation piece. The legend had it that the Japanese were lacking in native creativity and that their expansionist bellicosity was finally a sham because of their peculiar physiognomy, where their eyes were concerned—a "deformity" that made it impossible for them to aim a gun. As a teenager, I heard these stories, including one especially amusing piece about how the Japanese had built two large naval vessels, only to have them "turn turtle" when launched because the naval engineers had unwittingly omitted certain crucial factors in their equations.

In the early months of 1928, a U.S. Marine in Shanghai wrote to a friend, a student at Marquette University, who thought that part of the letter was of such significance that it should be published in the college paper, the *Marquette Tribune*. The informing lines were these: "The Japanese can't even shoot straight. The safest place to be is where they are aiming. . . . we have never been injured when the barrage was directed at us."

A principal source of this sort of put-down of the Japanese was the Street and Smith pulp magazines of the early thirties, especially a fifteen-cent pulp called *Flying Aces*. To what extent these publications nurtured a sense of Japanese as "the enemy" among some people is unknown, though the editor of *Flying Aces* well knew that the image of the "Jap," with slanting eyes, protruding front teeth, and scowling, lined visage, was highly marketable.

Historians, in their passion for "objectivity" have tended to skirt the presumably arid wastes of cultural history as manifested by the pulp magazine, perhaps because such a phenomenon leaves little that can be counted, sorted, and footnoted. Even so, the pulps represent a significant source of information where cultural history is concerned. For those interested in this aspect of history, the principal source is a collection at Bowling Green State University's Center for Popular Culture.

17

To Redeem the World

ON AUGUST 27, WOODROW WILSON, obviously needing nothing more at that time but rest, announced that he would tour the West to rally support for the Versailles treaty. The trip, said Mrs. Wilson, "was stoutly opposed by Dr. Grayson, who did not think the President could draw further on his strength without risking disaster." But Wilson, who would give no quarter to his opponents on the treaty, gave none to himself. In responding to Dr. Grayson, Wilson, according to his wife, delivered a brief lecture on commitment. Yes, doctor, he said, he was already tired and the trip would be extremely fatiguing, "but I feel it is my duty, and my own health is not to be considered when the future peace and security of the world are at stake. If the Treaty is not ratified by the Senate, the War will have been fought in vain, and the world will be thrown into chaos. I promised our soldiers . . . that it was a war to end wars; and if I do not do all in my power to put the Treaty in effect, I will be a slacker. . . . I must go."

Three days after Wilson announced his speaking tour, Senator Knox asked his colleagues, in effect, to wipe out all that had happened since 8:30 P.M. on April 2, 1917. Safety for the United States, he said, lay in "utter rejection" of the treaty; peace with Germany could be brought about by a Congressional resolution. Knox might have added that the war had been a great mistake.

The day of Wilson's departure, Tuesday, September 4, was gray and oppressive. At the White House, the president took his customary extended afternoon nap, marshaling his strength for the tour on which he would embark that evening. Shortly before 7:00 P.M., he, Mrs. Wilson, Dr. Grayson, and Joseph Tumulty emerged from a private room at the

Washington station to begin their walk to the concourse where the train awaited. There to see them off and to walk with them were economic advisers Bernard Baruch, Raymond T. Baker, and Norman Davis.

There was much joking and laughing as the group made its way toward the train. The occasion seemed almost festive, with Wilson wearing a straw hat, blue coat, and white pants. Mrs. Wilson smiled and looked regal, as always. A small crowd cheered and clapped as the party passed. "The President appeared to be in excellent health," said the *New York Times* the next day. Tumulty thought differently. Later, recalling that night's departure, he said that he had "never . . . seen the President look so weary as on the night we left Washington for our swing into the West." A few days before their departure, Tumulty had looked at Wilson and had made a mental comparison between the man he had known a few years previous and the one before him. "In those days he was a vigorous, agile, slender man, active and alert, his hair but slightly streaked with gray. Now . . . he was an old man." Wilson himself had told Tumulty, "I am at the end of my tether, but my friends on the Hill say that the trip is necessary to save the Treaty, and I am willing to make whatever personal sacrifice is required, for if the Treaty should be defeated, God only knows what would happen to the world as a result of it."

At the time, there was no special presidential train, so Wilson traveled on one that had been especially prepared for him. He did have his own car, the "Mayflower," which customarily was the last one on the train. Edith Wilson described the car in detail: Entering from the rear, one came into a small sitting room fitted with arm chairs and a long couch in front of which a folding table could be placed for meals. Then came her bedroom, containing a single bed and a lavoratory. Adjoining that was her husband's room, similarly equipped. Next was his work room, furnished with a desk and several chairs. And finally, two compartments that provided quarters for Grayson and Edith Wilson's maid, "a wonderful little Swedish girl named Siegrid" whose job was to press her mistress's clothes. There was also Brooks, whose principal recommendation, as far as Mrs. Wilson was concerned, was that he was "faithful." Brooks slept on the couch in the sitting room. Ahead of the "Mayflower" was a baggage car, diner, and a long line of Pullmans, carrying approximately one hundred movie cameramen, photographers, and newsmen.

Getting everything in order took some time, and it was not until 11:00 that the party in the "Mayflower" heard from down the track a brief toot then felt the first straining strokes of the pistons. In the president's car the trip began pleasantly enough. He, his wife, Tumulty, and Grayson sat chatting in the lounge where, shortly, someone sent in an order for "cool drinks." "Imagine our surprise," wrote Mrs. Wilson, "when instead of the regular porter, who should appear bearing a large tray but 'Little Jackson,' a coloured messenger in the Executive Offices." "Little Jackson" was wearing a white apron and a large white chef's cap, so large, in fact, that "we all laughed heartily, while he showed his white teeth in a pleased smile." Tumulty had planned it all, including the hat design.

The next morning Wilson made his first speech, in Columbus, Ohio. That evening he was in Indianapolis, and a big crowd was there to hear him, but Indiana's Republican governor, James P. Goodrich, who was only supposed to introduce Wilson, chose instead to address a few remarks to the audience. Shortly there were shouts of "Wilson, we want to hear Wilson." Goodrich waited a few moments for the noise to subside, "but when it was apparent that he had no intention of granting the request to introduce Wilson the cries were renewed with increased volume." Finally, Goodrich shrugged, turned away, and another person on the platform introduced the president.

The following morning Wilson's train reached St. Louis, where the president was to address a luncheon crowd at the Statler Hotel. Afterward, as Edith Wilson recorded it, "there was the usual stampede to 'shake hands with the President,' and the inevitable interviews with local politicians. Never a moment to relax and rest." That day, at the Statler and at the St. Louis Coliseum, Wilson spoke forcefully, saying there would be no compromise on Article X of the League Covenant, the article that pledged League members' armed assistance in resisting aggression, the article that isolationists had been assailing so bitterly.

From St. Louis, the president traveled to Kansas City and then to Des Moines, on September 6. In Des Moines, presumably to remind the country of the connection between the war and the League, the tour managers arranged a military setting for Wilson's arrival. As the presidential party left the train, a long line of soldiers stood at attention. Wilson reviewed them and then, behind a band playing patriotic airs, the soldiers marched to the coliseum, where they were given "seats of honor."

Aware of the mounting specter of communism in Europe and, as many believed, in America, too, Wilson told the citizens of Des Moines that America would have to act on the treaty, that Bolshevism was spreading across the world and peace was needed to stop it. Therefore, he said, those who opposed the treaty, Senators included, were aiding Bolshevism. It was, he declared, as if they were saying, "We have made a great promise to mankind which it costs too much to redeem."

Wherever he went, the crowds continued to gather to hear him. At one place in the Dakotas, because no building was large enough to hold the great audience, a large tent was pitched in a field. At Billings, Montana, Wilson was touched by an event that seemed to be a kind of happy omen for his mission. When his train had pulled away from the station, a number of boys carrying flags had trotted after it. As the train gathered speed, the boys ran faster, and one of them overtook the President's car and handed a flag to Mrs. Wilson. His companion, having no flag, looked unhappy, but then he put his hand into his pocket and produced a dime, which he thrust at the president's wife. Mrs. Wilson recorded this event in her memoirs, adding a sequel: nearly five years later, at the time of Wilson's death, she found a dime, wrapped in paper, in a separate pocket of his change purse. "I am convinced that it was the dime that little boy gave him on that September day in 1919."

From Billings, the train made its way through spectacular western scenery to Portland, to Tacoma, and then to Seattle, where the party detrained for two nights' stay in a hotel and where Wilson was to review the Pacific Fleet, a colossal piece of staging worked out by Navy Secretary Josephus Daniels. This courtly North Carolinian and his wife were at the station to greet the Wilsons, and together they drove through thronged streets to the dock from which they would be transported to the decks of the historic old battleship *Oregon.*

At the dock a naval launch stood by to transport the party to the battleship. By the time everyone had boarded, the craft was well down in the water; nevertheless, the engine was started and lines cast off. The helmsman, possibly distracted by the attention of everyone on the waterfront and on the fleet of ships, gunned the craft into a sharp turn that caused it to heel precariously. Unable to recover from the turn, he ran head-on into another launch. Finally, he was able to straighten out the craft and make his way to the *Oregon.* If the president had had the disposition of a tyrant, the helmsman would have been thrown to the sharks, but, unruffled, Wilson thanked the man for his efforts. Mrs. Wilson, never one to gloss over human frailty, said tartly that she "personally" would never have excused "the officers who had endangered lives in this way."

With the Wilson party aboard the *Oregon,* the old ship moved down the bay, passing the *New Mexico,* the *Mississippi,* the *Idaho,* the *Texas,* and the *New York.* From each ship, as the *Oregon* passed by, came the thunderous salute of big guns. Overhead, military planes dove and wheeled, engines buzzing, while over the water floated the strains of "The Star-Spangled Banner."

That night the president spoke at a dinner at the Hippodrome. Afterward, back in his suite on the top floor of the hotel, weary to the bone, he and his wife witnessed a spectacular sight in the harbor. Mrs. Wilson recalled the scene in her memoirs: "Straight out as far as the eye could see, lay the entire fleet, every ship ablaze with light. . . . It awed us both as we sat on a little roof garden and gazed silently."

The president's wife remembered those days on the Pacific Coast with particular poignancy. Composing her story some nineteen years later, she commented on how, as she wrote, "at this desk in a quiet room alone," the memories of those weeks of travel, "day and night, with their multitude of events," brought back memories that almost overwhelmed her. On the Pacific Coast great crowds were turning out to hear her husband speak. There were "luncheons, dinners, receptions, mile upon miles of driving in flower-laden cars; interviews; conferences and . . . committees of escort and entertainment."

In Los Angeles, the curtain dropped on an episode in Wilson's life that had threatened his planned marriage to his second wife. The Mrs. Peck with whom he had strolled and chatted back at Princeton and to whom he had written "letters," the Mrs. Peck whom Wilson had found so vital and stimulating, lived in Los Angeles, as Edith Wilson well knew. Always one to confront an issue, even if head-on, the president's wife invited Mrs. Peck to lunch, because of "the work scandalmongers had done" and her wish to "show my disdain for such slander." Mrs. Peck, "a faded, sweet-looking woman," obliged. Her conversation, wrote Mrs. Wilson, was almost wholly about her personal problems.

On September 22, the presidential train headed eastward. Mrs. Wilson was buoyed by the thought that soon they would be home again. But, as she said, with "each revolution of the wheels my anxieties for my husband's health increased. He grew thinner and the headaches increased in duration and in intensity until he was almost blind during attacks. Coming in from a reception or dinner I have seen him sit with his head bowed on the back of a chair in front of him while trying to dictate and keep abreast of his mountainous correspondence."

On September 23, Wilson delivered an address at the Salt Lake City Tabernacle. Fifteen thousand persons crowded into the building on that hot night to hear him. Afterward, at the hotel, Edith Wilson found that his clothes were soaked from perspiration. He changed, but they were soon wet again. Mrs. Wilson knew her husband was ill, but her entreaties to stop the tour brought only a negative reaction. The president thought he had "caught the imagination of the people," and he must carry on at any cost. The tide of battle was turning in his favor—or so he thought.

From Salt Lake City the train went to Cheyenne and then Denver, arriving at 10:30 P.M. on September 24. The next day, Wilson gave a morning speech in Denver's auditorium, then went back to the train for the journey to Pueblo and an afternoon speech. "This will have to be a short speech," he said, but to his wife it was his longest and most effective. Could Americans so soon forget that men had died in the war? Could they not understand that men had died "for something that vastly transcends any of the immediate and palpable objects of the War?" Wilson concluded by recalling the Memorial Day visit he had made to the American military cemetery at Suresnes, France. "I wish some of the men who are now opposing the settlement for which those men died could visit such a spot as that. I wish they could feel the moral obligation that rests upon us not to go back on those boys, but to see this thing through to the end and make good their redemption of the world."

Redeem the world! Who could redeem the world? Had the president gone mad? It may have seemed so, but he had not. His thinking was the logical consequence of an assumption lodged at the root of American history—namely that it was America's destiny to bring the world to that final perfection implied in the notion of Enlightenment progress. And he, Woodrow Wilson, had by the will of Providence and history's design, been assigned the role of architect of that final step.

History is always flaunting its great designs for humankind, and always, in the end, it lies. The man who just nine months previous had been lionized by Europe and who, seemingly, could command all, now stood with his back to the wall, pleading with Americans to sustain him through the last battle. But this prophet of the Enlightenment, exercising his last ounce of persuasive oratory on his fairground audience that warm afternoon in Pueblo, had lost. History had tired of its affair with progress and democracy. That dalliance had gone on long enough, and already it was setting up new illusions for humankind to pursue.

After the fairground speech, Wilson and his party returned to the "Mayflower," and soon the presidential car was in motion, rocking and clattering toward Wichita. It was not a relaxed moment for Wilson—no feet on a chair and a cold glass in hand. His headache throbbed with a new force. Dr. Grayson, anxious, thought that a little exercise would help his patient. The train was stopped a half hour while the Wilsons strolled in the cool Colorado evening air. They returned to the car, where dinner was served; Wilson ate well. His headache had retreated to the point where he thought he could sleep, and everyone, hoping for the best, retired to their respective parts of the train. Edith Wilson went to her room, adjoining his, and had the "wonderful" Siegrid comb her hair and give her a massage.

The hopeful mood ended abruptly when, at 11:30 P.M., the president knocked on his wife's door and asked if she would come to him. He was "very sick," he said; the pain had become unbearable. Siegrid was sent scurrying through the train to find Dr. Grayson. "I realized we were facing something terrible," Mrs. Wilson recalled. All night he turned and writhed from the pain, but as morning dawned he fell asleep. Two hours later he awakened, saying that he needed to shave to prepare for the Wichita speech. As Brooks performed this ministration, Mrs. Wilson, Dr. Grayson, and Tumulty laid out their strategy for dealing with the crisis. In the midst of their talk, the president appeared, shaven, dressed, but looking "oh, so piteously ill." The trip must be canceled and he must take a vacation, he was told. "No," he said, he would keep on. But Mrs. Wilson had made up her mind, and all his demurrers were vetoed. As the train slowed to enter Wichita, Wilson surrendered.

Once in the station, Tumulty left the train and announced to the reception committee that the president was ill and the tour was canceled. At 11:00 A.M., the train, with a pilot train ahead of it, began the seventeen hundred–mile trip back to Washington. Mrs. Wilson described the ordeal: "The hours dragged on: night came; brought no rest; another day; another bad night—and another dawn found me staring into the future, wide-eyed, wondering." The fight was over. She knew it and so did her husband. "He accepted the decree of Fate as gallantly as he had fought the fight; but only he and his God knew the crucifixion that began that moment—to stretch into interminable years, during which the seal he put on his lips, never to repine or voice a syllable of self-pity or regret, remained unbroken."

Wilson had suffered a "nervous breakdown," the *New York Times* reported on September 27. At the White House, he "wandered like a ghost" between his study at one end of a hall and his wife's room at the other. The pain in his head was such that he could not remain quiet to endure it. Three days later he was reported "slightly better," and, according to the *Times,* "there was nothing new to change the impression that the President is suffering simply from nervous exhaustion complicated by nervous indigestion."

Edith Wilson, too, thought he seemed better. Shortly after their return to Washington they took a brief afternoon ride and that evening watched a movie in the East Room. Then, as they prepared to retire, Wilson insisted that he would read to her a chapter from the Bible, as he had done nightly during the war. "He stood under the centre light in my room with the Book in one hand, the other resting on a table that flanked the big couch where I sat. His voice was as vibrant and as strong as I had ever heard it, and when he finished he put the Book on the table and stood while he wound his watch. We talked a little, and after he had gone to his room I saw the watch on the table and decided to carry it to him. He said: 'That worries me—to have left the watch there. It is not like me.' "

Concerned, Edith Wilson got up hourly to look in on her husband. Dawn came, and as he appeared to be sleeping normally, she turned to her own bed for a few hours of uninterrupted rest. At eight she looked in on him again and found him sitting on the side of his bed trying to reach a water bottle. She handed it to him and saw that his left hand hung loosely. He had no feeling in it, he said. Would she help him into the bathroom? She got him there with great difficulty and then, alarmed, she summoned Dr. Grayson. At that moment she heard the president fall. Running to the bathroom, she found him unconscious on the floor. Unable to lift him, she put a pillow under his head and covered him with a blanket. Shortly Grayson arrived and together they lifted him onto his bed. He had had a stroke; and one would suppose from the nature of his symptoms that in the half-year previous he had had a number of small strokes.

That afternoon, Grayson and four other physicians, including Dr. Francis Xavier Dercum, a neurologist from Philadelphia, examined Wilson. At 10:00 that night they issued a bulletin: Wilson was "a very sick man" whose condition had worsened. It was announced that he would have to stay in bed and cease handling executive duties. He would not be allowed to have callers, nor could he see anyone except members of his immediate family. His trouble? He suffered from "nervous exhaustion."

The next day, October 3, the president's family gathered at his bedside: Jessie (Mrs. Francis B. Sayre) came from Cambridge; Eleanor (Mrs. William G. McAdoo) arrived from New York; and his brother, Joseph Wilson, came from Baltimore. Margaret, who still lived at the White House, was away somewhere but was summoned to return. Wilson survived the night, and the next day Grayson stated that the president's condition appeared more encouraging. In fact, there had been a slight improvement, and a further "slight improvement" was announced on each of the next nine days. On October 10, Wilson sat up a few times.

Word nevertheless was circulating that the president was through. When Senator George H. Moses sent his own understanding of Wilson's condition in a letter to a friend, his view of the matter somehow got into the newspapers. The president had "suffered some kind of a cerebral lesion," Moses wrote. "His condition is such that while this lesion is healing, he is absolutely unable to undergo any experience which requires concentration of mind and the consequent suffusion of blood into his brain, the pressure of which would be likely to reopen this lesion. . . . Of course, he may get well . . . but if he does he will not be any material force or factor in anything." The next day Senator Gilbert Hitchcock, Wilson's Senate leader, characterized the report as a gross exaggeration. When Dr. Grayson was asked about it, he said that he and the other attending physicians had agreed not to answer questions based on long-distance diagnosing.

On October 16, Grayson was forced to confront a new crisis in his patient's condition: Wilson was suffering a return of the prostatitis he had had the previous spring. The next day his prostate became so enlarged that bladder elimination was impossible. There were more consultations, and two urologists were summoned. Catheterization was tried but was unsuccessful. There was nothing to do but operate. Grayson demurred. "The President can't stand one," he said. Mrs. Wilson agreed. The urologists drew pictures for her to illustrate the nature of the anatomical pathology that made the operation necessary. But Edith Wilson was adamant in her opinion that "nature will finally take care of things." And nature did. "The doctors went home to rest, and peace descended upon my spirit," she wrote. On October 26, the newspapers were able to report that the president was definitely mending.

Wilson improved only to a certain point. Senator Moses had been right that he would never again be of "any material force or factor in anything" insofar as firing the public's imagination in support of his vision of a world harmony. His body was worn out; hardening of the arteries had set in with a vengeance and would finally take his life.

Later on it would be said that, with her husband's collapse, Mrs. Wilson in fact became president, running the country as she saw fit. Having shown her ability in the past to deal with critical situations in her husband's life, she addressed forthrightly the problems raised by his illness and did what she thought was necessary. Pointedly, she asked Dr. Dercum if the president's mind had suffered. He assured her that "the brain was as clear as ever," then added: "Madam, it is a grave situation, but I think you can solve it. Have everything come to you; weigh the importance of each matter, and see if it is possible by consultations with respective heads of the Departments to solve them without the guidance of your husband." Thus, as Edith Wilson wrote, "began my stewardship. I studied every paper, and . . . tried to digest and present in tabloid form the things that, despite my vigilance, had to go to the President. I, myself, never made a single decision regarding the disposition of public affairs."

As to this last statement, one is inclined to think that, had she somehow been able to assume a role in setting presidential policy on the League issue, the results might have been better. There was no one in the Senate, including Lodge, who could be tougher than she; on the other hand, she could recognize the realities of a situation and deal with it in terms of its possibilities. Whatever the crisis, Edith Wilson did not flinch. Outwardly, and inwardly, she remained cool.

After his stroke the president was a fallen warrior, borne to the rear, so to speak, where from his bed he brought such strength as he could muster into the fight for the treaty. But there was little he could do. The Democratic senators who supported the treaty, led by Hitchcock, were unsure as to what they could do. On October 6, Hitchcock went to the White House to discuss with Joe Tumulty what strategy should be followed under the existing circumstances. Tumulty said he did not know. Hitchcock said he and the other Democratic leaders would, if at all possible, like to discuss the matter with Wilson, and if they could not, they would go ahead with their own initiative. Hitchcock wanted to get the voting over with. "I am anxious," he said on September 30, "for speedy action on the treaty and am willing to take my chances in a vote any time the leaders on the other side will agree to it."

But Lodge was not anxious for a vote. He well knew that time was his ally, for it continually produced new concerns to distract the American public and dim its memory of the solemnity of its commitment to world community when it entered the war. Lodge's tactic was to raise the specter of a new menace, that of Japan, which he likened to an "Eastern Prussia." With him stood the irreconcilable core of Republican senators who, in a rising crescendo of oratorical performance, denounced the internationalism of the treaty. The League, they passionately declared, would place America's purity on the block of a sordid internationalism, where foreign powers, given to intrigue and lust for power, would be able to achieve their soiled designs at the expense of American blood.

Other presidents, under the circumstances, might well have given Senator Hitchcock carte blanche to do with the treaty issue as he thought best. But Wilson was Wilson; were he at death's door, he would linger outside long enough to hold the line. Thus, on October 24, he let it be known that it would be his decision as to whether administration Democrats would support a Lodge version of the treaty.

On November 7 the voting began on the various reservations that Lodge and the Foreign Relations Committee were proposing to incorporate into the treaty. On November 13 the Senate voted to sustain the Lodge position on the vital Article X of the League Covenant. On November 18 the *New York Times* declared in an editorial that "the

Foreign Relations Committee . . . and Mr. Lodge have made a treaty of their own. Violently and in a hostile spirit they wrenched out of the compact signed at Versailles many substantive provisions."

The next day the Senate chamber was packed to capacity as Lodge presented a resolution for ratification of the treaty with reservations. Thirty-four Republicans and five Democrats voted for ratification; forty-two Democrats, following Wilson, voted against the resolution, along with thirteen Republican "irreconcilables." After some parliamentary maneuvering, the Senate adjourned, the treaty having been defeated. When word reached the White House, Edith Wilson went to her husband's room to give him the news. No doubt Wilson expected the results and had already resolved on a course of action. He remained silent for a moment, then said wearily, "All the more reason I must get well and try again to bring this country to a sense of its great opportunity and greater responsibility."

At Alice Longworth's home on M Street, there was rejoicing. A number of people, including Lodge, had gravitated there to exult over their victory. Among them was Senator Warren Harding and his wife, who went into the kitchen and scrambled a big plate of eggs for those who were hungry. The hostess, bubbling with excitement, moved from senator to senator, treating them with the favor of her electric personality and no doubt crowing over the defeat of her longtime, premier hate, Woodrow Wilson.

Four months later, on March 19, the Sixty-sixth Congress, after five weeks of debate, again voted on the treaty and again it failed. Not until July 21, 1921, with Warren Harding as president, did the war officially end for the United States, when a simple joint resolution of Congress rescinded Wilson's war declaration, made some four years previous.

And so Wilson's rocketing idealism, the light that was to make all the bloodshed of war into a sacrificial offering to end war, had turned to ashes. To Wilson the League of Nations had been the final form behind which humankind might work out an equitable destiny for all. But to achieve it he had bargained away at the peace table the very strength he might have used to rectify more immediate wrongs where boundary lines transgressed against national character. The formal character of the League would have admitted few means of treating one of the main causes of the war: superheated nationalism. The question remained— and still does—on what principle can humankind find its unity?

Of the many bubbles that arose from life after the war, seeming to shimmer in the light of a new dawn with the hope of something better for humankind, the biggest and, seemingly, the first to break was the League of Nations idea.

SOURCES

Aside from the newspapers indicated in the text, the principal source for the chapter was Edith Wilson's *My Memoir* (Indianapolis and New York, 1939).

FURTHER READING

In *Woodrow Wilson as I Know Him* (New York, 1921), Joseph P. Tumulty gives a detailed and colorful account of the Wilsons' trip. What seems to have impressed him most where Wilson's physical deterioration was concerned was Edith Wilson's determined and level-headed response to it. Perhaps here it is appropriate to name the poignant and readable book by Gene Smith, *When the Cheering Stopped: The Last Years of Woodrow Wilson* (New York, 1964).

18

Unrest and Tragedy

THE FAILURE OF the United States to ratify the Versailles treaty brought to an end the idealism that had been the standard by which the country had gone to war, a standard that in the early days of the conflict was made to illumine every effort and sacrifice. By September 1919, however, it was the shadow of the Bolshevik menace that was presumed to lie over the country that was the focus of national concern. Middle-class Americans were shaken by the strength of the revolutionary tide in Europe and especially by the vehemence with which it enforced a fealty to the gods it had enthroned. It was as if a new and virulent strain of diabolism had spread its hellishness into life. What had happened in Russia was incomprehensible but it could never happen in America.

Or could it? As fall approached, suburban America betrayed a fearful uneasiness as to what the answer to that question might be. Within the laboring class there were signs of deep restlessness. The nation's colossal industrial empire had been built on its abundant natural resources and a labor force made up mostly of immigrants who had sold their time and strength cheaply, simply to get a foothold in the upward flow of social possibility in America.

When the war came, with skyrocketing prices and longer working time, the workers' burden increased. With peace, the economic pressures, especially in rising food costs, did not abate. In August, Attorney General Palmer, feeling that high food prices were fueling radicalism, sent to the various federal district attorneys throughout the country a statement that sugar should not be retailed for more than eleven cents a pound and that its being "retailed for more indicates that either the wholesaler or retailer is making unreasonable profits."

Unreasonable profit making in the face of wartime scarcity was the game of many, and labor reacted. In September, members of the Boston police force took what to most people was the startling and radical course of organizing themselves into a union and then applying to the American Federation of Labor for a union charter. Once received, fifteen hundred men went on strike, on September 9. Samuel Gompers, president of the AFL, invited negotiations. Almost like a whirlwind, Governor Calvin Coolidge appeared on the scene, a man of strength demanded by the moment. Coolidge wired Gompers a cryptic message: "There is no right to strike against the public safety by anybody, anywhere, any time." Troops were brought into Boston to preserve order and the strike was broken. On November 11 the *New York Times* noted that Coolidge was receiving congratulatory messages from all over the country "for upholding Americanism." He was being "talked of for President."

The big crisis in labor occurred in the steel industry. Since the failure of the Homestead Strike of 1892, steelworkers had been without a union, but in September another attempt at industrial organization was initiated, principally through the efforts of William Z. Foster. With the nation sensitively attuned to the necessity of isolating the malignant virus of Bolshevism, Foster's leadership in the work of unionization represented the point of counterattack. He was known as a person of radical social vision, ruthless in his tactics—another Lenin, some may have felt. On October 1, newspapers prominently carried a statement of Judge Joseph Buffington, of the United States Circuit Court of Appeals, in which Foster was vigorously denounced as a "dangerous domestic enemy." Said Buffington: "There is in my town [Pittsburgh] a man, William Zebulon Foster, who is going among the foreign population, teaching the terrible doctrine of anarchy in his book—things that go to the destruction of the American Government. . . . He is a most dangerous leader and a dangerous domestic enemy."

Judge Elbert H. Gary, chairman of the board of directors of United States Steel, agreed with Buffington but stood on the higher ground of principle. Testifying before the Senate Committee on Labor Education in September, he declared that "the steel Corporation was fighting in defense of the rights of a man to work as a free man without dictation from a labor leader as to when and where and how he should work. At all costs . . . the corporation would maintain the open shop." Some three weeks later, at a dinner at the Commodore Hotel attended by a thousand people, among them King Albert of Belgium, Gary declared that the open shop was the "greatest question confronting the world." Another speaker pronounced Gary "a great leader against industrial Bolshevism."

Back in U.S. Steel's hometown of Gary, Indiana, Mother Jones, the legendary heroine of most of the causes of radical labor since the days of the Civil War, gave her view of the matter. Speaking to strikers at the Turner Hall, she took a deep breath and then said, "So this is Gary. . . . Well, we're going to change the name and we're going to take over the steel works and we're going to run them for Uncle Sam. . . . I'll be 90 years old the first of May, but by God if I have to, I'll take ninety guns and shoot hell out of . . . every damn scab you can lay hold on. We'll hang the bloodhounds to the telegraph poles. Go out and picket." Conscious of her colorful image and its place in history, Mother Jones was "pouring it on" during the closing chapter of her life.

But it availed her little. The temper of the country had hardened to support the position of Judge Gary and the Commodore banqueters. Wherever Foster went, he was "run out of town." In a letter to the Mahoning United Labor Congress, Senator Atlee Pomerene said that he backed all the negative observations that Ohio's Congressman John G. Cooper had made about Foster. "America would not tolerate the menace of a military autocracy in Germany," Pomerene declared. "She raised an army of 4,000,000 men to prevent it. This same spirit will not sit silently by and see industrial autocracy whether in the name of capital or of labor."

Whatever the character of the "negative observations" that Cooper had been making of Foster, they were in complete harmony with the general chorus of detraction that was raised around the labor organizer. Foster may have been a "Bolshevist," whatever that was, but if the cause he worked for in 1919 was to create an autocracy of labor, it was a cause aimed at meliorating the autocracy of management. It was not until the era of the New Deal, however, that steel workers got their union.

Meanwhile, in September 1919 the United Mine Workers announced its intent to call a strike for higher wages and shorter hours. Since the government had taken over the mines as a wartime measure, it was against the federal agency running the mines that the strike was directed. But it was President Wilson who responded to the miners. From his sickbed he issued a statement, on October 25, in which he said that the miner's strike was unjustifiable and unlawful. "When a movement reaches the point where it appears to involve practically the entire productive capacity of the country . . . the public interest becomes the paramount consideration." So it was in the public interest, the government said, to issue an injunction against the UMW's proposed strike. Eight hundred regular army troops were sent into the West Virginia coalfields, and the strike never took place.

A substantial number of people who were concerned about what was going on in the country believed that radicals of foreign origin were at the root of labor's discontent and that their creed was that of the "Bolsheviki." The *New York Times* of October 10 editorially observed that a count of the number of Bolsheviks in the country could not be taken, "but if it could . . . the total would amaze optimists who dismiss the menace to the country's industries, not to speak of its institutions." There were, at the very least, "many thousands" of them "who do not speak English" who had been "corrupted by pamphlet, circular, and fly-by-night sheet," plus those " 'intellectuals' and parlor varieties of the genus, who wear the cloak of respectability." These people, to be sure, comprised only a small percentage of the population, but "they are mad or malignant, and it would be a foolish mistake to underestimate their capacity for mischief."

A week later the *Times* was more specific, declaring, "50,000 aliens spread radicalism." A further alarming reflection came in a statement by Representative Albert Johnson to the House Immigration Committee. He insisted that "hordes of radicals and fully 10,000,000 Germans and Austrians were waiting to come into the country."

An alert police apprehension of the menace was not lacking—at least at Wierton, West Virginia. On October 7 more than one hundred fifty men, "declared by the police to have been members of the 'Red Guard of Finland,' " were rounded up, marched to the public square, and forced to kneel and kiss the American flag. After this ceremony, the men were driven out of town. It was only appropriate that the police officer who conceived of the flag-kissing idea was "formerly a United States Marine and a veteran of Chateau-Thierry." Two days later, "several thousand radicals" in New York City "tried to parade up Fifth Avenue as a demonstration in the guise of a protest against the Russian blockade." The parade was broken up by police, "with the aid of hundreds of civilians." In the action "police used their clubs freely," and "many paraders were soundly beaten."

Amid these alarms, Secretary of War Baker pledged full use of the forces under his command to put down the disturbances that had been racking the country since the armistice. "Our newspapers are daily filled with accounts of violent agitation by so-called Bolsheviki and radicals, counseling violence and urging action in behalf of what they call social revolution. The American people will not exchange the solid foundations of their social order for any of these fantastic programs. . . . We have an army of tried soldiers, of true Americans. They have seen too much disorder in the world to undervalue law and order in their own country."

These words, reflecting the high resolve of the secretary to resist those given to "violent agitation," no doubt warmed the hearts of his supporters, thinking, as they were, of "Bolsheviki" who were infesting the steel mills and coalfields. But there was violence of a different sort occurring in America, a kind that welled up from an impulse whose roots fed on a depraved form of community seeking. It is unlikely that Secretary Baker and his warm hearted audience gave much thought to the lynch mobs; they were most likely too busy contemplating the prospects of a Red takeover.

In the May 3, 1919, issue of the *New Republic,* an editorial entitled "The Lynching Evil" declared that since 1889 over three thousand men and women had been put to death by mobs, "a number comparable with that of authentic executions under the Red Terror in Russia. No other civilized state exhibits so shameful a record of lawlessness through a period of internal peace." The statistics may not have been correct, but that is scarcely the point. That such a thing, largely unremarked, could occur in a civilized society was more than shameful; it testified to a great moral wasteland in American life, to a moral blindness on the part of those who were integral to its religious and educational institutions. The year 1919 was one of the worst, with more than one hundred lynching victims.

The fall season seemed to be a time when this evil displayed itself with increased virulence. In Jacksonville, Florida, on September 7, two blacks were abducted from the city jail and lynched. A mob of fifty, looking for a black man who had been accused of assaulting a white girl, found that their intended victim had been taken to St. Augustine. Not to be denied the particular kind of psychic exaltation that attended mob violence, they seized two other blacks charged with murder, took them to the outskirts of the city, and shot them to death. Then, reported the *New York Times,* "they put ropes around the necks of the bodies and dragged them through the city streets. One body was dropped in front of a leading hotel."

Three weeks later, an even more grisly and insane mob action occurred in Omaha. During the night of September 27, five thousand men gathered outside the new five-story Douglas County Courthouse to demand that Will Brown, a prisoner held in the jail on the top floor, be handed over to them. As the mob grew, the mayor, displaying uncommon bravery, went to the courthouse to confer with the sheriff. After the meeting, he appeared at the courthouse door to address the mob and to appeal for order. The response was a yelling of, "Give us the nigger," to which the mayor responded, "I can't do it, boys." The mayor himself was then "seized by some of the rioters and rushed down Harney Street to Sixteenth, where stands a traffic box."

"Hang the Mayor; he won't give us the nigger," yelled some in the mob. Another shouted, "Lynch him," whereupon a rope was placed around his neck and he was dragged half a block to a trolley pole, over which the loose end of the rope was thrown. Twice the mayor was drawn up from the ground, but each time a policeman intervened to cut the rope. After the second attempt, several officers pushed the mayor into an automobile and drove him to a hospital. Back at the courthouse, the sheriff and his deputies were faring even worse. The mob had set fire to the building, forcing the sheriff to surrender the prisoner. Then, as the sheriff and the jailers prepared to leave, they were attacked and beaten.

Brown, who apparently was forced to run, was "riddled by a thousand bullets." His body was then placed over a fire of "red faggots" but "was not permitted to remain there long . . . and was soon being dragged through the streets at the end of a rope pulled by fifty members of the mob. This spectacle did not end until late in the morning hours, when what remained of the torso was hung to a trolley pole at one of the most important downtown intersections."

On September 30 the *New York Times* quoted a source that claimed to represent a body of opinion which held that the Omaha riot was a sign that the United States should not join the League of Nations, since the riot showed that the government could not "take care of things at home, much less go abroad." A week later, James H. Maurer, president of the Pennsylvania State Federation of Labor, who had several days previous been taken off a ship by federal agents just as he was about to sail for Europe, made a speech at New York's Lexington Theater as part of the opening rally of the Socialist party. Said Maurer: "We've taken so much democracy abroad that there is none left in the country."

SOURCES

This chapter is based principally on news items from the *New York Times*. The *Florida Times Union* was also consulted as a source for the Jacksonville lynching.

FURTHER READING

Most nation-states, it would appear, have their national history stained with some type of barbarous inhumanity. Where the United States is concerned, beginning in the 1880s and running through the 1920s, it was the atrocity of lynching. A number of books have been and continue to be written on the subject, including: John W. Caughy, *Their Majesty, the Mob* (Chicago, 1960); Jacquelyn Dowd Hall, *Revolt against Chivalry: Daniel Ames and the Women's Campaign against Lynching*

(New York, 1979); James R. McGovern, *Anatomy of a Lynching: The Killing of Claude Neal* (Baton Rouge, 1982); Arthur F. Raper, *The Tragedy of Lynching* (Chapel Hill, N.C., 1933); and Dennis B. Downey and Raymond M. Hyser, *No Crooked Death: Coatesville, Pennsylvania, and the Lynching of Zachariah Walker* (Urbana, Ill., 1990).

19

The Rebels

FOR A GROUP OF ROMANTICS who stood at the leading edge of change, where time, like a rolling wave, began its swell, there was only the thought to ride the wave forever. John Dewey's vision of calculated social advances abreast this wave did not strike them as exciting fare. They were rebels who wanted personally to move into the brilliant excitement of time's flow, to turn forever away from the vestiges of ordering myth forms that still bound them to established values and seemed to block the conduits of their souls where flumed those mystic calls to sensual joy. They rejected eternity and set their course as if, for them, time would never end. They were the prophets of the great excitement that gave to the decade of the twenties its unique character. Mostly, they were young and seemed to believe they would always be so.

In a review of Jean Untermeyer's book of poetry, *Growing Pains,* Floyd Dell, in the April 1919 issue of *The Liberator,* chided Untermeyer for qualities in her verse that he found not in keeping with the new spirit, the characteristics of which he named: "You are living in a glorious period of which the watchword—no, not the watchword, the key-note, rather—is Freedom; an age in which it has been discovered that the traditional rules of conduct in every department of life can be broken without any danger from divine—and not much from human—wrath; a time accordingly, which the younger generation—having already torn the locks from the doors, and taken the doors themselves from their hinges—is spending exultantly in battering down the front gate. Unquestionably that is the period in which you live."

Dell was one of many who, beginning around 1910, had moved out of midwestern cities and towns and into the holy place of the emancipated young, New York's Ninth Ward, Greenwich Village. A quiet backwater of a hundred or so square blocks below Fourteenth Street, it contained a number of stately homes built, before the Civil War, that by the turn of the century were being converted to flats. For twenty to thirty dollars a month, one could rent several large rooms with a fireplace or gas log and a cold water tap in the hall. In Greenwich Village the young bohemians could, in their phrase, "make love," drink wine, and celebrate in their poetry the wonderful passions of youth.

The Village had its sacred landmarks. When some of its better-known residents of the pre– and post–World War I era wrote of their days there, they recalled the saloon on the corner of Sixth Avenue and Fourth Street, the Golden Swan, with its backroom, the "hellhole." Harold Stearns remembered "a photograph of a nude lady looking out through the blinds of the window of a darkened room." He thought of some of the people with whom he had sat and gotten drunk at the table beneath the picture: "Eugene O'Neill and Art Young and Jack Reed (when he was in town) and Walter Franzen (whom we have lost) and Peggy Johns and Clara Tice and Thorne Smith and God knows how many of the others." Stearns said that he hated to think about all the liquor he had drunk at that table.

At 137 MacDougal Street was the Washington Square Book Shop, run by the Boni brothers. Next door was a small hall called The Liberal Club, styled "A Meeting Place for Those Interested in New Ideals." Beneath the club was Polly Holladay's basement restaurant. At some time, Walker Gilmer wrote, "with the permission of their joint landlady, Jenny Belardi," the bookshop and The Liberal Club were combined by knocking a hole through the wall that separated them. Thus, "a club, a restaurant, and a library provided the setting for budding Socialists and unpublished poets to mix with the famous, Emma Goldman, John Reed, Big Bill Heywood, Theodore Dreiser, Margaret Sanger, Henrietta Rodman, and Dr. A. A. Brill."

The remarkable thing about the Village bohemians was that with all their drinking and night-long talk, they still had time to fulfill their calling as evangelists of the new universe. Most of them seemed to have believed, with the fervor of converts, that a new age of freedom and sensual joy was theirs; and having purged themselves of bourgeois striving and having proclaimed their freedom from all forms of traditional morality, they were obliged to preach the good news of hope and deliverance. So in cold flats, where cupboards were frequently bare, they sat at their typewriters and hoped that theirs would be the work of authentic genius that would transform the world.

Among the rebels there was a disposition to regard the Russian

Revolution as a sign that a bright new age was at hand, a trait that in some, like John Reed and Mike Gold, took on the character of passionate commitment. In the meantime, still hanging around, ripe for the thrust of their clever barbs and jeering laughter, was an old America, a compound of bucolic backwardness and capitalistic crudity, both held intact by an outworn Puritan ethic.

It was largely persons of this bent who supplied the material for *The Masses,* a magazine that had begun in 1911 as an insignificant socialist publication emphasizing cooperatives. Striving to survive, in December 1912 the magazine's editorship was put into the hands of Max Eastman, a twenty-nine-year-old Columbia University graduate student and John Dewey's assistant. The new editor had been born on a farm near Canandaigua, New York; both of his parents were Congregational ministers. It appears that Eastman's mother was the dominant personality in the family, restless and driven, traits her son also possessed. Tall, blond, an engaging conversationalist, Eastman had that touch of managerial ability and social affability that cast a cloud on the purity of his credentials as an authentic Village type but that nonetheless served him well as the editor of *The Masses.*

Under Eastman, *The Masses* featured promising young writers like John Reed, Randolph Bourne, and Upton Sinclair; poets Vachel Lindsay, Amy Lowell, and Louis Untermeyer; and cartoonists Boardman Robinson, Robert Minor, and Art Young. Commentators on *The Masses* refer almost reverently to its blatant irreverence. Milton Cantor, in his biography of Eastman, calls the magazine "the gaily irreverent *Masses.*" Cantor quotes Mabel Dodge, Village queen, known for her generosity—her parlor was always available for radical discussions and her couch was available for more personal favors to radical heroes like Big Bill Heywood and John Reed—as remembering *The Masses* as "fearless and young and laughing at everything solemn and conservative." Many of its writers would gather in the evening at Mrs. Dodge's, where, says Daniel Aaron, they engaged in "happily subverting the social order by word and deed."

When the war came, *The Masses* opposed it. On July 5, 1917, Eastman received a letter from a New York City postal official telling him that the August issue could not be mailed because of the necessities of wartime security. With *The Masses* on its deathbed, Eastman received a cable from John Reed, then witnessing the October revolution in Russia, telling him that he would have exclusive rights to the story as Reed cabled it. Another magazine had to be started, so Eastman and his sister, Crystal, raised thirty thousand dollars and set themselves up in the front half of a third-story loft at 34 Union Square East, to put out their new publication, *The Liberator.* The first issue appeared in March 1918 and carried the first installment of Reed's story of the Bolshevik revolution.

In his book *Love and Revolution,* published in 1964, Eastman discusses both subjects, based on what he must have felt to be his uniquely rich experience in these areas. Love was, as the liberated Villagers regarded it, almost entirely a matter of sex, unfettered by the notion that its ultimate meaning could be found only in commitment. They talked on the subject as if it were something they had discovered, unmindful of the fact that the human race had been procreating, with unflagging zeal, for at least a million years. Love was "tender," "honest," and "brave"; and its course went like this: to meet; to pursue love's promise with all the innocence of spring's budding; to sing a hymn of joy (usually in the form of a bad poem) to its delight; to part when love waned—no bitterness, a tear or two for memory's sake, a tremulous smile, a good-bye.

Encounters and partings occurred on Village streets, but for some bohemians, who had taken flight from the insufferable atmosphere of American stuffiness, a Paris train station was the ideal place to bid farewell. Harold Stearns, the editor of the somewhat pompous *Civilization in the United States,* which Liveright published in 1921, left a poignant account of his parting from "Jessica": "And I was very happy with Jessica that spring; perhaps all the happier since she knew she would soon have to go back home, and we both knew, instinctively but surely, that that would be the end." Then the parting: "that day . . . I kissed Jessica goodbye as we stood on the platform of the Gare Saint-Lazare and, a moment later, she waved to me through the windows of the Le Havre express."

Eastman, perhaps of all the male Villagers, could be the most rhapsodic in describing his dalliances: "We lived a lifetime of five days together, Vera and I . . . sleeping in small rural hotels, roaming by the sea, exploring giant forests." Then the inevitable: "I can still call back the emotion of infinitude—readers who can be as romantic as I can will know what I mean—which filled me when I waved good-bye to her from the rear platform of the train east."

In 1919 Eastman lived comfortably with his sister and her husband in an old house on Washington Place, just east of Sheridan Square. His romantic affiliate at the time was an actress, Florence Deshon. They had met at a dance at Webster Hall, held on December 15, 1916. "We danced together while John Fox [John Fox, Jr., writer of Blue Ridge Mountain tales of feuds and romance] sat at a table sipping highballs. . . . We talked fervently as we danced, and our minds flowed together like two streams from the same source rejoining. She . . . was in exactly the same state of obstreperous revolt against artificial limitations which I had expressed in my junior and senior essays at college."

The affair went on for several years, but with an increasing number of indifferent moments, occasioned principally by what Eastman called the intrusion of his "other personality," the "Black Panther"—or, in language less romantic, periods of infidelity. The lovers parted, only to be reunited for a tragic moment at Christmastime, 1921. Deshon (a stage name—Eastman never knew her real one) had fallen on hard times. She could not find work. But, explained Eastman, he was "in no position to help her with a loan" since he was saving "every cent" for his projected journey to Russia. So Deshon, with her career seemingly ended, went back to her room and turned on the gas. Called to the hospital, Eastman was blood-typed and placed on a table as "Florence's dying young body was rolled in." His blood was transfused into her. "She was not pale; she was still vivid, but her breathing was racous and rapid, a fierce noisy effort of her body to get air." She died shortly thereafter, on the table beside Eastman.

In 1921 Eastman ended his association with *The Liberator* and went to Europe, first as an "observer" at the Genoa Conference, in February 1922, the first international conference in which the new Soviet government participated. From Genoa he went to Russia, where he lingered for two years, in an attempt, one is inclined to think, to take up the legend that John Reed had begun. But as a revolutionary, Eastman was pretty much a hothouse specimen. Reed had flown to the heart of the revolution, where it consumed his spirit and shortly his life; but Eastman, while in Russia, maintained a comfortable distance from the storm, preferring to deal with the subject from a more academic perspective while in the meantime enjoying a romantic dalliance and, for a period, consulting a psychiatrist.

In his latter years, Eastman came to the conclusion that revolution was an evil, the new absolute, the antithesis of his open universe. Did he then go on to redefine a human position on a higher ground, to work out a new and positive synthesis of his experiences? No. He died in 1969, denying his revolutionary vision. As for love, he seemed never to have really known it.

Eugene O'Neill, another Villager during the war years, was not a romantic. In 1916 George Cram Cook (called "Jig" by most) and his wife, Susan Glaspell, brought the Provincetown Players to the Village, settling at 133 MacDougal Street, several doors away from the Boni brothers' bookstore. For several years previous, the Players had, as a small colony of writers and technicians, been putting on their work in an old waterfront shed at Provincetown, Massachusetts. O'Neill had been one of them, and now he was with the group in the Village, helping with the production of his one-act plays.

During that harsh winter of 1917–18, Dorothy Day, who in the years to come would emerge, as many came to believe, as one of the great figures of the modern-age Catholic church, recalled how she had hung around the MacDougal Street playhouse. Mike Gold, editor of the Communist *Daily Worker* during the thirties, was her companion then, and it was he who introduced her to O'Neill. After rehearsal they would go to the Golden Swan's "hellhole." As Day related in *The Long Loneliness,* it "was on these cold bitter evenings that I first heard 'The Hound of Heaven' in an atmosphere of drink and smoke. Gene could recite all of Francis Thompson's poem, and would sit there, black and dour . . . 'And now my heart is as a broken fount, wherein tear drippings stagnate.' "

Frequently in those cold first months of 1918, just before dawn and after the Golden Swan had emptied, Day and O'Neill would walk over to his room near the East River. After turning down the covers of the bed, Day would nestle in with O'Neill, holding him to her like a child so as to stop his shivering. When he had gotten warm, she would walk back to her own room, stopping in at St. Joseph's Catholic Church to savor the warmth and silence. After a few hours of sleep, she would do several hours of work for Max Eastman. One of her chores was to pick up his mail at the post office and take it to his home. It was a job she did not like, for, as she recalled in 1978, Eastman had an Olympian manner about him and Florence Deshon was always hovering about to inspect the mail for signs of foreign female intrusion. Later, in the early afternoon, O'Neill would call to arrange another evening rendezvous.

"We stayed up all night because we did not want to be alone," Day said. It was this wanting to be together, the need for community, that brought the Village bohemians to a special closeness. If most of them thought they were going to find community in the special atmosphere of the Village, in sex, in the pursuit of revolutionary causes, O'Neill possessed an overpowering, paralyzing sense of the presence of what Ivan in Dostoevski's *Brothers Karamazov* called "the wise and dread spirit, the spirit of self-destruction and non-existence." There was no freedom in the community that came through power, or sensual indulgence, or in promoting the causes of history. Time was the enemy of community, for, inevitably, it destroyed all that abided in its domain. O'Neill, drunken, brooding, despairing, did not, like some of the glittering narcissists of the Village, delude himself into believing that community could be found in the excitement of time's unfolding. He did not find the new universe freeing; to the contrary, he thought it was bereft of every certitude for which his spirit seemed to hunger.

In an account of her association with O'Neill, Agnes Boulton relates a curious story about something that occurred just days after she met him. She had heard that there would be a party at the Golden Swan and, wanting to see O'Neill again and also to meet some of the young writers, among whose company she accounted herself, she went there. Once in the "hellhole," she stood tentatively aside, looking for O'Neill. Someone put a ragtime record on the phonograph and several couples began to dance. She saw O'Neill watching them, abstracted. After a moment, she went over to him. "Hello!" she said. "Remember me?"

"It's quite a party," he rejoined.

They stood a moment, looking at the growing number of dancers around them. Boulton observed that they were holding each other closely.

"It's a cold night—good night for a party! The iceman cometh!" O'Neill ran on, referring apparently to the fact that the weather had turned cold. Then his gaze fastened on Nina Moise, the director of the Provincetown Players, "a dark and trimly plump girl with a keen kind face." She was sitting with a plate of food in her lap. O'Neill smiled at her in a twisted way and then disappeared.

Boulton followed him with her eyes. She saw him go into another room that was empty and dark, and she watched as he turned up a bottle of whiskey and drank long. Returning, "he crossed dramatically to the end of the room and with a violent, sardonic, and loud laugh, pulled a chair up in front of the mantel over which the big clock ticked away the minutes. Everyone stopped talking. He stood on the chair and looked about at his audience. Then he quoted—it may have been a popular song at that time, I don't know—in a dramatic chant, full of meaning: '*Turn back the universe, and give me yesterday. TURN BACK—*.'" Then he turned and faced the clock, opened the glass door "and slowly and carefully with his sensitive spatulate fingers he pushed back the long hand of the clock, watching the small hand follow it." To O'Neill, time was the enemy, in whose grasp all creation would die. It was not the bearer of beatitude, as the revolutionaries of the world everywhere were proclaiming.

In 1941 O'Neill completed *Long Day's Journey into Night,* an account of his sense of the tragic hopelessness in which his early family life had moved. Edmund, who is O'Neill, at one point, in addressing his father, recites some lines from Baudelaire: " 'Be always drunken. Nothing else matters, that is the only question. If you would not feel the horrible burden of Time weighting your shoulders and crushing you to the earth, be drunken continually.' " Years later, Day observed of O'Neill, "I had the feeling he considered drinking his rehearsal for death."

In the spring of 1918, O'Neill and Boulton left the Village for Provincetown, where they were married. It was an up-and-down summer, with Boulton indulging her creative urge by writing for pulps like *Snappy Stories*. She probably was desperately trying to make money to pay off a mortgage on her farmhouse in New Jersey, where her parents lived and took care of her small daughter. With O'Neill and brother Jamie engaging in drinking bouts, it was not an easy business.

Yet between his drunken episodes, O'Neill persisted in a measured soberness and regimen of physical exercise that enabled him to write. When winter came, Boulton evicted her parents and her child from the New Jersey farmhouse so that she and O'Neill could live there until spring. The idea was that on the farm he would have the quiet he needed to write and, at the same time, be accessible to New York, where the Provincetown Players were rehearsing his play *Moon of the Caribbees*.

The winter passed drearily, with Boulton building fires and cleaning up after the several cats that roamed the house, one of which "got uncontrollable diarrhea when Gene was drinking." On New Year's Eve 1918, Boulton planned a little party for the two of them but gave up the idea when O'Neill settled down with the *Saturday Evening Post* (which he regularly read) and a bottle of Old Taylor. Boulton started on some Old Taylor herself, and as midnight approached she began to relate to O'Neill the plot of a drama that was running through her mind: *"There is a little country village, overhung with the indifferent moodiness of a somber night. At twelve o'clock midnight all about in isolated spots indicating taverns, churches and farms there is a comical medly of sounds which sound unutterably futile against the night's silence!"*

Boulton was obviously feeling the effects of the Old Taylor, but she persisted in the narration of her tragedy. Finally, O'Neill dropped the *Saturday Evening Post* and the story he was reading about a salesman, his home office, and a tractor. According to Boulton, the New Year entered happily. Her account of the opening moments of 1919 might have come from one of her manuscripts for *Snappy Stories:* "He got up, and for a second I saw the crazy, laughing light in his eyes; then I was caught and pulled tightly against him, his arms embraced me almost with desperation. I seemed to feel a tremor in that body against which my head rested, and then I felt him kiss my hair."

The summer of 1919 was one of O'Neill's best. When he and Boulton returned to Provincetown, the first person they met was an agent for O'Neill's father, who handed him a deed to a remote area of oceanfront property on which stood an old U.S. Coast Guard building, recently remodeled by Mabel Dodge. The elder O'Neill, feeling that his son was at last settling down, wanted to underwrite that hoped-for state by giving him a place where he could write. James O'Neill could not have chosen better. Peaked Hill Bar, as the area was called, was a place where the writer described himself as achieving "a true kinship and harmony with life."

With the responsibility of home-ownership came the prospect of another, more awesome responsibility: Boulton was pregnant, due in October. The days passed in almost idyllic succession. O'Neill would arise in the morning and eat his breakfast of a poached egg on toast—which he did, to Boulton's wonderment, by cutting and eating all of the toast not covered by the egg and then, in one gulp, the egg and the remaining toast. Then he went to his desk to write, a task he persisted at until 1:00 P.M. After that came exercise, lunch, a nap, and walks on the beach. All in all, Boulton wrote, "Gene was beautiful that summer, tall and brown and tender and smiling, working all morning, lying for hours in the sun, absorbing life and courage and hope from the sea." In October, their child, Shane, was born.

That summer O'Neill began to achieve national recognition as a playwright. In 1918 *The Smart Set* published three of his one-act plays, and in April 1919, Horace Liveright, gambling on another young writer, brought out all of O'Neill's one-act plays. It was a gamble that paid off. In June 1920 O'Neill won the Pulitzer Prize for *Beyond the Horizon,* his first Broadway-produced play.

The prize was awarded on June 3, and for O'Neill it seemed to have meant something more than $1,000 in prize money and the recognition it brought to this work. Less than two weeks later, his father was admitted to a New London hospital, dying of cancer. For the old actor, who had repeatedly been stung by his son's persistent, unreasoning, and venemous hostility, and who could only have reacted with dazed wonderment at his son's rejection of himself and most of what he held to be true, the prize brought some light to his last days of suffering. He died on August 10, believing that Eugene would turn out all right.

Chastened by his father's suffering, O'Neill sentimentally wrote to a friend, repeating his father's dying observation that his long years of acting had all been froth. Those words, said O'Neill, "are written indelibly—seared on my brain—a warning from the Beyond to remain true to the best that is in me though the heavens fall." When the playwright himself died, also after much suffering, on November 27, 1953, he could indeed say that he had remained true to the best that was in him.

After O'Neill's death, Dorothy Day, his close companion in those early months of 1918, wrote a six-page, typewritten statement on O'Neill that she called "Told in Context." Her principal point was to comment on the sometimes-voiced opinion that O'Neill was not interested in religion. It was her conviction that religion was at the center of his life struggle. She believed he was tortured by those questions to which only religion could provide an answer, and they were so crucial to him that he dared not believe there could be an answer. "His whole life seemed to be like that terrible dialogue of Ivan with Alyosha [in *The Brothers Karamazov*] and the problem of evil, and God's permissive will." But, she observed, there was no time with God, and she prayed that O'Neill had found "the Light."

SOURCES

The sources for this chapter are principally reminiscences and biographies. Harold Stearns, *The Street I Know: Reminiscences of Greenwich Village* (New York, 1935); Walker Gilmer, *Horace Liveright, Publisher of the Twenties* (New York, 1970); Daniel Aaron, *Writers on the Left* (New York, 1961); Milton Cantor, *Max Eastman* (New York, 1970); Max Eastman, *Love and Revolution* (New York, 1964); Dorothy Day, *The Long Loneliness* (New York, 1952); Agnes Boulton, *Part of a Long Story* (New York, 1958); Arthur Gelb and Barbara Gelb, *O'Neill* (New York, 1962); and Doris Alexander, *The Tempering of Eugene O'Neill* (New York, 1962).

FURTHER READING

My book *Dorothy Day: A Biography* (New York, 1982) includes segments on Max Eastman, Floyd Dell, Mike Gold, Maxwell Bodenheim, Agnes Boulton, and Eugene O'Neill. When I last visited with Day in 1978 at Maryhouse, the Catholic Worker House of Hospitality on Third Street in New York, she could look out over the Village area from the window of her room, several stories up. During this visit she recalled the time during the winter of 1918 when one of her duties as interim editor of *The Liberator* had been to take Max Eastman's personal mail from *The Liberator* office to his home on Washington Square—a distasteful occupation so far as she was concerned. It was, after the performance of this office, that she would meet O'Neill at the Golden Swan.

20

Autumn

IN THE FALL OF 1919 the final scenes of the drama "Over There" were played out. Herbert Hoover came home on September 13 and got a full-page tribute in the *New York Times.* He was praised for his "wonderful aptitude at making correct decisions in an emergency," which could "be traced to his training as an engineer."

On October 8 the *Leviathan* docked at army transport pier A in Hoboken and discharged members of the military who had remained in France to see to the packing up and return home of the American Expeditionary Force. Among those descending the gangway to the dock was General John Pershing, slim, erect, and stepping briskly. Members of the press surged forward to take pictures and note his views. "At last in a clear, light space, Pershing stopped and told the cameramen to 'shoot.'" Some begged him to salute, and he bantered, " 'Oh, no; I can't perform.'" After the pictures reporters began to question him. One, a woman, asked: "General, aren't you going to give us an interview? We stayed up all night to meet you." In response, "Pershing fixed his keen gaze on her a moment, then . . . replied, 'I can't possibly believe it of any one who looks so perfectly fresh as you do.'"

Three days later, riding a horse, Pershing led twenty-five thousand helmeted veterans in a parade. Observing the festivities was a visitor from Belgium, Desideratus Cardinal Mercier. Of the stream of visitors America received from Europe that fall, Mercier was, as a result of his public denunciation of the German army for burning the library of the University of Louvain, the most celebrated. On September 17 he was honored at a gathering of notables in the grand ballroom of the Waldorf Hotel. "With bowed head and hands clasped as though in grateful prayer, his shoulders enfolded in an American flag, he received from 700 men and women of many creeds one of the most remarkable demonstrations." Speaker after speaker honored him at the city-sponsored banquet.

Archbishop Patrick Hayes introduced Mercier: "We shall long remember . . . how you stood like a lone sentinel in Belgium, the frontier of civilization, and for the Constitution of the United States. . . . I think you will realize how a great country exists and goes forward without denying God, as the Germans seem to do." And more in the same vein throughout the evening, to the point where one might suppose for that moment that the declared universality of the Catholic church ended at the American shoreline, if not at the walls of the banquet room of the Waldorf.

On September 29, Princeton University bestowed an honorary degree upon Mercier, and immediately afterward, an "unscheduled" event occurred. "Led by their cheerleaders," fifteen hundred students sent the locomotive cheer "thundering back and forth across the auditorium" —for " 'Mercier,' and then for 'Belgium.' The distinguished primate's face was wreathed in smiles at this spontaneous outburst and when at the conclusion of the ceremonies, the entire student body and faculty rose and sang 'Old Nassau,' he seemed to have entered entirely into the college spirit and nodded his head in time with the rhythm of the song."

As Mercier made the rounds, his king, Albert of Belgium, and his queen arrived for a three-week tour of the country, which included a visit to the ailing Woodrow Wilson. In New York the Belgian king drove a car around the city, stepped one evening "to the edge of a flag-draped platform in Madison Square Garden" to be cheered by "10,000 members of the American Legion as a soldier brave, and a comrade in arms," and then arose the next morning at daybreak to hail "an old taxi," to be driven to the Columbia Yacht Club. There, he donned helmet and goggles, got into a Martin bomber hydroplane, and was flown over the city.

The following month the British cruiser *Renown* arrived, bearing Edward, Prince of Wales, who on the previous June 23 had reached the age of twenty-five. A reporter described him as "a good-looking youngster, with golden fair hair and blue eyes, clean shaven, medium height [and] slightly built." He was said to be a "great admirer" of feminine beauty and was "very fond of dancing, especially the fox trot, and the one-step."

On the evening of November 18, the prince attended part of a performance of *Samson and Delilah* at the Metropolitan Opera House. His appearance was scheduled after the third act; it was shortly after 10:00. "The succession of boxes, with their rich red hangings, that have come to be known as the 'Diamond Horseshoe' were filled. Tiaras glinted and gleamed as the facets of gems caught the lights with the turning of the fair wearers, training glasses to observe other fair wearers. Against the vividness of the women's gowns, the startling hues of slowly moved ostrich feather fans, was the contrast of men, almost effaced they would have been, except for the occasional splash of the color from a sash of some foreign order."

While the audience waited and talked, the singers backstage likewise waited and talked. Florence Easton, Caruso, Amato, and Laurenti waited, occasionally curiously peeping from behind the curtain at the empty Morgan box, decorated with laurel ropes, white chrysanthemums, and American Beauty roses. "Then, at a signal from the orchestra pit, came a long roll of drums and Moranzoni's baton lifted and 'God Save the King' came welling up. At that point Edward, in full dress with the blue sash of the Order of the Garter across his chest, stepped into the box. 'Three cheers for the Prince of Wales,' shouted a plump, gray-haired man, who sprang to his feet in the second row of the orchestra."

The next day the prince went by special train to Washington to visit the sick president. Mrs. Wilson received him, served tea, and then took him upstairs to see Wilson. "At first he seemed as embarrassed as many another young boy would be to see an older man in his sickroom. He sat beside the great bed nervously pleating his trousers." On Saturday, November 22, the *Renown*, with the prince aboard, left for home.

Such visits were doubtless intended to refresh the sense of wartime comradeship that had existed between America and its Allies and perhaps they did. As for what might be regarded as its counterpart, the anti-German feeling, it may have begun to moderate, but the thrill its indulgence had produced had not been forgotten. German opera was again the issue. At a mass meeting, called by the Manhattan Naval Post of the American Legion, a resolution committee addressed the threat at hand: "Whereas certain citizens are planning the production of German opera in the German language by German singers in New York," it was resolved that "the New York County Organization of the American Legion hereby goes on record as being thoroughly opposed." The production of German opera represented "propaganda for German kultur," the occasion for its spread "through all the underground channels which were employed . . . in the recent war."

The Star Opera Company nonetheless persevered in its plan to stage a performance at the Lexington Theater, even though Mayor Hylan opposed it. The opera was performed on the evening of October 20 and during the course of the performance one of the singers, Herman Weil, was the target of some eggs thrown from a box. Weil nimbly dodged them and laughed at his assailant while he kept singing. Outside, a crowd of sailors, soldiers, and civilians had gathered and, according to the *New York Times,* its members tried to commandeer an army motor truck at the corner of Park Avenue and Fifty-first Street, "to aid in a protest against the singing of opera in German." Mounted police charged the mob and broke it up. The next day the mayor ordered the Lexington closed and Harry B. Hertz, manager of the Star Company, said he was quitting, that the odds were too great to continue.

The persistence through the fall of 1919 of anti-German sentiment that had produced the wartime ban on German music and the German language indicates how strong and unreasonable were the wartime passions that still burned. The closing of the Lexington Theater was one incident only, but it was a sign that the national derangement lingered.

One musical event that October went unchallenged. On the twenty-fifth, eighteen-year-old Jascha Heifetz played a violin recital at Carnegie Hall. The reviewer for the *New York Times* knew his man: "Without the allurement of what is ordinarily considered a 'magnetic' personality, with the reserve that keeps back the disclosure of any personality whatever, . . . and with a total absence of anything suggesting the ostentations of the virtuoso, in hair, cravats, or postures in performance, he has centered upon himself a public admiration that can feed upon nothing but his beautiful performance." Heifetz played it safe: the feature rendition for the evening was Caesar Franck's sonata for piano and violin.

There was a moment of national glory that fall, a return of that "old feeling," of the sort to which the country had been treated the previous spring when the NC planes had begun their flight across the Atlantic. On October 9, Lieutenant Belvin Maynard left New York in an Army DeHaviland, carrying in the front cockpit a mechanic, Sergeant Klein, and Klein's "Belgian war dog, 'Trixie.' " Maynard made the trip from New York to San Francisco and back in ten days. "Aviation records will be searched in vain for such a performance as his: 5,400 miles of flying at more than 100 miles an hour in spite of . . . troubles that only the stoutest resolution could overcome," declared the *New York Times* editorial on the flight. "Inspiring is the story of the substitution of the motor from . . . [another Army plane] with the local farmers turning their automobile headlights on Sergeant Klein working furiously as the night wore on. . . . 'The best mechanic in the air service,' says Maynard of Klein. 'The army's best pilot,' declares Klein." As for Trixie, the Belgian war dog, "It was she whose coat kept the tired Klein warm in frosty altitudes. . . . When did another dog fly 5,400 miles . . . to prove so handsomely its fidelity to man?" Heroes all!

Even as Maynard was making his flight, there were heroes of a different sort who were putting their exalted status to sordid use. Except for motherhood and the flag, no institution stood more for what was good and true about America than baseball. The World Series of 1919, set to begin on September 29, was anticipated with what seemed to be more than the usual eagerness, perhaps because it was the first series of peacetime and because the Cincinnati Reds had somehow managed to rise above their accustomed lowly state and finish the season as the National League champions. Still, as the baseball historian Richard Crepeau writes, "The Cincinnati Reds had come into the 1919 World Series as definite underdogs, because the [Chicago] White Sox were regarded as one of the great teams of all time."

This estimable ranking of the White Sox was due in part to the outstanding fielding of Shoeless Joe Jackson and, especially, to the pitching of Eddie Cicotte. So fearful was the latter that Christy Mathewson, an oldtime Giants pitcher, said what he had been hearing suggested that all the Chicago manager, Kid Gleason, had to do was "to send Eddie Cicotte to the box to face the Reds lonehanded in the opening game, and then wait for the . . . Reds . . . to fan the air and go down in defeat." The opening game was to be at Cincinnati. It was noted that it would be Umpire Billy Williams's fifth series, but one other umpire, who would have worked with Williams for the fifth time, would not be there: Frank O'Loughlin, known as "Silk," had, ten months previous, "answered the call of the Great Umpire."

The night before the opening event, several trainloads of Chicago fans arrived, among whom were 250 members of the Weedland Bards, a singing cheering squad of sorts. Its "chief bard" was Joe Farrell, who led his men in singing their newest chant: "Oh, Sox, bring home the rocks, no hostile knocks, no dreadful shocks shall scare you. Sox! bring home the rocks!" As expected, Cicotte pitched the first game for the White Sox, but contrary to what the fans of the sport had predicted, he did not prevail. "Hostile knocks" were so numerous in the fourth inning that Gleason took Cicotte out of the game. When it ended, Cincinnati had scored nine runs to Chicago's one. "As a baseball game, it was so one-sided that the heralded White Sox looked like bush leaguers," declared the *New York Times.* The next day Chicago lost again and the Cincinnati fans began to think it was their team that was the premier baseball organization of all time. Back in Chicago, however, the White Sox won the next game behind the pitching of Bantam Dick Kerr, throwing his "left-handed tangents."

Cincinnati won the fourth game, taking a three-games-to-one lead. Cicotte reportedly had "begged manager Kid Gleason . . . to let him go in against the Reds. Eddie wanted to vindicate himself for his failure in the opening clash in Redland, which clouded Sox hopes. He implored and beseeched for another chance." Gleason "turned a sympathetic ear to Eddie's supplications and the flinger . . . went against the Reds." But the dark spirit that had come to possess Cicotte took over and he "failed again. . . . A wild throw to first," and then, after a single, "Cicotte made even a worse blunder than his wild heave. Jackson ran in and stopped Kopf's hit in short left. Jackson made a beautiful throw to the plate and Duncan saw that it was useless to try to pass third. As the ball was going serenely to Schalk at the plate, Cicotte ran over and tried to intercept the throw. It was a careless bit of baseball. The ball hit Cicotte's uplifted gloved hand and it deflected off, . . . rolling wild to the backstop." With the next game, the Reds took the pennant.

When emotions had settled, many who reflected on the 1919 World Series began to feel that something had been wrong. No doubt Cicotte's erratic playing caused some to wonder. There were rumors that gamblers had bought certain players. But the thought was too fantastic. Crepeau writes that John B. Sheridan of *The Sporting News* denied even the possibility of such a thing: "For a man to throw a game he would have to be willing to do 'terrible things.' . . . Such a man would die of 'his own self-contempt.' " Nonetheless, rumors persisted, and in December, Ray Schalk, the White Sox catcher, said that when the baseball season started next year, seven White Sox players would be missing. Later, Schalk denied that he knew of any wrongdoing.

It was not until a year later, when a Cook County grand jury, convened to investigate a charge of a fix in a Cubs-Phillies game, reached back to include the games of the 1919 World Series. On September 28 Cicotte and Jackson admitted to the grand jury that they had contributed to throwing four games. Six teammates were implicated. Gamblers, it was said, had paid the eight players $100,000 for their services.

The rest of the story, which Crepeau quotes, is told by James T. Farrell in *My Baseball Diary*. Just after the confessions of Cicotte and Jackson, Farrell went out to Comiskey Park for a White Sox game with Detroit. It was a muggy day and the crowd was subdued. Cicotte pitched, and the Tigers could do little with him. After the game Farrell went under the stands and stood by the steps leading down from the White Sox clubhouse. A small crowd always collected there to watch the players leave. But on this Sunday there were 200–250 boys waiting. "Some of the players left. . . . A few others came down the steps. And then Joe Jackson and Happy Felsch appeared. . . . They were sportively dressed in gray silk shirts, white duck trousers and white shoes. They came down the clubhouse steps slowly, their faces masked by impassivity."

A few fans called out to the pair, but neither acknowledged the greetings. They began walking away but the crowd followed close behind. Someone said, "It ain't true, Joe." There was no response. The two continued to walk slowly, while behind them the crowd took up the cry, "It ain't true, Joe." Jackson and Felsch walked to the Thirty-fifth Street side of the ballpark and got into their cars, parked in a soccer field behind the right field bleachers. "I waited," continued Farrell, "by the exit of the soccer field. Soon Felsch and Jackson drove away in their 'sportive roadsters.'" And thus, it may be added, an image was provided for the conclusion of the year 1919 and the beginning of the decade of the twenties: a year of morbidity riding off in a "sportive" car.

Despite the baseball scandal, the gold of fall still came. "In the old days," mused a *New York Times* editorial writer, "the most any of us knew of war was learned in intercollegiate contests. . . . Could any one love his country more or strive for it more loyally than the undergraduate who loved and strove for his alma mater? . . . Every Autumn the college made a call upon all that a man could give of heart and brain and sinew." The man called to give his all was, of course, the football player—he who stood in the way of assuming the hero's mantle, the occasion of which could bring young hearts as close to the ecstasy of community as ever could be reached within time's domain. On November 15, sixty thousand people packed the Yale Bowl in New Haven to witness Princeton's defeat of Yale for the first time in eight years. Joe Scheerer was the Princeton hero, in the judgment of the *Times* sportswriter. "He it was who won the game for the Tigers. . . . Joe Neville's lateral pass to Kempton went wild. Sheerer, a substitute half back, plunged his way through the mad scramble of Yale players, picked up the truant pigskin and dashed 22 yards for a touchdown."

It was a golden moment for the Orange and Black. "These are the . . . moments which one never forgets," the *Times* writer continued. "The game was played in a glorious autumnal setting. The russet countryside about the bowl could be seen for miles."

SOURCES

The first section of this chapter is a recapitulation of the daily news and, as the text indicates, the *New York Times* is the source. In retrospect, one of the more significant events of fall, in the light of later revelations about it, was the 1919 World Series. The source quoted is Richard Crepeau's *Baseball: The Diamond Mind* (Gainesville, Fla., 1980); see also Eliot Asinof, *Eight Men Out: The Black Sox and the 1919 World Series* (New York, 1963).

FURTHER READING

Of great interest is Harold Seymour, *Baseball: The Golden Age* (New York, 1971). A work of fiction by Harry Stein, *Hoopla: A Novel* (New York, 1983) centers on the Black Sox affair.

21

December

AT THE BEGINNING of December 1919, the NC-4, transatlantic flyer of six months previous, began a recruiting tour of the eastern and southern states. On December 3, the *New York Times* observed that the president's health was improving. His handwriting was "much firmer." Two days later the Senate Foreign Relations Committee decided to appoint a subcommittee of two members "to confer with Wilson on the Mexican crisis and ascertain his views upon any action the Senate might take in regard to a break in relations with the Mexican Government." This action of the committee, a news item explained, was to determine "whether the President is able to perform the functions of his office."

With respect to this episode in the closing days of the president's fateful year, Edith Wilson, as usual, had the final word. In her *Memoir* she tells of the visit of Senators Gilbert Hitchcock and Albert Fall: "Senator Fall entered the room looking like a regular Uriah Heap, 'washing his hands with invisible soap in imperceptible water.' He said to my husband, 'Well, Mr. President, we have all been praying for you.' 'Which way, Senator?,' inquired the President. . . . Mr. Fall laughed as if the witticism had been his own. . . . When the oil scandals sent Mr. Fall to the penitentiary I could not but recall that this was the man Mr. Henry Cabot Lodge had delegated to pass on the mentality of Woodrow Wilson."

In November 1919 congressional elections had been held. One of the districts in which a representative would be chosen was Milwaukee's Fifth, which included half of Milwaukee. The constituency consisted mostly of German-born or German-descended persons. Victor

Berger, the incumbent, was the editor of the Socialist *Milwaukee Leader* as well as a prominent member of the American Socialist party. Because of his antiwar editorials in the *Leader,* Berger had been indicted in 1918 under the Espionage and Sedition Acts. In February 1919 he was sentenced to twenty years in prison, but on appeal his sentence had been set aside.

Berger's opponent in the November race was a man named Bodenstab, a name that, according to the *New York Times* news interpreter Charles Selden, made it impossible to have "clean cut Americanism" an issue— such as would have been the case had Berger's opposition had "an American name," preferably attached to "a Mayflower descendant if they could find one." Nevertheless, Selden concluded, there were signs that "Milwaukee apparently has hopes of Americanizing herself in the end" thanks to the war-time decrease in the number of German-language classes.

When the election was held, Americanization failed by some five thousand votes of bringing Bodenstab into office. The *New York Times* had declared on October 27 that "Victor L. Berger . . . is not entitled to any seat in the House of 1919, whether he was elected or not." The House of Representatives would refuse to seat him, not "because he is a Socialist, but because the House believes he was disloyal during the war." The newspaper thought that there was "no doubt that Mr. Berger, Mr. Hillquit, Mr. Lee, and the whole reigning clique of the Socialist Party in this country led it into the path of disloyalty."

In mid-December the chairman of the House Elections Committee, Representative Dallinger of Massachusetts, said that when Berger presented himself to be sworn in, "I shall then object, as I did the previous time." So Berger stayed out. His response was that he did not care much whether he was reseated or not. But he took his re-election to be the first genuine sign of an awakening democracy "since the days of the struggle for the emancipation of the black race."

As it became clear that Berger would not be seated, the governor of Wisconsin announced that the Fifth Congressional District of his state would go unrepresented until the regular 1920 election. He did "not believe in spending any more of the people's money" in holding another election. Thus the disfranchising of the people of Milwaukee's Fifth District became another unfortunate consequence of the continuing prejudice left by the war.

Finally in that year of tumult—of an ideal of international equity and comity all but wrecked, of the existence in national life of a noisy and arrogant national self-congratulation, of a general contempt for the humanity of blacks that on occasion manifested itself in the satanic form of the lynch mob—a new element of discord that produced much suffering occurred as the Christmas season approached. A roundup of alien radicals was begun.

It started in New York on November 7, "the psychological moment to strike," since it was "the second anniversary of the Bolshevist revolution in Russia." Justice Department agents, aided by the New York munici- pal police, "dealt the most serious and sweeping blow it has yet aimed at criminal anarchists." The news account did not say where "the blow" was dealt, only that it was at a "building" and that a group of "Reds" were "merely studying English when the police arrived." Further news indicated that "a number of those in the building were badly beaten . . . during the raid."

On November 22, at a House Committee on Immigration meeting held on Ellis Island, it was said that most of the country's anarchists were in New York, including the trainload that had come east the previous spring on the "Red" special, "cursing and blaspheming the country." As the hearings proceeded, seventy-three "radicals," inmates of "Room 203," began a hunger strike to compel immigration officials to remove a wire screen barrier that separated them from their visitors. Announcing this move, a statement was sent to the Congressional Committee:

> Gentlemen: Whereas we, inmates of Room 203, having been subjected at the time of our arrest to cruel beating and insults on the part of the agents of the Government of the United States which permitted such an outrage:
> Whereas: we have received a formal slap in the face from the com- mission of the Island, a certain Mr. Uhl, who broke a promise given to us by the Commissioner to the effect that the barriers that had been lately placed between us and our friends and relatives would be removed,
> We, the undersigned, declare that we are:
> Resolved that so long as we hold dear our inalienable rights to press to our breasts our children and relatives when they come to visit us: so long as a wire net barrier placed between us and our visitors shall remain at the time of our visit, so long as our comrades held in Room 210 shall have not been transferred to Room 203—until then we refuse to go to hearings, and we declare a hunger strike.

To which Commissioner of Immigration Byron H. Uhl responded: "The affair doesn't worry me the least bit. They can go without food as long as they like." Perhaps the Commissioner relented, for the matter did not appear again in the press.

On Saturday night, December 20, some 249 alien "reds" were told that on the following morning they would leave for Russia. They took a vote and elected Alexander Berkman as their spokesman. Emma Goldman, Dora Lipkin, and Ethel Bernstein "sat with emotionless faces." All were silent for a time, then Berkman stood up "studying the faces keenly through his abnormally large tortoise shell rimmed spectacles." "Comrades," he said, "let us sing," and he launched into the "Internationale." Afterward, "lugging their grips and old-fashioned, foreign-looking portmanteaus, their Old World tin trunks," the company congregated in the big room in the south wing of the main immigration building. Putting down their luggage, they sat, some "with hands under chin, elbows on knees; some read books . . . a few strummed melancholy Russian peasant strains on their guitar." Berkman sat apart, "tying twine around a paper bag of oranges."

The next morning, at 6:00, the old ship *Buford* sailed for Russia with the radicals aboard. "Splashing and rasping in the silence of the empty bay, the anchors came up to the bow, the *Buford's* bow swung lazily Eastward, a patch of foam slipped from under the stern" and the voyage had begun. The next day the *New York Times* hailed the *Buford's* departure because it had "given us the sweet sorrow of parting at last with two of the most pernicious of anarchists, Emma Goldman and Alexander Berkman."

Berkman had been released from the Atlanta Federal Penitentiary on October 1, after serving out a sentence for violating the Espionage Act. On December 2 he was in Chicago and, along with his long-time friend Emma Goldman, went to a farewell dinner party friends were giving them on the occasion of the imminent deportation. As they ate, reporters dashed into the restaurant to tell Berkman that Henry Clay Frick, the man Berkman had tried to assassinate, had just died. "What have you got to say?" asked the reporter. "Deported by God," Berkman answered.

The next day Goldman and Berkman boarded a train bound for New York, to comply with an order to surrender there on December 5. As the *Buford* sailed out of New York's harbor on December 21, Goldman glanced out a porthole and saw that they were abreast of the Statue of Liberty. As she relates in her autobiography, *Living My Life,* her thoughts were bitter. Yet ultimately, she lost her faith in revolution itself. "Its manifestations were so completely at variance with what I had conceived and propagated . . . that I did not know any more which was right. My old values had been shipwrecked and I myself thrown overboard to sink or swim."

On December 18, in New York, the thermometer hit zero and snow began to fall, assuring the city of a white Christmas.

SOURCES

This chapter, a sort of recapitulation, has the *New York Times* as its principal source. In their respective autobiographical accounts, so frequently used in this work, Edith Wilson and Emma Goldman conclude this tale in a posture of which they would no doubt approve: Edith Wilson heaping scorn on Senator Albert Fall and Emma Goldman rejoining Alexander Berkman at the conclusion of their American odyssey. See Edith Wilson, *My Memoir* (Indianapolis and New York, 1939); Emma Goldman, *Living My Life* (New York, 1970).

22

Apocalypse or Progress?

TO MANY PEOPLE OF THE World War I era, the magnitude and appalling bloodletting of the war suggested the character of an apocalyptic event. For Americans, especially those who in 1918 had read Blasco Ibanez's *Four Horsemen of the Apocalypse,* it was a simple and deliciously exciting occupation to depict the "Hun" as the Evil One of the apocalypse. It made the wartime business of killing Germans a holy endeavor. To a few thinkers, however, the proposition that the war was the result of a singular German guilt might have been regarded as producing only a dark cloud of passion that masked a deep truth. Something had gone wrong at the heart of history.

The Russian thinker Nikolai Berdyaev was one of the main proponents of this position. In 1919–20 he delivered a series of lectures in Moscow at the Liberal Academy of Spiritual Culture to a group of intellectuals concerned with examining how spiritual values might survive in those days of profound upheaval. Fifteen years later, Scribner's published these revised lectures under the title *The Meaning of History.* Berdyaev's position, so at odds with the dominant theme of progress in American thought, was something of an arcane commodity in the life of higher learning, but he did influence a small circle of religious thinkers. "There can be little doubt," he wrote, "that not only Russia but Europe and the world as a whole are now entering upon a catastrophic period in their development. . . . Volcanic sources have opened in the historical substrata. Everything is tottering."

In *The Fate of Man in the Modern World,* written in the early thirties in France and then published in America in 1963, Berdyaev restated the theme of his Moscow lectures: "It has become a banality to say that we live in a time of historical crisis, that a whole epoch is ending, and a new one, as yet without a name, is beginning." The post–World War I world was not witnessing simply a judgment upon an epoch; it was witnessing a judgment upon history itself. "The apocalypse is not merely a revelation of the end of the world: it is also a revelation of the inner events of history," Berdyaev wrote. A philosophical-historical revolution was necessary, not for the survival of history, but for the survival of the person, free to exercise fully his or her creative endowments. Freedom, Berdyaev believed, was not an endowment concerned ultimately with the movement in time called "progress." It was a condition that permitted the reach for the beauty and truth that were the goals of the life of spirit.

But Western thought had hoisted the flag of "progress" over time and then, with increasing insistence, had pressed upon it to quicken its pace so as to attain the heaven it promised, a heaven where no craving of sense would go unsated, and where the caress of time's flow, through science, would remove all wounds of mind and spirit. This was the vision of Western liberalism, which in Marxism had been made direct, categorical, and transcendingly urgent.

Yet, argued Berdyaev, the pursuit of this alluring, compelling vision has been filled with intimations of catastrophe ahead. The fatal undoing of the Enlightenment vision had come from its assumption that the data of creation were finite and that, finally, they could be organized into a completed order of beauty and freedom. But data of the phenomenal world were inexhaustible; "facts" went to infinity, increasing and feeding on themselves with an ever-growing acceleration. That final "objective reality," assumed by nineteenth century evolutionary thought to exist, was never reached. Yet its pursuit mounted in tempo, fed by the fever of its internal necessities. Time had placed its promised vision always beyond the goal that was thought necessary to attain it, strewing all the while with an accelerated expansion of interactions the path that presumably led to its own beatitude.

The result for contemporary life had been catastrophic. The ordering consequences of humanizing traditions had been lost to life. Increasingly, sense and power had become the ends of existence—the spirit of "bourgeosity," Berdyaev called it. History's process had become so dominated by the irrational that the work of the intellectual came to be directed toward stabilizing a myth form that would give order and meaning to existence. Indeed, it had come to be almost a matter of keeping the process away from the abyss toward which it so radically inclined. The intellectual could no longer be permitted to think, but instead must count and sort.

What escape was there from this perverse and malignant action, working at the heart of history's process? Berdyaev's hope was not in an intellectual reordering of life in which the values of spirit would subdue time's wanton course. To him, the Christian, it would come through a new and striking appearance of truth—a Second Coming, that would sign the end of historical Christianity, with its record of complicity with time and death, and bring into brilliant apprehension a clear vision of the exalted level to which God had destined humankind.

In America in 1919 there was little disposition to examine the spiritual and philosophical causes of the war just ended. For professors and churchmen the continuing turbulence of history's flow provided new menaces immediately at hand on which they could offer their insights and treat with their eloquence. They, and the American middle class, lived in a mood made rich and vibrant with the expectation of new miracles of progress. Perhaps the tragedy of the war was of such magnitude that few could comprehend it.

It therefore seems almost anachronistic that leading the nonfiction sales of 1919 was the pessimistic work of the American historian Henry Adams—his autobiographical *Education of Henry Adams,* first published privately in 1907 and then publicly in 1918. Adams had died on March 27 of the previous year at the age of eighty, but had he lived through 1919, the vigor of the cult of progress would, perhaps, have provided him further fuel to sustain his mood of grim humor at what he seemed to believe was the descent of civilization into chaos.

Born in Boston on February 18, 1838, Adams could scarcely have been provided with more sumptuous endowments with which to nourish the life of the scholar than those he possessed. A descendant of presidents, a member of a family in which intellectual precocity was an unexceptional trait, a beneficiary of the most advanced education that nineteenth-century America and Europe could offer, he became at the age of thirty-two an assistant professor of medieval history at Harvard.

Adams began his teaching, as a Harvard professor presumably should, according to the most advanced theory so far as the study and use of history was concerned. History was an unfolding of progress, and the history professor's mission was to gather all the verifiable facts that could be had relating to the subject and then to recite them to his class in a manner that was as entertaining as possible. The facts were not invoked to support some preconceived large design; design and meaning would arise out of the facts, unbidden, as increasing numbers were brought to bear on the subject.

But Adams soon found that professing was not to his taste. In a chapter of *Education* that he entitled "Failure," he described his seven years at Harvard. The trouble, he wrote, was that he had already decided that history was "in essence incoherent and immoral." It "had either to be taught as such or falsified," and he wanted to do neither. "He had no theory of evolution to teach, and could not make the facts fit one. He had no fancy for telling agreeable tales to sluggish-minded boys, in order to publish them afterwards as lectures." And thus "barred from philosophy and bored by facts," he found his position increasingly intolerable. Later he would say that "nothing in education is so astonishing as the amount of ignorance it accumulates in the form of inert facts."

If Adams had "no theory of evolution to teach," if he could not see history as an irresistible unfolding of progress, he nevertheless seemed to have thought that the historian, faithful to the spirit of an objective ideal, might still find some "law" of history. After all, what right had he, still in his thirties, to declare that history was chaos when the most luminous minds of the time were declaring that a careful and honest method of assembling and verifying facts would lead to "objective reality"? Who, for example, even passably informed on the great minds that represented the flowering of nineteenth-century German scientific thought, did not know of Ernst Haeckel, professor of zoology at the University of Jena for nearly fifty years, who had affirmed evolution and a monism at the center of the life process, one that, identified and understood, would explain existence? Adams knew him and thought of him as "the oldest and clearest and steadiest spokesman of nineteenth-century mechanical convictions."

After leaving Harvard, Adams, searching for a law of sequence in history, "published a dozen volumes of American history for no other purpose than to satisfy himself whether, by the severest process of stating, with the least possible comment, such facts as seemed sure, in such order as seemed rigorously consequent, he could fix for a familiar moment a necessary sequence of human movement." The results "satisfied him as little as at Harvard College. Where he saw sequence, other men saw something quite different, and no one saw the same unit of measure."

Adams had passed his sixtieth year when he completely left off his search for a "method" of history that would lead to that fabled goal whose existence was piously professed by all properly trained students of history—"objective reality." Finding himself "lying in the Gallery of Machines at the Great Exposition of 1900, his historical neck [having been] broken by the sudden irruption of forces totally new." Standing by a huge dynamo, "scarcely humming," he was overwhelmed by a sense of the universe in a mode that was the same as the one with which he viewed history. It was one completely beyond any reach of the human sense to measure and order it. It was "supersensual, irrational"—a mystery of seething, random energy, of rays bombarding one another in a seemingly infinite nihilism.

Confronted by this intellectual dead end, Adams effected a speculative maneuver that flew directly into the face of the evolutionary, progressive view of history. "The historian was thus reduced to his last resources. Clearly if he was bound to reduce all these forces to a common value, this common value could have no measure but that of their attraction on his own mind. He must treat them as they had been felt; as convertible, reversible, interchangeable attractions on thought. He made up his mind to venture it; he would risk translating rays into faith."

Thus Adams, with this seeming display of the scholar's logic, was able to conceive a radical alteration of phase from the random, explosive nihilism of time-bound energy to the focus of eternity. Was this whimsical game playing? Not if, as Adams saw, the mysterious rays of radioactive force denied science and he was thus relieved of the logical necessity of reducing all force to an equation. The logic of the phase made plausible the "risk" of translating rays into faith.

How, then, could he feel the force of faith as an "attraction on his own mind?" "He could not say; but he knew only since 1895 he had begun to feel the Virgin . . . as force." She was "the animated dynamo; she was reproduction—the greatest and most mysterious of all energies." He had come to this feeling through his study of French cathedrals: "at Chartres . . . was the highest energy ever known to man, the creator of four-fifths of his noblest art, exercising vastly more attraction over the human mind than all the steam engines and dynamos ever dreamed of."

How curious that this highly intelligent American of Puritan descent, educated in the highest traditions of Enlightenment lore, should have become so alive to a force that was so alien to his tradition and education. The Virgin Mary had recently appeared to some children at Lourdes, Adams interjected. Ignorant children—one could understand that—but Henry Adams? Had an ancient memory made its way through the venemous turbulence of a thousand years of history to lodge at last unscathed in his consciousness and thus transfix him? It was the memory of a time not vexed by "progress," a time of unity when the subject came before the object, the pursuit of which had taken the human quest, with an ever-accelerating momentum, to the outer limits of creation.

Over this vision of unity the Virgin reigned. It was She, not colliding electrons, that was force. She was "The Woman." Her force was in the potential of her creativity, and she was never more potent than as the Virgin. "All the steam in the world could not, like the Virgin, build

Chartres," wrote Adams. "Symbol or energy, the Virgin had acted as the greatest force the Western world ever felt, and had drawn man's activities to herself more strongly than any other power, natural or supernatural, had ever done." He continued: "The Woman had once been supreme," but "evidently America was ashamed of her. When she was true force, she was ignorant of fig-leaves, but the monthly-magazine-made American female had not a feature that would have been recognized by Adam." Adams, unjustly perhaps, blamed this on his Puritan forebears: "anyone brought up among Puritans knew that sex was sin. In any previous age sex was strength."

But Puritanism, in a way that it itself never understood, was a fracturing of that unity the Virgin bespoke. When that alien force of random energy began to intrude itself into the consciousness of persons, first under the promise of its beneficent law-abiding guise—that is, under the governance of "natural law"—that promise seemed to add vitality to the Puritan mind. But the Virgin knew that where rays had become gods, she could no longer be goddess. As Adams said, she was Queen because of her own force; "she was the animated dynamo; she was reproduction—the greatest and most mysterious of all energies."

Did Adams think that there could be a new major intellectual synthesis of history's process, and that it could be redirected again toward unity and away from chaos? No, like Berdyaev, he saw history hastening toward chaos with an increasing acceleration. "If this view was correct," he wrote, "the mind could gain nothing by flight or by fight; it must merge in its supersensual universe, or succumb to it." So, Adams seemed to say, there was no hope. All one could do was keep one's head above water as long as possible, but expect in the end to go under. Once the force of the Virgin had been a barrier to chaos, but Adams did not think that force would again enter into history. He seemed to have felt that it would be unseemly to bring her radiance into the darkening light of a time when alien powers had taken hold of life and, demonlike, would destroy the last vestiges of her power.

Why did this curious and difficult book sell so well in 1919? The reviewers professed to be ecstatic about it, recommending it to anyone who had any cultural pretensions at all, but almost universally they failed to comprehend what Adams was saying. "It is a book of unique richness," gushed an unnamed reviewer for the *New York Times Review of Books,* "of unforgettable command and challenging thought, a book delightful, whimsical, deep-thinking, suggestive, a book greatly worth waiting for." *Publishers Weekly* rated it highly "for its wise philosophy of life, its deep understanding of human nature, its pervading charm of style and mood." It deserved "an abiding place among those rare volumes that are a personal joy of cultural minds." Francis Hackett, in the *New Republic,* tried to deal with some of Adams's theorizing, but after pondering aimlessly as to what was meant by "supersensual multiverse," he retreated to join the chorus. The *Education,* he concluded, was "an original contribution, transcending caste and class, combining true mind and matter."

So in 1919, Americans who considered themselves cultured spent five dollars for *The Education of Henry Adams* and doubtless read it with as much befuddlement as those who had written the reviews. After all, who in 1919, sensitive to the new vision of existence, could be brought to believe that anything other than a new universe of exciting promise lay just ahead—one where the beatitude lying in the promise of eternity might be brought into time? Adams seemed not to believe it, but apparently his Virgin removed from him the attraction of believing it.

T. Jackson Lears, in *No Place of Grace,* says that the meaning of Adams's Virgin transcended the Schoolmen's rational philosophical and theological structuring of the twelfth and thirteenth centuries. If so, her meaning certainly transcends the counting and sorting that has become the rational process of Berdyaev's Inquisitorial slavery.

William James, whose life in a number of ways ran parallel to Adams's—wealthy and cultivated family, best European education, a Harvard professorship—was enchanted by the new universe of process where all was open and nothing finally predictable. No Virgin had cast a spell upon him, to lure him toward eternity with her force. The fullness of existence could be achieved, he professed in his essay on pragmatism, published in 1908, by those who took positions at the forefront of the rolling wave of time and who availed themselves of whatever choices lying at hand seemed best to give meaning to existence. When James read a book that posed an absolutist formula as the final reference for life, he would liberally notate its margins with expressions of his low opinion of the author's intelligence. One wonders what his marginal inscriptions would have been had he read Adams's *Education.* Surely, the "force" of the Virgin would have been incomprehensible to him, but he and Adams would have agreed profoundly that the universe was open and in process. It was where the process was headed that separated the two. Adams saw the person, bound to the process, accelerating into chaos. James saw the process as endlessly open, beckoning to the person to go where he or she would in a perpetually expanding array of choices.

In 1919 Professor John Dewey of Columbia University made it his work to infuse the open choice position of James into the substance of American life, especially into educational philosophy. Dewey, a philosopher, agreed with James that philosophy's traditional concern with absolutes served no earthly purpose. For Dewey, the work of the philosopher was to stand at the advancing edge of history's process and issue procedural directives to guide that process toward an ideal of an enlightened and open human unity. Dewey was the era's master synthesizer of process, standing with one foot in history's action and with the other in the headquarter's tent as he reflected on directives to be given to his generals—namely, the personnel of the nation's colleges of education. Eventually, his directives would be caught up in such phrases as "education for democracy," "learning by doing," "child-centered," and, above all, by daring to be "innovative" and "experimental" when facing the exigency of making a way through the roadblocks that time was forever erecting for persons and institutions. In addition to his philosophizing and teaching, Dewey provided a continuing comment on the social process in the *New Republic.*

The year 1919 was not an especially good one for Dewey. Always the advocate of a detached and scientific sorting of elements in favor of only those that led to a convergence bringing all into the completely harmonious process of the democratic community, he forsook logic for the higher truth of patriotic certitude and in 1917 become a spokesman for the Great Crusade. It was, after all, a war to end wars, which made it a legitimate pragmatic choice. But not so, according to the thinking of Randolph Bourne, who had been a Dewey student at Columbia. Bourne wrote in the October issue of the *Seven Arts:* "To those of us who have taken Dewey's philosophy almost as our American religion, it never occurred that value could be subordinated to technique. ... It is the outstanding lesson of the whole war that statesmen cannot be trusted to get this perspective right, that their only motto is, first to win and then grab what they can."

Bourne, only thirty-three years old, died of flu a few days after the armistice. By then Dewey could certainly see plenty of evidence that supported Bourne's position, and by mid-June 1919, after the publication of the peace treaty with Germany, all of Dewey's hopes turned to ashes. Yes, he said, the war had been a catastrophe, but, nonetheless, he had been right. The use of unlimited armed force on behalf of an ideal was still a sound position. He was not to blame for the way affairs had turned out; rather, the American people were to blame for going off on an emotional binge and neglecting their obligation to be thoughtful. Peevishly, Dewey told the editors of the *New Republic* in the spring of 1919 that if it continued to publish Bourne's essays, he would cease his contributions.

In 1919 Dewey, turned sixty, had a nagging backache and was so out of sorts with his young critics, especially with Nicholas Murray Butler for what Dewey regarded as his conformist pressures on the Columbia faculty, that he took a sabbatical from teaching. With the liberal world of the *New Republic* he retained his stature, and for the next thirty years he continued as the ultimate authority to be invoked in support of "progress."

As to the outcome of Dewey's cause there had never been any question. The world had long since been under the spell of progress, and the notes of apocalypse sounded during World War I, with the "Hun" as its fire-breathing agent, and reverberating in 1919 as the "red scare," were transient excitements. Also of passing moment, one may now suspect, was Wilson's endowment of the League of Nations issue with the overtones of apocalypse. Could any mechanical structure, the product of academic formulation, have moderated those dark and virulent passions that festered in people's spirits after the war? Could the cause of the League, like that of communism, have been made to appear as a vital source of human unity and community?

After 1919 the word "apocalypse," if ever adverted to, was raised mostly in those piney-woods churches of the rural South where sat congregations rapt in their expectation of Armageddon—congregations whose only knowledge of progress was that it had passed them by. The ultimate paradox in the theme of apocalypse, as it was understood in the presentiments of Berdyaev and Adams was that progress itself, when defined only in objective terms, was the engine of apocalypse. The nineteenth-century social philosophers had assumed that progress would lead to a final "equilibriation," in which all parts of the equation had been placed in order and from which perfect harmony would follow. But for Adams, the historian, there was no such thing as getting all the "facts" of history. The data of creation continued to infinity, and as humankind ventured out among them to organize its own kingdom, it increasingly became entrapped by them. The system became god and the person its servitor. During the decade of the thirties the apocalyptic vision of Berdyaev and Adams had a broadly approximate restatement in the writings of the Parisian Simone Weil.

Today, possibly, it is beginning to be recognized in the increasing depersonalization and time-fettered trivialization of existence that something has gone wrong in life. Were those who reviewed Adams's *Education* in 1919 able to revise their copy, they might recognize conditions of life that would give them more depth of discernment in their comments on what Adams had said. But in that year after the first great war, the new miracles of technique fell on life amid great excitement and joyous acclaim. It was these miracles, not the memory of war's horror, that possessed their spirits. And yet, even as they stood facing a new era, life then was, for the most part, still held together by those threads of tradition and remembrance that spoke of community and eternity. It is the loss of these threads that has put the dark shadow on our own time.

SOURCES

The essential sources for this chapter are the books discussed in the text. Additional sources on Henry Adams include that R. P. Blackmur, *Henry Adams* (New York, 1980); T. Jackson Lears, *No Place of Grace: Anti-Modernism and the Transformation of American Culture* (New York, 1981); and my own "Henry Adams, the Doctrine of Progress, and the Virgin," in *New Oxford Review* (March 1989). The source on Randolph Bourne, in addition to those included in the text, is Carl Resek, ed., *Randolph S. Bourne, War and the Intellectuals* (New York, 1964). The source for material on John Dewey is Charles F. Rowlett, *Troubled Philosopher: John Dewey and the Struggle for World Peace* (New York, 1977).

FURTHER READING

Henry Adams's *Education of Henry Adams* was privately published a decade before the war began, so the war had nothing to do with his apocalyptic presentiment. Historians of American intellectual history have tended to linger over Adams, but some—R. P. Blackmur, for example—have had difficulty in accepting *Education* at face value. The obscurantist dimensions of his work are charged to his being Henry Adams—whimsically obscure and clever. No Adams, some seem to say, could have given himself over to rapturous musings about Chartres Cathedral and, of all things, to some kind of visitation from the Virgin.

The difficulty in accepting this kind of criticism of Adams's treatment of either the Virgin or the apocalyptic principle that derives from it is that it does not fit the facts. From the time he wrote *The Education of Henry Adams* until the end of his days, he kept alive in his life the memory of the Virgin. As for his apocalyptic principle—that accelerating increase in mechanical interractions intruding themselves into life would blur the ideals of truth and beauty and turn the creative act into a mechanical repetition—it cannot be said other than it is a truth of our time.

For a good history of the concept of "progress," see John Bagnell Bury, *The Idea of Progress* (London, 1920).

Index